A SOCIAL PSYCHOLOGY OF PREJUDICE

A SOCIAL PSYCHOLOGY OF PREJUDICE

DOUGLAS W. BETHLEHEM

Department of Psychology,
University of Leeds

CROOM HELM
London & Sydney

© 1985 Douglas Bethlehem
Croom Helm Ltd, Provident House, Burrell Row,
Beckenham, Kent BR3 1AT

Croom Helm Australia Pty Ltd, Suite 4, 6th Floor,
64-76 Kippax Street, Surry Hills, NSW 2010, Australia

British Library Cataloguing in Publication Data

Bethlehem, Douglas
    A social psychology of prejudice.
    1. Prejudices
    I. Title
    303.3'85   HM291

    ISBN 0-7099-3265-0

Printed and bound in Great Britain
by Billing & Sons Limited, Worcester.

CONTENTS

Preface

PREFACE

This book is intended primarily for students (in the widest sense) of psychology and of social science. To get the most out of the book, the reader needs some background in psychology, and to know the elementary probability theory and statistics that such students normally learn in their first and second years of study. The reader should know enough to appreciate the importance of statistical 'significance'. He or she should be familiar with the concept of correlation, should know how correlation is commonly measured, and should appreciate the meaning, implications, and particularly, the limitations, of such measures. Except to the mathematically very gifted or sophisticated, formulae and equations involving symbols always look very daunting at first sight. My very firm advice to the reader is, 'Do not allow yourself to be daunted.' Going through a formula or equation slowly, bit by bit, often reveals it to be far simpler than it at first appeared. All the formulae in this book are very simple, requiring nothing more of the reader than the most elementary algebra. Students can easily brush up on their elementary algebra by referring to some simple text. And even students unfamiliar with conditional probability will find no difficulty with the few references made to conditional probability, mostly in connection with stereotypes.

The book is simple, clear, and straightforward. That does not mean it is quick and easy to read in the sense that some over-simplified texts are. I respect students far too deeply to think that they are satisfied with over-simplifications and the avoidance of difficulties. Students, in my experience, are not afraid of taxing their intellects. The book deals with a mass of evidence, seeking to order and clarify it. Occasionally it deals with some mildly complex ideas: where it does, the student who is interested in prejudice will do well to make the necessary effort. That is the only way to achieve both the knowledge that will enable him or her to go further, and the intellectual satisfaction which is the chief reward of study. Students not familiar with the nature of science will do particularly well to read the second half of chapter 1 with care.

For this book is one of psychology mainly in its scientific and scholarly mode. Psychology has reached a very exciting ledge in its climb to greater heights. The importance of the scientific approach is coming to be appreciated, and the nature of science is becoming more widely understood. I hope the reader will find in this book no unsupported statements and no unbridled speculation.

And yet speculation there is, in fair quantities. For, as has been averred, this book is scientific, and science aims at the framing of hypotheses (to use Newton's celebrated phrase) by way of inductive speculation. But the speculation is bridled by consideration of the aims of science, and by what philosophers have educed about its limitations. The aims of science are to explain and predict classes of interesting phenomena – in psychology's case, behaviour and 'mental events'. The method by which it is done is by the induction or invention of hypotheses, principles, laws, theories, models – call them what you will – which explain as much as possible as precisely as can be. Philosophers, notably Sir Karl Popper in this century, have told us how we might proceed towards scientific knowledge, though we may never attain the tedium of certainty.

William James wrote, in the introductory chapter of his textbook of psychology, in 1892, 'If critics find that this natural-science point of view cuts things too arbitrarily short, they must not blame the book which confines itself to that point of view; rather must they go on themselves to complete it by their deeper thought' (p. 3). Now, nearly a century later, we are able to appreciate the nature and meaning of science at a deeper level than James was able to. Part of that deeper appreciation of science is an even more lively appreciation of its limitations.

My own very firm view is that science is by no means the most important thing in life. And further, if the student wishes to 'know about people', to understand the human heart (to use an old-fashioned metaphor) she or he will do better to study works of literature and art than to read psychology. Psychology is nothing if it does not strive to be a science, but science will never be everything.

It is with that thought in mind that I hope the book will be read. It is not pure science, for the study of prejudice demands that we go outside that domain into other scholarly domains, notably that of history. Cultures are moulded by time, and the cultural phenomena relating to ethnic relations are understandable only in historical terms. The reader will find chapter 3 (giving an historical perspective) different in style from the rest of the book, in being less formal and easier to read. This abrupt change of style may jar on some. But history is vitally important in our understanding of the forms prejudice takes, and lends itself to a lighter style than does the formal and scientific material which makes up most of the book. Inter-sexual manners are also touched on. But the growing tip of the book is in the inadequate and weakly reaching towards clearly framed theories and hypotheses, which, however sickly they now appear, are nonetheless infinitely worth cultivating, for their own sake and for what they might grow into.

* * *

I come now to a series of unrelated points.

First, one of the biggest gaps in our knowledge of the social aspects of prejudice, is detailed knowledge of the effects of prejudice on persons against whom prejudice is directed. Certain of the principles in chapter 6 have implications in this regard. Common sense and common experience tell us that prejudice sometimes leads to bitterness, anger, low self-esteem, and a 'chip-on-the-shoulder' attitude, as well as material loss, on the part of members of minority groups. More empirical work is necessary here.

In dealing with racial/ethnic minorities in Britain and the USA, it is difficult to know what choice of words to make. The terms 'black', 'brown', 'non-white', 'coloured', 'Afro-' (American), 'Caribbean', 'Asian', all have some currency, and practically any choice will seem inadequate and offensive to some. To those who experience offence, I apologise in advance: no offence is intended.

One of the effects of the volume of the studies

of prejudice that have been done in the USA has been to leave the impression that ethnic prejudice is a specially American phenomenon, and white Americans have been inclined to castigate themselves unduly for their collective shortcomings in this connection. I have purposely chosen to emphasise studies done elsewhere than in America (and elsewhere than in Britain too, for that matter) in many instances. It is important to be aware that prejudice, and the principles explaining it, are universal. On the other hand, I have felt it important to go into some detail regarding demographic and social facts in connection with minority ethnic groups in Britain, as these are less well known than corresponding information in the USA.

The reader will find a very extensive list of references at the end of this book. I have read far more than appears in that list. Unfortunately, what is published does not always yield important information. And quite often one finds that the empirical work does not support the conclusion stated by its author, but is useful in supporting or corroborating other principles or conclusions. Reading the scientific literature requires careful perusal of the work and an independent assessment of its implications.

My thanks are due to my colleagues Professor Anthony J. Chapman and Dr Noel Sheehy, for reading and commenting on parts of the original manuscript: not that they are to be blamed for any of what follows. I would also like to thank my very patient and understanding editor, Mr Tim Hardwick.

Last, I borrow the words of the greatest (notwithstanding his own disclaimer) framer of scientific hypotheses, Sir Isaac Newton, and 'heartily beg that what I have here done may be read with forbearance and that my labours in a subject so difficult may be examined, not so much with a view to censure, as to remedy their defects.'

Chapter One

PREJUDICE AND RELATED TERMS; SCIENCE AND PREJUDICE

Prejudice has assumed great importance in social psychology, because of its connection with racial discrimination. In particular, many social psychologists have felt concerned about the anti-Semitism, anti-black, and anti-oriental discrimination, which has been a feature of societies in which 'White Anglo-Saxon protestants' form a majority, and has been a great disadvantage to members of these minority groups. The most influential study of the subject, and indeed a study that has had as much influence as any in social psychology, was the study which culminated in The Authoritarian Personality (Adorno, Frenkel-Brunswik, Levinson, and Sanford, 1950/1964), which was begun during the second World War at the instance of the American Jewish Committee, who were concerned, for obvious reasons, with anti-Semitism.

This concern with social discrimination led to a bias in the study of 'prejudice', so strong that 'prejudice' was often defined in such a way as completely to ignore the original meaning of the term. Harding, Kutner, Proshansky, and Chein (1954) say: 'By "prejudice" we mean an ethnic attitude in which the reaction tendencies are predominantly negative. In other words, a prejudice is simply an unfavourable ethnic attitude' (p. 1022). Kutner (1952, p. 2) defines it as '. . . a readiness to respond to an individual or a group in terms of a faulty and inflexible generalization, the net effect of which is to place that person or group at a disadvantage.' And Allport defines it as 'an avertive or hostile attitude towards a person who belongs to a group, simply because he belongs to that group, and is therefore presumed to have the qualities ascribed to the group.' (1958, p. 8)

All these definitions, which are typical of

definitions in the literature, agree in confining the term to 'negative' or 'avertive' or 'hostile' judgements, and the first does not directly refer to beliefs or opinions. Allport does take some pains to justify his definition, taking into account the dictionary definition of the word. The <u>Concise Oxford Dictionary</u> (fourth edition) gives us 'preconceived opinion'. The dictionary thus gives us a definition which embraces much more than is commonly done by psychologists. Neither does there seem to be any good reason for confining the definition to an 'unfavourable ethnic attitude'. This kind of definition gained currency simply for historical reasons, not for any rational reason. Its use obscures the important consideration that our prejudices are not confined to ethnic groups, and that they do not necessarily or invariably entail unfavourable judgements or opinions. One can be prejudiced in favour of black Englishmen, as well as against them; and one's prejudices can concern motor-cars and tinned soup as well as ethnic groups. I suspect that I, and many other social psychologists, are prejudiced against people we classify as 'racists'. Hence, I take the definition of prejudice to be: 'an opinion or belief held by anyone on any subject which, in the absence of or in contradiction to, adequate test or logically derived conclusions or comparison with objective reality, is maintained as fact by the person espousing it, and may be acted on as though it were demonstrably true'. This definition is not very different from Hazlitt's written in the early nineteenth century: 'Prejudice, in its ordinary and literal sense, is <u>prejudging</u> any question without having sufficiently examined it, and adhering to our opinion upon it through ignorance, malice, or perversity, in spite of every evidence to the contrary' (1852/1970, p. 83). His classic little essay on the subject is well worth reading: the work of psychologists on the subject would be less confused if his essay were widely read.

The fundamental problem of prejudice, from the point of view of the cognitive psychologist, is to explain how it comes about that people make judgements and apparently believe things, or act as though they believe them, in the absence of adequate evidence. From the point of view of the person interested primarily in groups, the focus of interest is how prejudice affects the relations between members of different groups, and the part played by a person's identifying with a particular group in the formation of prejudices. These 'group' questions are dealt with in chapter 6.

Some observations about prejudice and its definition are called for. That prejudices may be favourable or unfavourable, and they may concern any kind of object has been said. But it is wise further to note that we are all prejudiced, since not even by the most liberal definition of the terms, can any of us be said to have subjected many of our opinions to 'adequate test' etc. Life is too short for us to find out or check everything for ourselves. The question then arises, when is prejudice important? The answer is a value judgement. The implied answer of many social psychologists is that one area in which it becomes important is when innocent people are made to suffer, as is the case when people hold prejudices about members of other ethnic groups. The impetus for research on prejudice in social psychology has come from the emotional commitment of many social psychologists to non-racialism, or to redressing what they see as the wrongs non-white people have suffered at the hands of Whites.

Further, let it be observed that the definitions which include the term 'attitude' are not so different from the definition suggested as may at first appear. Recall that 'attitudes' are defined in terms of 'feelings' and that attitudes usually have beliefs and action tendencies associated with them. The co-relation between feelings, beliefs, intended behaviour, covert behaviour, and overt behaviour, is made clear below.

SOME TERMS RELATED TO 'PREJUDICE'

Let us look at some allied terms, which are often used interchangeably with prejudice.

Ethnocentrism

Ethnocentrism means a tendency to glorify the ingroup while denigrating outgroups; usually there is an implicit suggestion of the ingroup being at the centre of a series of concentric circles, each circle representing an outgroup, attitudes towards which become increasingly more unfavourable as the number of circles between it and the inner-most circle (ingroup) increase in number. In fact, as will be seen, ethnocentrism is usually measured by an 'E scale', and a look at this scale shows it to be a fairly direct measure of ethnic prejudice. Operationally, that is, the terms 'ethnocentrism' and 'ethnic prejudice' are the same.

Intolerance
Intolerance refers to a tendency to disapprove of things one dislikes: it is conceptually quite distinct from 'prejudice' though empirically it may be that intolerant people are very often also prejudiced.

Dogmatism
Dogmatism refers to the tendency to assert untested opinions in an arrogant or authoritative way. (There has been only one major, published attempt to measure dogmatism, by Rokeach, 1960. His dogmatism scale, designed to measure the extent to which people's belief systems are 'open' or 'closed', is of dubious validity.) The similarity of dogmatism to prejudice is clear, the special feature of dogmatism being the expression of a prejudice in an authoritative or arrogant way.

Rigidity
Rigidity means the relative inability to shift from one line of thought or hypothesis to another, when dealing with any problem or task. No really satisfactory measure of this quality has been produced, so it is to some extent doubtful whether it is the case that some people are more rigid than others - that is whether a trait of rigidity exists. In fact, a large number of putative measures exist, but all are open to criticism, as to their reliability or validity. One such test is the 'water-jar test' of rigidity. This test consists of a number of simple arithmetic problems which can all be solved in the same way, followed by one which can be solved either in that way or in another, simpler way: the response supposed to indicate rigidity is a solution of the task in the same way. Leavitt (1956) in a review of this test concludes:

1. After eight years of research, evidence for the validity of the water-jar test is still lacking.

2. The water-jar test is a poor test _qua_ test (p. 369).

A variety of pencil-and-paper tests are available, but the evidence for their validity is lacking. The problem is partly that the term has often been defined loosely. There is strong evidence that emotional stress increases rigidity in the sense that the term is used here (Ainsworth, 1958; Luchins & Luchins, 1969; Ray, 1965). That partly explains why people seem to stick most closely to their prejudices at times of stress and conflict.

Stereotype

Stereotype is defined in the Shorter Oxford English Dictionary as something 'continued or constantly repeated without change.' In psychology this 'something' is a response of some sort, and we are most interested in cognitive 'responses'. It means to respond (by categorizing, or by behaving in the same way towards) to a group of discriminable stimuli as though they were identical. In other words, stereotype is the assumption of considerable similarity between members of groups or categories where such groups are defined in terms logically and empirically unrelated to the characteristics assumed to be common to members. The term is a metaphor from the printing trade: originally it meant a metal plate, which always produced the same image on paper. Its present use was originated by the American journalist, Walter Lippmann, early this century (Lippmann, 1922/1956). Classic measures of stereotypes (Katz & Braly, 1933/1961) consisted of a list of adjectives, with instructions to respondents to mark those that applied to certain groups - Jews, black Americans, etc.. This technique has been criticized (Brigham, 1971) on the grounds that Mann (1967), among others has shown that people are not as inconsistent as this kind of test makes them appear: not even the most prejudiced white person thinks all black people are lazy, dirty, etc. It is probably better to ask respondents to say what proportion of the group have the characteristics in question, if one is interested in individual responses. If one is interested in groups' responses, however, and does not draw strong inferences about individuals from it, the Katz and Braly approach is perfectly adequate. Bethlehem (1969) used a series of bipolar rating scales (e.g. altruistic - selfish; cold-hearted - warm-hearted as a measure of stereotype. A number of measures have been used as indices of intra-group agreement about what traits characterize the outgroup. Katz and Braly (1933/1958) for instance used the smallest number of adjectives that would have to be included to account for 50% of their subjects responses. More sophisticated indices have been suggested by Freund (1950) and by Lambert and Klineberg (1959). They all produce indices that are high when subjects agree with one another about what adjectives characterize the outgroup.

More recently it has been suggested that one should concentrate, in measures of stereotypes, not on the characteristics ascribed to a particular group, but on the characteristics ascribed with a particularly high probability to members of that group and with lesser probabilities to members of other groups. A good way of measuring this difference is in terms of the likelihood- or diagnostic ratio.

In terms of conditional probabilities, the multiplication rule tells us that

$$P(A\&B) = P(A|B)P(B) = P(B|A)P(A)$$

(NOTE: 'A&B' - say 'A and B'; 'A|B' - say 'A given B'.)

Dividing through by $P(A)P(B)$, we see that

$$P(A\&B)/P(A)P(B) = P(A|B)/P(A) = P(B|A)P(B)$$

The conditional probability of an event, B, given that event A has occurred, is

$$P(B|A) = P(A\&B)/P(A) = P(A|B)P(B)/P(A)$$

$$= P(B)\{P(A|B)/P(A)\}$$

That is, to find the probability of event B, given that A has occurred, we multiply the probability of event B by the probability of event A given B over the probability of A. Or we can multiply the probability of event B given A over the probability of B, since we have shown that

$$P(A|B)/P(A) = P(B|A)/P(B)$$

Hence

$$P(B|A) = P(B)\{P(A|B)/P(A)\} = P(B)\{P(B|A)/P(B)\}$$

The terms $P(A|B)/P(A)$ and $P(B|A)/P(B)$ are known as

likelihood or diagnostic ratios. These ratios tell us the factor by which we must multiply the simple probability of an event when we know that that event is conditional on another event.

To illustrate the application of the above: McCauley and Stitt (1978) asked students to estimate a number of probabilities and conditional probabilities, to do with the known stereotypes of Germans. They estimated, among other things, the percentage of the world's population who are efficient [P(efficient)] and the percentage of Germans who are efficient [P(efficient¦German)]: this latter is akin to the usual meaning of stereotype. They were then able to calculate the diagnostic ratio

$$P(efficient¦German)/P(efficient)$$

i.e., the probability that a person is efficient given that he is German divided by the probability that anyone in the world is efficient. If a person judges that Germans are more likely to be efficient than just anyone, this diagnostic ratio will be greater than 1. That is, it tells us that knowing a person is a German <u>increases</u> the (subjective) probability that he is efficient relative to just anyone. To give another example, let A stand for 'university lecturer' and B for 'lazy', and let us suppose that the probability that a university lecturer is lazy $P(B¦A)$ is .8, and the probability that a random person whose occupation we don't know is lazy is .2. Then

$$P(B¦A) = P(B)\{P(B¦A)/P(B)\}$$

Hence

$$.8 = .2(.8/.2)$$

The diagnostic ratio (.8/.2) is 4. That is, given that we know that a person is a university lecturer, we are much more sure that he is lazy than we would be if we did not have that information. McCauley and Stitt (1978) show that it is indeed the case that for characteristics which form part of Americans' stereotype of Germans, as indicated by a previous study, (efficient, extremely nationalistic, industrious, and scientific minded), diagnostic ratios calculated in this way are greater than 1, and for other, non-stereotype characteristics (e.g.

superstitious) the diagnostic ratios are less than
1. They suggest that this diagnostic ratio

P(characteristic|ethnic etc. group)/P(characteristic)

should be used as a measure of stereotype.
This idea, though probably close to the
intuitive ideas of many people, is a departure from
the definition of stereotype quoted above. It would
mean that if a person had the view that a very high
proportion of Jews are dishonest, and that a very
high proportion of members of other outgroups are
also dishonest, then 'dishonest' would not be
counted as part of his or her stereotype of Jews,
even if he or she avoided all financial transactions
with Jews. The meaning of the term would be altered
and we would need a new one to replace it, because
stereotype in the old sense is a useful concept.
The diagnostic ratio is a good measure of what
people see as the characteristics peculiar to a
particular group.

Intolerance of ambiguity
Intolerance of ambiguity, like rigidity, is an
ill-defined term, without an adequate test to serve
as an operational definition, but which is
frequently used as an explanatory concept. Budner's
(1962) scale would seem to be of questionable
validity. It is best defined as relative inability
to tolerate feelings of uncertainty, since this is
what most people seem to mean when they use the
term. Perhaps 'intolerance of uncertainty' would be
a better term.

Social distance
Social distance is best defined in terms of the
scale, originated by Bogardus (1925) which measures
it (Table 1). With modified items the scale has
been extensively used, and has been shown useful in
non-Western cultures in rather more modified forms
(Brewer, 1968; Mitchell, 1956; Bethlehem &
Kingsley, 1976). MacCrone (1937/1957) introduced a
useful modification in asking respondents whether
they would admit 'Any', 'Most', 'Some', 'Few', 'No',
members of a given ethnic group to a particular
level of intimacy. Triandis (e.g., 1967) factor
analysed modified social distance scales, and found
a variety of factors in social distance, each factor
influenced by different aspects of the group (or

persons) being responded to. This point will be returned to later but here it is sufficient to note that, while these findings refine the concept of social distance, they by no means invalidate the somewhat more blunt but robust social distance scales commonly used.

TABLE 1: A Social Distance Scale
(after Bogardus, 1925)

According to my first feeling reaction, I would willingly admit members the following groups (as a class, and not the best I have known, nor the worst members) to one or more of the following classifications:

Black
Jews   Americans   Students   etc.

To close kinship
by marriage

To my club as
personal chums

To my street as
neighbours

To employment in my
occupation

To citizenship in
my country

As visitors only
to my country

Would exclude from
my country

Relation between the Concepts

Let us now examine the relation of the various terms to prejudice, ethnic and otherwise.

Dogmatism's relation to prejudice will be returned to later, but by definition they are very similar, and empirically Bethlehem (1969) found a positive relation. Ethnocentrism is not distinct in practice from prejudice. Rigidity and intolerance of ambiguity are thought to relate to prejudice, because a rigid mode of thought implies an inability to reconsider judgements (and hence to jettison prejudices for better based opinions) and intolerance of ambiguity results in the acceptance of firm, unqualified opinions before the examination of evidence. Stereotyping is, by definition, a form of prejudice. Social distance is a logical consequence of a negative attitude to a group, and both are implied by prejudices against members of a group. But social distance does not seem to imply prejudice or a negative attitude, since it is logically possible to have intense feelings in favour of an ingroup without being against outgroups. And it would seem logically possible to have a negative attitude towards an outgroup ('I don't like them') without making unwarranted judgements about them (being prejudiced).

Relation between Measures

In fact various measures of prejudice, negative attitudes, and social distance are taken in practice to be measures of the same thing, and are used interchangeably. There is fairly strong evidence for the relationship. MacCrone's (1937/1957) results indicate that there is a perfect relation between Whites' attitudes to black South Africans and social distance, when group means are taken (the groups including English speaking students at a liberal university, Afrikaans speaking students at a small Calvinist university, etc.). Here tau = 1, N = 5, p < .02. (The reanalysis of MacCrone's results was done by the present author.) Bethlehem and Kingsley (1976) found, using group results again, a strong relation between prejudice and social distance. Orpen (1971) found, among white South African students, a correlation of 0.5 between social distance and a measure of attitude to black people. Campbell, in a PhD thesis (cited by Harding, et al., 1969), found that measures of social distance, prejudice, attitude and hostility, correlated .52 among college students and .58 among high school students. Hence we can accept that measures of prejudice, social distance and attitude, can in practice be used interchangeably.

PENCIL-AND-PAPER MEASURES AND ACTIONS

The relation between measures of attitudes etc. on the one hand, and behaviour, on the other, is an important one, and hence is given a major section to itself. Psychology is about the explanation and prediction both of <u>behaviour</u> and of experience.

Many years ago LaPiere (1934) called the relation into question, and his theme has been taken up rather naively by others since. Since the study has been influential in affecting attitudes to attitudes, and is often misleadingly quoted, it is presented in some detail.

Between 1930 and 1932, he tells us, LaPiere (1934) enjoyed travelling all over the United States with a Chinese-born couple. It sounds surprising today, but at that time Chinese came out lower on social distance scales completed by white Americans than almost everyone, including American Indians, Jews, and Negroes. He and they stayed at the best hotel in a small town (the receptionist merely lifting his eyebrows by way of comment); a phone call to the hotel two months later to ask if they would accept a reservation for 'an important Chinese gentleman' elicited the local equivalent of 'No way!' LaPiere was intrigued.

Thereafter, in the course of their travels, they visited 67 hotels and 'auto-camps', and 187 restaurants and cafes. Sometimes they arrived dusty from the road, sometimes clean; sometimes the Chinese approached the receptionist first, some LaPiere did; he even cultivated a 'crab-like gait', so as not to overawe the receptionists. Only during one request for accommodation, and at one meal, was the reception 'definitely, though temporarily, embarrassing', and at only one auto-camp, and an insalubrious one at that, were they refused accommodation.

Yet when he wrote to the establishments they had visited six months after visiting them in each case, and to other hotels, restaurants etc. which they had not visited, to ask if they would accept Chinese as guests, only 1 out of 79 hotels etc., and 1 out of 187 restaurants and cafes, replied unequivocally that they would. A very few wrote back saying they weren't sure, and over 90 per cent of those replying stated unequivocally that they would not.

LaPiere concluded that though the average

American businessman may have an unfavourable verbal attitude to whores, confronted with such a lady of pleasure 'in a Paris brothel' (sic), he may well succumb to her charms. In other words, verbal attitudes, he inferred, are not predictive of actions.

What he does not emphasise are the roles played by the professional lady's charms and the anonymity conferred by Paris - each so far from Babbitt's home town. He does mention in passing that his Chinese friends were young, 'personable', 'charming', 'skillful smilers', and that they spoke without foreign accents. He also notes that receptionists are not employed to refuse business for their establishments. But he did not develop these themes.

His inference - that attitudes do not predict behaviour - has been much quoted, and his paper frequently mentioned in support of that inference. To accept that inference today is very naive. First, when LaPiere wrote, the sophisticated measures of attitude we have available today were in their infancy: his measure of attitude was a phone-call or letter asking a direct question. Surely no-one has ever supposed that what people say and what they do are always identical!

Secondly, a more sophisticated appreciation of the meaning of the term 'prediction' is current. To 'predict' is to reduce the uncertainty about something which is not yet known, not to say precisely in every minute detail what will occur. Hence, if two measures reliably correlate with one another, the one is said to <u>predict</u> the other. Evidence quoted below shows that measures of attitude do relate to behaviour of various sorts.

Before turning to that evidence, let us briefly look at some of the - fairly obvious - reasons why attitudes and actions are not perfectly related, and remind ourselves that no-one who gave the matter a moment's thought would ever have supposed that any measure of attitude would predict behaviour perfectly. Measures of attitude usually measure attitudes to one object only: there may be many other attitudes a person holds which are relevant. Hence, a white person in, e.g., South Africa may have a very positive attitude to Blacks, but may nonetheless discriminate against black people, because not to do so would put him or her in trouble with the police - and most people have a negative attitude to prison! And it may be impossible for a person to be more than superficially friendly with a

person of another race in South Africa, since the
system of segregation makes actual contact very
difficult. Again, the relation between an attitude
and an action may not be very clear: lots of people
dislike the thought of killing animals (i.e. have a
negative attitude to killing animals), but are very
fond of a lamb chop. And finally, people may be
reluctant to express attitudes they hold, because to
do so would be socially unacceptable: for instance,
it is becoming more and more unacceptable to express
strong racist attitudes in most countries.
Heinemann, Pellander, Vogelbusch, and Wojtek (1981)
showed that while their German students expressed
positive feelings towards physically handicapped
people, when actually in a room with a person in a
wheel-chair, they appeared to observers (who
observed and rated their behaviour on video film
taken secretly) to be more uncomfortable than when
in a room with a physically normal person, and they
sat further away from the physically handicapped
person. Thus there is a slight disharmony in that
case between expressed attitude and observed
behaviour.

Hence the relation of a measured attitude to
behaviour is never likely to be perfect. But many
investigations show that the relation is there.

Attitude and Overt Actions

Green (1972) representing himself as a student
working part-time for a publisher, asked white
students at an American college to pose, as part of
a group, for photographs to be published in various
books and magazines. They were asked to sign a
contract agreeing to let the photographs be widely
published (in a nationally distributed popular
magazine), or to allow it to appear in magazines
with more restricted circulations of varying
degrees. Independently, a measure of their
attitudes to black Americans was obtained. He found
that measured attitudes to black Americans did have
the expected relation to the <u>behaviour</u> of signing
an agreement to appear in a photograph with Blacks
and to allow the photo to appear in various
publications. Gaertner (1973) arranged for
registered members of New York's Conservative and
Liberal parties to be telephoned by an apparently
white or black caller, who said that he or she was
trying to reach a garage to repair their car, but
apparently had the wrong number, and had run out of
change, and asked the receiver of the call to phone

13

the garage for them. Conservative Party members (who can be expected to have less favourable attitudes to Blacks than Liberals) discriminated more against Blacks than Liberal Party members did. Bethlehem (1977) found that the less favourable the attitude of one Zambian ethnic group were to another, the less likely it was for members of those ethnic groups to be sitting together in the dining hall of the University. Warner and deFleur (1969) found that attitudes to black people held by white students did affect the behaviour of signing and returning a letter committing them to certain acts, like giving to a charity for the benefit of black Americans, or 'dating' a black person. (As with the Green investigation above, factors like the publicity of the behaviour also had an effect.) Bagley (1973) found that landlords and landladies in the Netherlands who discriminated against Blacks in the matter of offering accommodation had a higher score on a prejudice scale than those who did not so discriminate. Melamed (1970) found the expected significant relation between a measure of attitude to social integration between the races in South Africa and actual willingness to go to the university refectory with a black student. (The subjects were white South African students.) Press, Burt, and Barling (1979) found that among South African five-year-old children, both black and white, scores on a racial preference questionnaire correlated with the number of sweets given to children of the other race in an experimental situation.

The above selection of studies clearly shows that measures of attitude - which, it may be remembered, correlate with measures of prejudice, and social distance - do predict actual overt behaviour. Though, of course, the prediction is and always will be, less than perfect.

Covert and Involuntary Actions

A number of studies have shown that involuntary responses are predicted by expressed attitudes. Vidulich and Krevanick (1966) measured attitudes to black Americans in a sample of white students. They showed a set of photographs to the students while measuring emotion (as indexed by the GSR). They found that students with negative attitudes towards Blacks showed greater emotional response (than students with positive attitudes) to photographs showing Blacks and Whites interacting, but not to other photographs. Porier and Lott (1967) showed, with white American students, the expected correlation between attitude to Blacks and the tendency to show emotion (as expressed by the GSR) when the electrodes were adjusted by black, in contrast to white, experimental assistants.

CONCLUDING COMMENT

This volume is on prejudice. The evidence in the preceeding pages shows clearly that measures of prejudice relate strongly, in practice, to measures of negative attitudes and of social distance, and that paper-and-pencil measures do predict actual behaviour.

Perforce, the emphasis in the social psychology literature being what it is and has been, most of what is written, the reader will find, is about attitudes of members of one ethnic group towards members of other ethnic groups. But, for the reasons given when discussing the definition of prejudice, the general sense of the term needs to be given greater emphasis, and for that reason the influence of prejudice on thinking will be discussed in the next chapter. No-one can escape his or her past, so we will turn thereafter to a consideration of the historical development of the attitudes and prejudices of white people to black.

SCIENCE AND PREJUDICE

But first a word from our sponsor. It was said in the preface that this book is scientific and scholarly in orientation. This latter half of Chapter 1 will serve to outline the nature and meaning of science, for the sake of completeness; the form of much of what follows arises from the nature of science as outlined here.

This section is not meant as a comprehensive introduction to the philosophy of science. That is a large subject, and the interested reader will find many books dealing with it. I hope enough will be said to make clear even to a reader new to the subject what science is about. Particularly to a reader new to the subject, the ideas may seem a little difficult at first; but they will repay close attention.

The nature of science starts with a definition of its aims: science is an activity whose aims are to explain and predict the phenomena in which the scientist is interested. To a degree, these aims are arbitrary. If one is not interested in explaining and predicting, one simply does not pursue science. But they are not entirely arbitrary aims: if we do not accept these clear aims, we are left without any satisfactory idea of what we should be doing. Once we have accepted these aims, certain consequences follow, which provide us in outline with a way of evaluating what we are doing - whether we are doing it well or badly. Of course, science and its aims are not the only things in life. Far from it: science is a small part of what is important. Art and philosophy, religion, literature, history, the daily acts of living - no-one in their right minds would deny that these things come before science. Science is an adjunct, if a very important adjunct. Its importance lies in the intellectual satisfaction it offers, and in the offshoots of technology it throws up. Science is the intellectual game, technology the set of techniques for accomplishing goals outside of science, techniques which often come out of scientific activities. It is the author's firm belief that psychology must primarily be a scientific discipline, or it degenerates into mere moral and political attitudinizing, of a kind which requires no special education or learning. It must primarily be scientific, but be not only scientific. The reader will find an entire chapter on history, and much reference in the forthcoming pages to matters other than mere science. But science provides the framework of thought in the book.

Two further points need to be made: one is that social psychology is being treated here as a natural science. The author does not acknowledge any essential difference between 'natural' and 'social' science (the point is developed in 'Social Psychology as the scientist views it', Bethlehem, 1980). This is not to say that humanity is being debased, or that the author does not acknowledge free will. It is merely to say that while we are being social psychologists - between 9.00 a.m. and 5.00 p.m. on weekdays as it were - it is useful to accept the working assumption that behaviour is determined and predictable. The reader is asked to bear that in mind. The importance of art and the humanities has already been stressed.

The second point is that what is to be outlined in this section is an ideal view of science. It is not a description of what scientists actually do, or have done, or how scientists think. A grasp of the logic of science is essential, moreover, if the reader is to understand the structure of much of what follows; and social psychologists must understand science if social psychology is to advance at a reasonable pace in the near future. As the actual practice of science comes to approximate more and more to the ideal, with a spread of knowledge and interest in the philosophy of science, scientific practice will become more efficient. This remark applies to all branches of science.

The Aims of Science

It has been said above that the aim of scientific activity is to <u>explain and predict</u> the phenomena in which we are interested - in our case, prejudice. This aim is somewhat arbitrary, but adopting these aims gives us a useful focus, and allows us to consider clearly the problems involved.

To <u>explain</u> something means to state the general principles from which a particular event can logically or mathematically be derived. To illustrate a simple explanation, consider the question, 'Why did the air in the bicycle pump diminish in volume?' The explanation might be

> Whenever pressure is exerted on a gas, it diminishes in volume; and the person using the pump put pressure on the air in it. Therefore: The air diminished in volume.

This explanation becomes a <u>prediction</u> if we change the tenses involved ('Will the air in the pump diminish in volume . . . ?'). Explanation and prediction are simply the same thing seen from different points of view.

The above is a very clear explanation, and not many explanations in practice are so simple and clear and precise. Few explanations in psychology even approximate to this ideal: but that does not mean we should give up trying.

The reader should note that we do not use the term '<u>cause</u>' in explanation. We deduce (logically) or derive (mathematically) an explanation. It was pointed out long ago - in the eighteenth century - that there are so many problems associated with the term 'cause' that it is best avoided.

In practice, as has been said, few explanations

are as clear and precise as the example above. Most predictions are of the kind 'X increases the chances that Y will occur'. Nonetheless, that kind of prediction is useful: it tells us something, even if not everything. If a measure of something X reliably correlates with a measure of something else Y, then X is said to predict Y, even if the correlation is far from perfect.

The student is earnestly advised to remember that the aims of science are to explain and predict what we are interested in, the definition of explanation, and that in practice we accept less than perfect explanations and predictions.

Theories, Laws, and Hypotheses

The explanations used in science are called theories, laws, and hypotheses. These terms are very similar in meaning: an hypothesis is an explanation which is small in scope and of which we are not very confident; if the hypothesis should grow, or if we become more confident of it, then it may come to be termed a 'law'. A theory is wider in scope, and may contain definitions and axioms or unprovable assumptions. Ideally, several laws might be derived from or explained by a theory, and several hypotheses from a law. The point to remember that 'theories', 'laws', and 'hypotheses', are all variants of the same thing. Here is an example of a mini-scientific system:

I   THEORY/LAW
    Behaviour is learned as a function of its
    effects.

II LAW/HYPOTHESIS (derived from the above)
    (a) Rewarded behaviour is repeated.
    (b) Punished behaviour occurs less and less
    often.

III HYPOTHESES
    (a) If I give these rats food for turning
    right in a T-maze, they will turn right in the
    maze more often.
    (b) If I smack my son for snatching his
    sister's sweeties, he will snatch the sweeties
    less often.

Note that at levels I and II we are dealing with generalizations. And that is what a scientific law is: a law is simply an assertion of a generalization, and it is scientific to the extent that we can test it. (Testing, proof, and disproof, are dealt with below.) The hypotheses at level III are closer to 'facts': we can place the rats in mazes, reward them for turning right, and see whether <u>as a matter of fact</u> they do turn right more often.

Of course every parent knows that the occasional smack (none of us parents is perfect!) puts a stop to some behaviours, if only temporarily. We know how we feel if we are punished, and suppose that others feel the same way. <u>Scientific</u> understanding comes from being so familiar with scientific explanations that we do not have to think consciously about them before making predictions based on them. <u>Human</u> understanding comes from feeling with others, and is helped by literature, art, and so on. Obviously the latter is very, very, important - perhaps the most important thing in social life. But do not turn to psychology to gain it: psychology has sparer aims.

The outline of a scientific system of explanation above covers the many sciences where the scientist is faced with uncertain measures and varying forms of the same thing - as in most of psychology. Where the processes in which the scientist is interested tend to be the same in the vast majority of cases - as in some aspects of biology and biological psychology, such as the study of the relation of (normal) brain and behaviour - there is less need for formal laws. There are thus 'two cultures in psychology' (Bethlehem, 1984); some forms of biopsychology are part of one, and scientific social and cognitive psychology are part of the other.

A word may be said here about teleological theories or laws - that is, laws expressed in terms of purpose or function. For example, the purpose or function of the heart is to ensure that blood reaches the various cells in the body, or the purpose of a rat in pressing a lever is to obtain food. This kind of law can be incorporated in a formal system (in the latter case, the generalization 'animals will do whatever is necessary to obtain food' may be taken as a kind of 'law'): it need not be purely mentalistic - that is, it may not rely only on a vague feeling of empathy of hearts and rats. And it may provide us with a moderately satisfying explanatory and predictive theory: all theories are imperfect.

Testing, Proof, and Disproof

A theory or law is <u>tested</u> by comparing it, or derivations from it, to reality. To hark back to our mini-scientific system above, we can actually put rats in the T-mazes, reward them appropriately, and see what happens. If they turn right, as expected, the law (Level IIa) and the theory (Level I) is <u>corroborated</u> (NOT <u>proved</u>). If the rats do not do as expected, then IIa and I are <u>disproved</u>. In practice, people do not give up a good theory or law easily, and would probably say the rats were schizophrenic or the reward was insufficient, or something, and try again. Note that if IIa is corroborated, that strengthens our belief in I, and, since IIb is also derived from I, our belief in IIb is indirectly strengthened by corroboration of IIa. Much evidence adduced in favour of laws etc. is of this indirect kind.

Another and very important point is that, while a theory can be disproved, it can never be <u>proved</u> <u>right</u> beyond doubt. The eighteenth century philosopher Hume pointed out that a generalization cannot be proved. Take the generalization 'All swans are white' (this is a standard example). We cannot prove this to be true: even if we examine all swans in the world - which would not be possible - we could not examine the swans not yet born. Yet even one red, green, black, etc., swan, proves the statement wrong. What we can say, is that the more frequently the generalization is tested (by looking at swans and noting their colour) and corroborated, and the more unlikely places we go to and the more far flung kinds of swans we observe, the more different people look at varieties of swans in varieties of places, the more confident we feel in the generalization. Just the same considerations apply to more obviously scientific, and more complex, generalizations (which we call theories, laws, hypotheses).

A swan may be white or (conceivably) any other colour. A problem may arise in testing the generalization about swans, in that people may disagree over whether a swan they observe is actually white or not white (it may be, say, the colour of clothes washed in Brand X washing powder in the commercials). This brings out the importance of stating theories in as clear and unambiguous form as possible, and providing <u>operational definitions</u> of important terms. An 'operational' definition is one which specifies the operations or sets of procedures we perform to decide whether a quality is present or absent, or in what degree it is present. For instance, in the swans example, we may say that a swan is considered to be white if we use a spectrometer in the routinely accepted way and obtain a reading of between x and y. In psychology, an operational definition of intelligence might be the score on an accepted test administered in the accepted way, and the operational definition of ethnic prejudice a score obtained on this or that scale designed to measure prejudice or some related concept. Maths and stats are important in science, very substantially because measurements (expressed in numbers) provide clearer and less ambiguous operational definitions than do words, and because in fields like psychology and biology and medicine where measures are subject to a great deal of variability, our hypotheses can only be tested statistically.

In rare and happy circumstances, where we have two theories which explain similar phenomena, we can do a crucial experiment to decide which is the better: in general, that involves finding two contradictory predictions, one from each theory, and seeing which one actually occurs in fact. In practice, this kind of crucial experiment is very rare in any science and almost unknown in psychology.

Almost as rare as a crucial experiment to decide between two theories, is a test which is accepted as disproving a theory once and for all. This is especially so in psychology, because theories are so imprecisely formulated as to make it very difficult to offer any test at all. Part of the aim of this book is to state theories and hypotheses in a reasonably clear form. In practice, then, theories are seldom simply rejected as wrong (once they have got beyond infancy); often they are modified in the light of new evidence. The lesson of this section is to beware of ad hoc modifications - that is, modifications which are obviously made simply to save a theory from being extinguished by the facts, rather than genuinely to improve it.

Scientific Theory beyond the Laboratory
Science, especially psychology, often comes in for the criticism that what happens inside the laboratory is not necessarily what happens outside it. This remark applies, of course, not just to

formal laboratories, but to scientific investigations carried out in any setting. This kind of remark is to be ignored, not so much because it is untrue, as because it is irrelevant. Some experiments are carried out as direct analogies of what happens in real life. But even with those, and certainly with other experiments, the basis of applying what is said to other situations whether in the same or different settings, is the inference we draw from the experiment or the generalization that is associated with it. It is wrong to think of experiments as simple analogies. We explain and predict the behaviour of gases under pressure by reference to the scientific law or generalization associated with the situation (that the volume of a gas is inversely proportional to the pressure on it – Boyle's Law). We do not say that what happens in my bicycle pump is the same thing as what happens in a deep sea diver's lungs. And if asked to predict what will happen to the gas in (say) an aerosol tin when taken to a very high altitude by rocket, a prediction would be made not by reference to my bicycle pump, but by reference to Boyle's Law. Similarly, if we want to know whether a person who scores high on an intelligence test is likely to be prejudiced against members of outgroups, we do not predict by reference to some friends of mine who seemed quite intelligent and expressed such-and-such a view in my laboratory, but by reference to the generalization (see below, chapter 6) that 'intelligence . . . [is] negatively related to prejudice'. The term 'external validity', which refers to how closely analogous an experimental set-up is to some 'real life' situation is a confusing irrelevance. Science does not proceed by analogy, but by hypothesis, law, and theory.

Theory and Practice
In practice, theories are and should be kept on if they are useful in explaining and predicting, or if they are useful in guiding research, even if they are known to be severely wanting. We don't throw a theory away, until we have a better one. Almost any theory, that is not obviously wrong, is better than nothing.

It may be useful to note that theories change subtly over time. Indeed, the very meaning of our terms and every-day words, no matter how precisely they are defined, change. Language, and science grow, change, develop. The word 'prove' provides a nice example. 'The proof of the pudding is in the eating', says the old proverb. It is meaningless today: when the saying came into use, the word 'prove' meant what we mean by 'test': you <u>test</u> the quality of the food by tasting it. ('The exception proves the rule' is totally meaningless, as the saying is commonly used today: it is a contraction of a lawyers' maxim.) And scientific terms change, sometimes subtly, with changes in knowledge and understanding. 'Attitude' meant a physical posture at first; the word was taken into psychology as a metaphor to mean the way in which a person mentally regarded something; with the advent of a firmly founded measure of attitudes (by Thurstone) in the 1920s the term came to mean a particular measure of a particular feeling; and the further work on attitudes since has meant that we look on attitudes rather differently now, recognizing that they have many dimensions, only one of which is captured in the traditional measures. Hence, while it is necessary to accept a fairly simple version of philosophical realism – the view that words describe real things existing in a real world – while being a scientist, it is nice to appreciate that this is another limitation of science.

It is the goal of science to produce ever better theories: theories that predict more, and a greater variety of, phenomena, more accurately, and are open to test, and are corroborated. But, although we strive towards an ideal, we have to make do with what we can get. Thus, we explain the relation of personality to prejudice by reference to a theory expounded in 1950 – the theory of the authoritarian personality. It has to do until we have something better, even though it clearly has shortcomings. Theories predict with greater or less accuracy: but as long as they allow us the satisfaction of offering some kind of explanation, of reducing uncertainty even a little about the future – and, remember, that is what to <u>predict</u> means – they are worth having. The more clearly stated and formal a theory is, the more easily testable it is, and the more satisfying and useful. Psychology has got to produce clear theories if it is to advance.

CONCLUSION

Science is an intellectual game that challenges us

to explain and predict interesting phenomena. To play the game, we have to accept a simple form of determinism and a simple form of realism. But as people, we recognise the limitations of science: recall the words of the wise William James, quoted in the preface. The game is infinitely worthwhile, both for the satisfaction it brings in itself, and for its applications to problems outside itself. Psychologists became interested in prejudice because they were concerned with the human suffering it brought about. In dealing scientifically with it, we make use of techniques of measurement which have their roots in the desire of a physicist-philosopher to prove that mind, body, and all things in the universe, are part of a single great unity (I am referring to G. T. Fechner). There is a useful and creative tension between pure science and problem-oriented research. Pure science provides us with a store of theories which may be applied to practical problems when the time is ripe. There is nothing so practical as a good theory. Good theories can best be developed by a self-conscious regard for the logic of scientific theory. Without that, anything may pass for social psychological theory: crude fascists and crude communists can both claim the sanction of something they call 'science' for their prejudices and dogmas. 'Anything goes' means 'anything stays'. A young priest in E. M. Forster's <u>A Passage to India</u> gets himself into a tangle speculating whether monkeys, jackals, wasps, and even bacteria and mud, may expect to enter heaven: 'We must exclude someone from our gathering, or we shall be left with nothing', comments the author.

I hope that the above will not only render the attitude of this book intelligible, but will whet the appetite of the student to read and think further about the nature of science and its application to social psychology. <u>Bon appetit</u>!

Chapter   Two

THE INFLUENCE OF PREJUDICE ON
REASONING AND JUDGEMENT

LOGICAL THOUGHT

Some Formal Logic

Prejudice has been defined in chapter one.
Basically, the term means believing something which
has not been shown to be true. Hence, as has also
been said, the fundamental problem relating to
prejudice for cognitive social psychology is to
explain and elucidate how it is that people come to
hold opinions which cannot really be justified.

The question of how knowledge and opinion can
be justified, and where they derive from, is one of
the fundamental questions in philosophy, and one
which western philosophers have been thinking about
and arguing over for thousands of years. Briefly,
we may say that knowledge may either be a priori or
empirical. A priori knowledge is what is axiomatic,
what is obviously true and cannot be proved by
reference to anything but itself. Empirical
knowlege, on the other hand, is knowledge based upon
experience or perception of objects and events.
Thus, if I see an apple, the knowledge that 'That
apple is green' is an example of empirical
knowledge. Obviously much of our knowledge, our
opinions and belief, come through observation and
experience.

The other kind of knowledge, the a priori,
includes knowledge of <u>relations</u> between objects
and ideas. For example, to say that one line is
<u>parallel</u> to another is to say something about the
<u>relation</u> between two lines: parellelism cannot be
perceived directly in the way that the lines
themselves can. A priori knowledge also indicates
knowledge of truths which are so basic that they
cannot be proved, but which seem so necessarily
right that it is impossible to conceive of a world

where they would be untrue. They are almost matters of definition, but matters of definition which we wish to apply in the real world. For example, it cannot be proved that a straight line is the shortest distance between two points, or that conclusions correctly drawn from true premises are necessarily true: but is it possible to conceive of a world where the shortest distance between two points on a flat surface is drawn, and it turns out not to be a straight line? Or where one might accept as true that 'All dogs are mammals' and that 'Rover is a dog', but not accept that 'Rover is therefore a mammal'? Now, the major organising systems involving relations between ideas are systems of logic, mathematics, and statistics. Pure mathematics and statistics are systems of logic applicable to specialised fields of ideas.

This chapter will be concerned with showing how and where people's judgements as to matters of truth and fact fall short of what would be required by formal logic, mathematics, and statistics. Logic, maths, and stats, provide us with <u>normative</u> models for judging the truth of certain conclusions: that is, they give us a means of comparing inferences which people do in fact reach in certain circumstances, and their judgements about whether conclusions are valid or not, with the conclusions and inferences which are logically justified. It will be shown that people do indeed draw conclusions which are not justifiable in terms of logic and mathematics, and which often contradict the logical conclusion; that these erroneous conclusions are not by any means random; and that they are frequently congruent with the preconceived ideas of the people involved - in other words, that prejudice does influence reasoning. To accomplish this, it will be necessary to outline some classical formal logic, with which the reader is unlikely to be familiar. Then conclusions from experiments designed to find out whether people think logically will be sketched, and (since people do not think logically) extra-logical influences affecting reasoning will be outlined. A roughly similar plan will be followed after that with statistics.

Logic has sometimes been taken as providing a description of the thought processes by which people make inferences. But this extreme view seems untenable, since the very existence of commonplace errors seems to disprove it. Perhaps, though, people do think logically sometimes, and apparent fallacies are due to deficiencies in cognitive processes other than logical ones: some of these deficiencies - like misunderstanding premises - are discussed below. It is plain that people sometimes do try to think logically. The first four chapters of Stebbings' classic little book (1961) provides a nice introduction to classical formal logic. Since the reader may not be familiar with formal logic, a brief introduction will be given here in order to make the research on the influence of prejudice on reasoning understandable.

Classical logic, from Aristotle's time until quite recently, dealt largely with propositions (i.e., assertions which might be true or false) in four forms. Here are examples of them.

1. All students are intelligent people.
2. No lecturer is lazy.
3. Some psychologists are scientists.
4. Some philosophers are not logicians.

These propositions are simple sentences, having a subject and a predicate joined by a copula (is or are); each contains a word indicating whether all, no or some members of the class referred to by the subject or predicate (i.e., students, intelligent people, lecturers, lazy people, etc.) are being talked about, and each is either affirmative or negative (i.e., it either includes the words 'no' or 'not', in which case it is negative, or it does not include these words, in which case it is affirmative). The words used need some simplifying and explaining, because some have particular meanings in logic which are not the same as the meanings they are accorded in everyday life. It should be said that these meanings are not simply arbitrary, but are necessary in order to make the logical system internally consistent.

The copula 'is' or 'are' is often taken to mean 'is equivalent to', but in logic, 'is' or 'are' means 'is (are) included in the class of'. Thus 'All students are intelligent people' means 'All students are included in the class of intelligent people'.

'Some' in logic does not mean, as it usually does in everyday life, 'some are and some are not', but rather 'some' means 'at least one and perhaps all'. Thus 'some psychologists are scientists' means 'At least one and perhaps all psychologists are included in the class of scientists'.

The subject or the predicate is said to be 'distributed' if it refers to all the members of a

27

given class, and 'undistributed' if it does not refer to all the members of the class. Thus, the subjects of the propositions 1 and 2 are clearly distributed, and the subjects of propositions 3 and 4 are clearly undistributed. The distribution of predicates is more problematic. The predicates of propositions of the type exemplified by 2 and 4 above are usually held to be distributed (that is, the whole class of lazy people and the whole class of logicians are referred to), and the predicates of propositions 1 and 3 are held to be undistributed. Where the subject is distributed (propositions 1 and 2) the proposition is said to be <u>universal</u>; where the subject is undistributed (3 and 4) the proposition is <u>particular</u>.

Euler, an 18th century mathematician, suggested a method of representing various possible relations between subjects and predicates in diagrams. These diagrams are referred to as Euler's circles. (Students of mathematics will be familiar with the similar Venn diagrams). Unfortunately the diagrams do not wholly correspond to the types of proposition above. Euler's circles are particularly useful in helping us to arrive at conclusions from two propositions which share one term. Two propositions of the type illustrated above, sharing one term (called the <u>middle term</u>), and a conclusion regarding the terms which are not shared, is known as a <u>syllogism</u>. Here are four examples:

1. All students are intelligent people.
   All receivers of grants are students.
   Therefore: all receivers of grants are intelligent people.

2. No lecturer is lazy.
   All students are lazy.
   Therefore: no student is a lecturer.

3. Some psychologists are scientists.
   All psychologists are empiricists.
   Therefore: some empiricists are scientists.

4. No logicians are metaphysicians.
   All metaphysicians are philosophers.
   Therefore: some philosophers are not logicians.

All four syllogisms are valid (and their validity can be illustrated by a little manipulation of

Euler's circles or Venn diagrams for those familiar with them). But syllogisms can be very difficult for one not acquainted with Euler's circles, or not used to formal logic. And they can be made more difficult by adding irrelevant premisses. They are particularly difficult when 'X' and 'Y' are used in place of words (e.g. instead of 'Some philosophers are not metaphysicians', 'Some X is not Y' can be written). Investigations of the errors made when people attempt to assess the validity of syllogisms, or when they draw conclusions from two premisses, (e.g., Chapman & Chapman, 1959; Morgan & Morton, 1944; Roberge, 1970) reveal that students get about a third of invalid syllogisms right, and about half the valid ones, when the terms used are Xs and Ys and Zs. Some of the non-logical rules which appear to guide subjects in drawing conclusions (and which partially explain the errors made) follow.

1. <u>The atmosphere effect</u>. A negative premiss creates a negative 'atmosphere', and a particular premiss creates a particular 'atmosphere'. Specifically, when one or both premisses are negative, subjects will tend to draw a negative conclusion; and where one or both premisses are particular, subjects will tend to draw a particular conclusion.

2. <u>Invalid conversion</u>. Subjects are inclined to convert 'All S is P' to 'All P is S' and 'Some S is not P' to 'Some P is not S', especially when they are dealing with unfamiliar material. Both these conversions are invalid according to the rules of logic, but are commonly done because the copula is taken to mean 'is equal to' by analogy with mathematics, instead of being given its proper meaning of 'is included in the class of'. It will be obvious that these conversions are nonsense if you will consider for a moment the nonsense of converting 'All dogs are mammals' to 'All mammals are dogs', or 'Some mammals are not dogs' to 'Some dogs are not mammals'. The conversion seems right because in everyday language these conversions can often be made sensibly: 'Some dogs are not vicious creatures' and 'Some vicious creatures are not dogs' are both true statements. The second seems to follow from the first, though logically it does not. Revlin and Leirer (1978) attribute the bulk of

logical errors to this kind of mistake.

3. <u>Probabilistic inference</u>. In everyday life, and in scientific investigations, we make inferences in terms of (subjective) probabilities. One basis on which such inferences are made is that it usually seems probable that things which have some salient property in common are the same; this mistake is common, and gives rise to the need to remind ourselves that all that glisters is not gold. Classical formal logic cannot deal with probabilities of this kind, but subjects often make this kind of probabilistic inference, with the middle term as the property held in common. Take, for example, the two propositions, 'Many socialists advocate a greater regard for human rights' and 'Some people who advocate a regard for human rights are communists'. It seems reasonable, if one accepts the two propositions as true, to conclude that 'Some socialists are communists'. In fact, that may be true. But the conclusion does not follow from the two premisses. Substitute 'poor people' for 'socialists', and 'millionaires' for 'communists', and the point is obvious.

The evidence shows clearly that people make errors when trying to argue in terms of syllogisms or to judge whether syllogisms are correct. It may be that these errors are due, not to failure in subjects' logic, but to failure to appreciate the special meanings that words (like 'some', 'are', etc.) acquire when used in formal logic, or to failure to bear in mind that <u>formally valid</u>, not <u>true</u>, conclusions are required by the experimenters. Whatever the reason, people do make errors, and it will be shown in the next section that these errors are influenced by their prejudices.

Inferences in formal logic can also be made from so-called hypothetical propositions: for instance 'If a student works hard, then he passes'. Another way of saying that is: 'A student's working hard <u>implies</u> he passes'. Two valid inferences can be drawn from this hypothetical statement. Given 'the student works hard', we can infer that 'he passes', and given 'He did not pass', we can infer 'he did not work hard'. Two common <u>errors</u> are: to infer from 'he passed' that 'he worked hard' (he could have passed by pure luck); and to infer from 'He did not work hard' that 'he did not pass' (again, he might have passed by pure luck). Logical errors in arguments of this kind have also been found to be influenced by prejudice.

The Influence of Prejudice on Reasoning.

This question is worth considering at this juncture because reasoning is so fundamental in our lives. If it is the case that prejudice influences the reasoning process in some way, to distort the conclusions we reach, then it is clear that presenting reasons as a way of influencing opinions is unlikely always to be successful, and people will be able to support their prejudices by quasi-logic, and hold to their prejudices all the more firmly for this apparent support. And common experience leads anyone who devotes a moment's thought to the matter, to the conclusion that people do not arrive at conclusions by logical processes, and that even when they think they do their conclusions are often not logical at all.

Philosophers have long wondered whether the laws of logic are a description of the mental processes by which we arrive at conclusions. It has just been asserted, it is hoped convincingly, that they are not; and the very existence of logical fallacies in thought is sufficient evidence that they are not. Nonetheless, as has been said, the laws of logic are in some sense fundamental. It is not possible to conceive of a world in which for instance the conclusion 'All dogs are warm-blooded' does not follow from the statements 'All dogs are mammals' and 'All mammals are warm-blooded'. The conclusion, once the two statements are accepted, must be true - and its truth is not dependent on an empirical examination of the temperature of dogs' blood. But if logic is fundamental, why do people not reason correctly? Let's first look at evidence showing that they do not, and that the fallacial reasoning is congruent with their prejudice, and then return to that question.

Janis and Frick (1943) found that 19 postgraduate students in an American university were more likely to make errors when asked to judge whether syllogisms were logically sound when the conclusions agreed with their preconceived opinions. (In this and in other experiments of this kind, subjects are asked to judge whether the conclusion presented follows logically, not whether it is consonant with their opinions; a measure of their opinions is taken at another time, to see whether the mistakes they make are consistent with their prejudice). They found that students were more likely to say that an unsound argument was sound than to say that a sound argument was unsound when the conclusion was in accord with their preconceived opinion; and conversely, that they were more likely to say that a sound argument was unsound than that an unsound argument was sound when the conclusion contradicted their preconceived opinion. (Following the last sentence may have given you a headache: logic is like that!) In other words, the students were clearly influenced in their judgements of the soundness of arguments by their prejudices, even though the syllogisms did not have to do with very emotive issues (their topics dealt in range from oriental art, to sailors' ability to swim), and though the subjects were postgraduate students.

Thistlethwaite (1950) investigated immediate inference of the kind 'If a student works hard ...'. Some of his arguments dealt with black Americans, and some of the conclusions of the arguments presented denigrated black people. He found that black students in a Southern state, and Whites in Northern states, made fewer errors on these arguments than white students in Southern states. (These error scores were calculated relative to error scores on non-emotional items, to control for differences in ability to cope with formal logic). Prentice (1957) found (using American students as subjects) that the E and F scales (two scales measuring prejudice and hostility to ethnic minorities) related in the expected way to errors made in judging the soundness of syllogisms' conclusions, when the syllogisms had to do with ethnic groups. Feather (1964), working in Australia with external students attending a 'vacation school', found that students with positive attitude to religion tended to make errors in judging the soundness of syllogisms consonant with their religious bias, and an interaction showed this tendency to be especially marked among students with very strong pro-religious attitudes. Lastly Thouless (1959) found the expected pattern of errors with adult students on a weekend course in Cambridge.

Not all investigations have found the expected effect. Thouless failed to find evidence of prejudice affecting judgements of validity of syllogisms with full-time students in Cambridge, even with a harder test: test sophistication and intelligence are two possible factors accounting for this negative result. Feather (1964, 1967) failed to find it with his <u>mildly</u> anti-religious students. Nonetheless, the important point to bear in mind is that the evidence seems very clearly to support the hypothesis: <u>there is a tendency for people to evaluate arguments as logically sound when the conclusion agrees with their prejudices, even when the argument is unsound, and as unsound when the conclusion contradicts their prejudices, even when it is sound</u>. That is not to say that this distortion <u>always</u> or <u>universally</u> occurs — hence the term 'tendency' in the hypothesis. Evans (1982, p.227) suggests that 'belief-bias effects in syllogistic reasoning are relatively weak when compared with, say, atomosphere/conversion effects', but, even if he is correct — which I doubt — he is referring only to laboratory studies, where people are trying to think logically, where strong feelings do not often enter, and where the effects of different biases can at least be partially separated. In 'real life' it cannot be doubted that prejudices affect the inferences people make much more markedly, no doubt working through 'atmosphere/conversion effects' very often.

Henle (1955, 1962) considers how this distortion comes about, and she investigated the steps in the reasoning processes of subjects by interviewing them. Her suggested reasons closely parallel, in some instances, the kind of convolutions in the thought processes of Rosenberg's (1960) subjects when they found their feelings changed as a result of hypnotism and no longer consonant with their opinions. Some possible reasons are (more than one may operate at a time):

1. <u>Lowering the criterion</u>. Persons familiar with the theory of signal detectability will know that the effect of motivation is to change the postion of the criterion — that is, if a person <u>wants</u> to detect something, he will accept a smaller amount of evidence as indicating its presence than if he does not want to detect it. Similarly, it seems that people may accept a smaller amount of evidence as implying the truth of something they <u>want</u> to believe than they would demand for something they wanted not to believe.

2. <u>Selecting and omitting of premisses</u>. Particularly where arguments are rendered confusing by superfluous or very long premisses, and people cannot think of the whole argument at one time, they can select among the premisses. This selection can

be made consciously or unconsciously, on the basis of which premisses seem to support the favoured conclusion.

3. <u>Adding premisses</u>. People sometimes implicitly add steps to an argument, which favour their conclusions. Unless a psychologist is probing their thought processes, this process is likely to remain implicit.

4. <u>Altering meaning of statements</u>. Advertisers want us to make this sort of error when they make statements like 'Many doctors agree . . .'. They want us to alter the meaning of this statement, which may be true, to 'Doctors agree . . .' or 'All doctors say . . .'.

5. <u>Neglect of logical requirements</u>. Very often, even in an experimental situation where people have been particularly asked to arrive at a logical conclusion, the dictates of logic are forgotten, and they arrive at a conclusion by other means. This may be the most common reason for people endorsing conclusions which accord with their opinions rather than looking for the soundness of the argument in the experiments quoted above.

Evidence for paragraphs 2, 3, 4, and 5 can be found in Henle's two articles (1955, 1962), but it seems almost unnecessary to seek this evidence. A few moments reflection about the last argument in which you were involved will, I am sure, recall many of the mechanisms mentioned above in operation. Even the most rational of us, if we will admit it, occasionally argue irrationally to arrive at the conclusion we favour. And the scope for illogicality is greatly increased by the universal practice of arguing from unstated premisses, very often to implied conclusions: for this reason, as philosophers have been aware for centuries, it is seldom possible to fault someone's reasoning in 'real life'. And indeed, it would become impossibly tedious to state most of one's premisses and conclusions explicitly. Ordinary conversation would be impossible. Psycholinguistics addresses itself to the important fact that people take as given by a sentence far more than is either clearly asserted by the speaker, or follows logically from the assertion. The elucidation of the 'psychologic of implication' (Nosanchuk, 1980) or 'pragmatic implication' (Harris & Monaco, 1983) in everyday conversation is receiving increasing attention. Argument often boils down to making people state some of their premisses explicitly - and then agreeing to differ, as often as not.

Let us briefly allude to some other experiments by way of making clear the potential effect of people's prejudices on judgements which are more closely related to the 'real world' than the logical tasks referred to in this section. Much more will be said on the subject later in the book. Miller and Hewitt (1978) showed black and white students, male and female, videotapes of the beginning of an actual trial where the accusation was one of rape of a thirteen-year-old girl. A summary of the evidence was given. It was found that when the victim was said to be the same race as the subject, whether black or white, the subjects were twice as likely to say they would have convicted on the evidence as when the victim was of a different race from the subject: the evidence being, remember, exactly the same. Noel and Allen (1976) showed that the same editorial from a student newspaper was judged poorer in quality when attributed to a Mexican American (or to a woman) than when attributed to a white (or a man), by white adults. The pages dealing with prejudices against women show how prejudice affects judgements of the quality of work attributed to men and women.

Conclusions and Implications

People tend to accept as logically valid those arguments whose conclusions reflect their prejudices. They do so for a variety of reasons, such as being willing to accept a smaller amount of evidence as conclusive in those arguments than in others; omitting from consideration, or misperceiving the meaning of, premisses; simply ignoring the requirements of logic; and through being prone to a number of errors and error-inducing tendencies, such as atmosphere effects and invalid conversions.

These conclusions have distressing implications for those of us who would like a more rational world. They are too obvious to be spelt out here, perhaps, but one that stands out is that they point the futility of rational argument in altering prejudices.

We can state as a formal hypothesis then:

Hypothesis:
> People tend to accept as logically valid those arguments whose conclusions reflect their prejudices, and invalid those whose conclusions contradict their prejudices.
>
> And add as a rider: Some reasons for the distortions that occur in logic are that people (a) accept a smaller degree of evidence as implying the truth of propositions they agree with; (b) people select, omit, and add to premisses in order to support conclusions compatible with their prejudices; (c) people alter the meanings of statements in order to make the statements conducive to the support of their prejudices; (d) people sometimes simply ignore the requirements of logic; and (e) people are prone to a number of errors and error-inducing tendencies through which conclusions conformable to their prejudices come to be drawn.

'STATISTICAL' JUDGEMENTS

Logic, Probability, and Statistics

It has been pointed out that in classical logic a term might either be distributed or undistributed - that is, it might refer to <u>all</u> or <u>none</u> of the members of a given class, or to <u>some</u> of them. <u>Some</u>, it may be recalled, means (in classical logic) 'at least one and perhaps all'. These are the only quantifiers available. And they are totally inadequate to deal with many of the problems which call for judgements to be made: they cannot make use even of terms like 'a few' or 'many' or 'almost all' - all of these are simply compressed into 'some' - let alone precisely calibrated numerical quantities. We turn to probability and statistics to take us beyond this limitation of classical logic.

The mathematical theories associated with probability and statistics are, as has been said above, systems of logic which can be applied in the real world to aid in questions of judgement - that is, where we make decisions in conditions of uncertainty. Like formal logic, probability theory and statistics provide us both with algorithms by which to reach conclusions, and with a means of evaluating conclusions reached by less formal means - i.e., they provide a normative method of decision making.

Probability theory and statistics can be traced back at least to Galileo's time (Galileo, 1962. The paper, on gambling with dice, was written early in the seventeenth century). The original impetus came from a practical interest - how to improve one's success rate in gambling games, gambling being the archetypal situation in which judgements - decisions in conditions of uncertainty - are called for. There is now hardly any sphere of activity in which statistical theory cannot profitably be applied. Hence, it is of interest to psychology to investigate whether, when people make judgements, that they make use intuitively of roughly the steps which would be followed by a formal statistician, or, at least, whether the judgements that people arrive at are roughly justifiable in terms of formal probability and statistical theory.

People as Intuitive Statisticians and Intuitive Scientists

In the 1950s and 1960s a fair amount of work was done, indicating that non-statistician subjects are quite capable, when presented with samples of stimuli, of making (intuitively) good estimates of the mean, median, and mode, of samples of non-emotive stimuli, in laboratory conditions. However, even under laboratory conditions and with simple, clear, stimuli, people showed no clear appreciation of the statistician's concept of variance, which is so important in sampling theory. (The evidence was reviewed by Peterson & Beach, 1967.) People are not good intuitive statisticians except in very restricted circumstances and for very simple parameters and decisions. The literature on ethnic stereotypes and prejudice would have been sufficient in itself, to make that plain. But in the 1960s, social psychology was becoming interested in the general question of how people arrive at assumptions about the characteristics of other people, on the basis of which they predict their behaviour. That is, social psychologists came to see the importance of the question of how good ordinary people were at an informal science of person perception. This area of investigation now goes under the misnomer 'attribution theory', and the first formal statement in the area seems to have been Jones and Davis's 'Theory of Correspondent Inferences' (1965).

These two traditions merged in the brilliant, pioneering work of Amos Tversky and Daniel Kahneman in their explorations of the types of bias to which people were prone when making judgements which could be made on the basis of formal statistical reasoning. In their first significant step on this frontier (Tversky & Kahneman, 1971) they showed that even psychologists at a mathematical psychology conference were prone to serious biases in their intuitive statistical judgements. Since then, the kinds of bias to which people are prone, and the 'heuristics' - i.e., the intuitive rules or guiding precepts or strategies - which lie behind the statistical decisions of ordinary people have been explored and tentatively classified. It should be emphasised that these are <u>tendencies</u> - it is not the case that everyone is subject to these biases all the time. They are very strong tendencies, however. Research is being done to discover under what circumstances the influence of the heuristics is attenuated (e.g. Ajzen, 1977), but it is fair to say that the evidence points to the heuristics having a very robust influence.

The kinds of error to which people are prone in statistical judgements will be gone into, then errors in the intuitive assessment of correlations, and then the importance of this work for the question of prejudice will be dealt with - but fairly briefly, because the relevance is fairly obvious.

Some Heuristics which Bias Judgement

1.   <u>Representativeness</u>.   When judging the probability that an object or event <u>a</u> is a member of a category or set <u>A</u>, people are prone to be unduly influenced by how similar <u>a</u> is to what they think of as the typical member of <u>A</u>. In an experiment which has become a classic, Kahneman & Tversky (1973/1982) told people that they had one hundred descriptions, 30 of which were of engineers and 70 of which were of lawyers. When given a random description, and asked whether it was of an engineer or a lawyer, the people made their judgements very largely according to whether the description seemed more typical of the stereotype of an engineer or the stereotype of a lawyer: they were very little influenced by the information that

70% of the population from which the descriptions were drawn consisted of lawyers, and only 30% consisted of engineers - making it much more likely that any random description would be of a lawyer rather than an engineer. In general, people are more influenced by any information which seems to point to 'representativeness' than by any intuitive approximation to sampling theory.

2. <u>Availability</u>. When judging the probability or frequency of occurence of an object or event, people are prone to be unduly influenced by how easy it is to recall or imagine the object or event. Thus people overestimate the incidence of newsworthy causes of death, such as homicide, car accidents, and poisonous bites or stings, and underestimate the incidence of such more mundane causes of death as diabetes and strokes (which seldom get into the news media), because the media coverage makes the former causes of death more readily available to the memory.

3. <u>Prior Theories</u>. When estimating the extent or degree to which events are predictable from or covary with other events, people are unduly influenced by their prior theories concerning the relationship between the events. One set of prior theories which is especially troublesome in this connection is those theories involving <u>cause</u>. People in general seem to have a very strong tendency to order the world in terms of <u>cause</u> and <u>effect</u>, and even scientists, more than two hundred years after Hume (1748/1955) pointed out the problems the concept of 'cause' involves, find it hard to resist overuse of the term. In general, people estimate a strong correlation between two types of event where events of one type are supposed to <u>cause</u> events of the second type.

4. <u>Other biasing tendencies</u>. In addition to the three biasing 'heuristics' just referred to, there are other factors which distort judgement. For example, once people have made an estimate of any kind, they find it difficult to modify or alter that estimate significantly: they tend to act rigidly, to <u>anchor</u> their later estimates to their first one, so that subsequent estimates are unduly influenced by the first one, even when the first one

is patently groundless. Another is a tendency for people to be more <u>conservative</u> in their estimates of probabilities close to 0 or to 1 than statistical theory would demand: that is, people are reluctant, when estimating the probability of an uncertain event, to make estimates very close to 0 or very close to 1. And yet another is the tendency for people to be <u>over-confident</u> regarding the estimates they make.

Tendencies Biasing General Cognitive Processes

We will depart briefly from direct consideration of intuitive statistical judgements, and consider biasing tendencies in general cognitive processes. We do so both because these obviously affect prejudice in themselves, and because, it will be shown, they affect a particularly important form of statistical judgement - the intuitive detection and assessment of the strength of covariation (expressed in statistics as various indices of correlation such as the contingency coefficient whose significance is assessed by the familiar chi-square significance test, and the Pearson product-moment correlation coefficient).

Biases in Interpreting and Coding the Evidence of our Senses.

The act of perceiving anything means that we put a <u>meaning</u> to what we see, hear, etc. That is, we <u>code</u> the sense data, and the coding can only be done in terms of the <u>schemas</u> available to us. It is a fairly common observation that people see what they want to see, and there is plenty of formal evidence to back this observation up.

Anyone who has ever discussed a football or boxing match with a rival supporter knows that different people see the same event very differently. Hastorf and Cantril (1954) showed <u>the same film</u> of a football match between Dartmouth and Princeton, two American universities, to students at the two universities. As expected - but it is nice to have it formally demonstrated - each side attributed more fouls to the other side than their own, and judged the fouls by the opposing team as being more flagrant than fouls by their own team. Asch (1948) gave identical quotations to groups of American students, but attributed them to different sources. For instance, he presented the following statement to the American students: 'Those who hold and those who are without property have ever formed two distinct classes'. But some students were told that the author of the statement was Karl Marx, others that it was John Adams (one of the leaders of the American Revolution). He found that students who were told the author was the hero John Adams were inclined to agree with the statement, while those who were told that the author was the demon Marx were inclined to disagree. Asch attributes the difference to a difference in the interpretation – in the very meaning – of the statement, in the light of its supposed authorship. Duncan (1976) showed white Californian students videos of a black and a white student having a discussion. Towards the end of the video the discussion became heated, and different groups of students saw either the white student on the video push the Black, or the Black push the White, or a Black pushing a Black, or a White pushing a White. The incidents had been carefully rehearsed to be precisely the same. Nonetheless, the observers who saw the Black doing the pushing rated the shove as being more intense and violent, than the ones who saw the push done by the White. Moreover, those who saw the Black doing the pushing attributed the cause to be personality and disposition of the black person, while those who saw the White doing the pushing attributed the cause to the situation. Similarly, Sagar and Schofield (1980) found that both white and black American children (about 12 years old) rated identical behaviour as more 'mean' and 'threatening' if it was performed by a Black than if the same behaviour was performed by a White. Kruglanski and Freund (1983) showed that, under conditions of time pressure and when they thought their judgements would be scrutinised by others, Israeli teacher-training students gave higher grades to essays thought to have been written by an Ashkenazic Israeli child (i.e., an Israeli of European descent, the dominant Jewish cultural group in Israel) than if the identical essay was supposed to have been written by a Sephardic Israeli (of Spanish, African, or Arab descent) child. The chapter on sex differences presents evidence that the sex of the supposed originator of a piece of work alters people's evaluation of that piece of work, at least in some circumstances. Jones and Russel (1980) showed that people that believed in ESP (extra-sensory perception), after witnessing a test of ESP in which there was no objective evidence that ESP had occurred (the 'receiver' had to guess which card the 'transmitter' was looking at, and the correct guesses were only at a chance level of accuracy), nonetheless asserted that ESP had occurred, whereas sceptics regarding ESP did not.

Preconceptions affect attributions of the cause of behaviour as well as coding of behaviour and of events themselves. Duncan's (1976) experiment has been referred to above: undesirable behaviour by a Black was attributed to his personality, whereas the same piece of behaviour by a White was attributed to situational factors. Taylor and Jaggi (1974) gave Hindu clerks in India brief descriptions of desirable or undesirable pieces of behaviour - for example, of a person helping or refusing help to a child who had received a small injury in the playground. The person doing the behaviour was described either as a Moslem or as a Hindu. It was found that good behaviour by a Hindu (i.e., a member of the ingroup) and bad behaviour by a Moslem were ascribed to internal, personality factors (e.g. the Hindu is of a generous disposition) whereas bad behaviour by a Hindu and good behaviour by a Moslem was attributed to situational factors. Kulik (1983) showed that if students shown videotapes of introverts and extroverts behaving in the expected ways (i.e., an introvert hesitantly beginning a conversation, or an extrovert talking loudly and spontaneously to another person, while waiting together on a bench), led to the behaviour being attributed to the personalities of the actors, whereas if they behaved in unexpected ways the behaviour was attributed to situational factors. Hence we can conclude (a) that in the very act of perception people tend to adjust what they see to align with their existing schemas and prejudices; and (b) that inferences regarding the personalities of other people based on observations of their behaviour tend similarly to be influenced by existing schemas and prejudices.

Distortions in Memory. Our memories are notoriously subject to distortions. In this section it will be shown formally that these distortions occur - and are probably far more serious than most people realise - and that they frequently distort our views in the direction demanded by our expectations and prejudices.

Loftus and her colleagues have been concerned to show how far memory is open to distortion in quite simple ways, and how great an effect this distortion has on eyewitness testimony. In one series of experiments (Loftus, Miller, & Burns, 1978) students saw a series of slides depicting a car accident involving a pedestrian. Half the students saw a stop sign in the pictures and half saw a yield sign. Subsequently they were asked a series of questions, including the question 'Did another car pass the red Datsum while it was stopped at the stop sign?' or '. . . while it was stopped at the yield sign?' Half the students asked the question including the phrase 'stop sign' had actually seen a stop sign, and half had in fact seen a yield sign; and the same applied to students who were questioned about the 'yield sign'. When the students were afterwards shown slides of the red Datsun at a stop sign and at a yield sign, and asked to choose which they had previously seen, it was found that the questions had introduced distortions in memory. Students who had seen one sign, but had been asked about a different sign, were significantly likely to choose the sign included in the question rather than the one actually seen. Following experiments in the series indicated that it is the actual memory, not just the verbal response, that the misleading information in the question affects, and that misleading information embedded in the question had a greater effect when presented a week after the original slides were seen than when presented soon after the original slides were seen. In another experiment (Loftus & Palmer, 1974), students saw films depicting motor accidents. The independent variable was the phrasing of a subsequent question. Some were asked 'How fast were the cars going when they hit each other?' Others had similar questions, but with other words - 'smash', 'collided', 'bumped', 'contacted' - substituted for 'hit'. Estimates of the speed of the car varied significantly depending on the wording of the question: the term 'smashed' in the question yielded the highest estimate of speed, and the term 'contacted' the lowest. In a subsequent experiment, students were asked after seeing another film, 'Did you see any broken glass?' (In fact, no broken glass was shown in the film.) Students who had answered a previous question involving the word 'smashed' were more likely to say 'yes [I did see some broken glass]' than students whose earlier question had contained the word 'hit' or who had not answered a previous question.

Snyder and Uranowitz (1978) gave a brief potted biography of an imaginary woman to students to read.

Some of them were subsequently told that she was now (i.e. some time after the biography ended) a lesbian, others that she was sexually 'normal'. A week later they were given a recognition memory test. The students who were told - after reading the biography - that she was now a lesbian made the kind of errors in their memory test which were obviously influenced by their knowledge that the woman was now a lesbian. The errors of the other group were consistent with the picture of a woman of 'normal' sexual habits.

Chapman and Chapman (1971/1982) found that when people read lists of paired associates, and were asked to estimate from memory the frequency with which various pairs had occurred, they overestimated the frequency with which commonly associated words (such as 'bacon - eggs', 'lion - tiger') had occurred together. Their demonstrations that people grossly misremember the frequency of occurrence of expected sign-symptom pairs in projective tests will be referred to in some detail below. Hamilton and Rose (1980) conducted a series of three experiments leading to conclusions congruent with the work of Chapman and Chapman. In the first, sentences in which adjectives describing people of various occupations were presented. The adjectives were paired equally often with each occupation. Nonetheless, subjects estimated the expected pairs (e.g. salesman - talkative) as having occurred more frequently than unexpected pairs (e.g. accountant - talkative). In the second experiment, expected pairs of words did actually occur more frequently together than non-expected pairs: their frequency was exaggerated in the students' memories. In the third experiment, the effect of pairing words which stood out by the incongruity of their pairing (e.g. 'quiet - salesman') was investigated. The frequency with which these types of pairs occurred was underestimated when they occurred no more frequently than other pairs of words - in other words, the memories of the subjects adjusted the data to suit their implicit schemas or expectancies. The conclusion seems clear, and it is a terribly important one both in the context of prejudice and in other contexts. Memory is untrustworthy and malleable, and what shapes it is our expectations and prejudices.

Intuitive Assessments of Covariation

A number of investigations have been conducted to

find out whether people are capable of detecting, and assessing the degree of, correlation between two variables in data presented to them. (The student may do well at this point to refresh his or her memory with the bare outlines of correlation by referring to any statistics-for-psychology or statistics-for-social-sciences textbook.) The evidence shows fairly clearly that people are not good at intuitive judgements of correlation. Peterson and Beach (1967), reviewing evidence available to that time, found that people concentrated on one or two cells when presented with 2 X 2 tables summarizing information and asked to estimate degree of correlation. This is a shortcoming which has repeatedly been found since. Smedslund (1963) presented student nurses in Scandinavia with cards on which letters representing symptoms and others representing diseases were associated to various degrees. They were asked to assess how far symptom A was diagnostic of disease F - in effect, for the correlation between the two, whose significance would formally be assessed by a chi-square test. He found that neither in the nurses' responses to the task, nor in their answer to questions afterwards, was there much sign of their comprehending, even vaguely, the underlying concept of correlation. The evidence they looked for was overwhelmingly the cases in which both the symptom and the disease were present, ignoring the important cases of when the symptom was present but the disease absent, or the symptom absent but the disease present. It is not surprising that the more demands the data make on the memory, the more people are likely to rely on simplistic strategies, like the strategies used by Smedslund's subjects, of basing the assessment of correlation on an estimated frequency of positive, confirming, cases. (This point was demonstrated by Shaklee and Mims, 1982, who asked students to estimate the covariation of different sorts of stimuli presented on slides; some of the students had their memory loads increased by being asked to attend to and remember certain irrelevant information on the slides.) Ward and Jenkins (1965) presented American students with data relating to the seeding of clouds, and rainfall. They were asked whether the data led to the conclusion that seeding clouds had any 'control' over rainfall - in effect whether there was a correlation between seeding and rain. They found that when the data was presented item by item, students appeared totally unable to detect a correlation, relying on assessments of the relative frequencies of seeding followed by rain and seeding followed by no rain. When the data was presented in the form of a summary 2 X 2 contingency table, however, students were better at taking the appropriate information into account, although they grossly overestimated the degree of correlation. Inhelder and Piaget (1958), using clearly stated problems and clear, simple, data (up to twenty four instances of blue eyes and blond hair, brown eyes and brown hair, etc.) found that some adolescents had some notion of correlation, but a very unclear one.

The experiments of Ward and Jenkins and of Smedslund looked for evidence of an intuitive appreciation of correlation in situations where the familiar chi-square test might be appropriate. The next experiment presented data which were appropriate for the Pearson product-moment coefficient of correlation. Jennings, Amabile, and Ross (1982) presented students at one of the top universities in the United States with three sorts of data, and asked them to estimate the degree of correlation present in the data. The three sorts of data were: (a) simply pairs of numbers; (b) drawings of men of various heights holding sticks of various heights; and (c) letters having different positions in the alphabet and tones of varying duration. They found the individual differences in the estimates of correlation were very great, and that moderate to moderately high correlations (Pearson product-moment correlations of 0.2 to 0.6) were hardly detected by the subjects; higher correlations were detected, but their degree gravely underestimated. In other words, the subjects displayed the tendency to conservatism mentioned above.

On the other hand, when subjects were asked to estimate the degree of correlation between actually occurring variables, such as the correlations actually found between students' self-ratings of ambitiousness and their self-ratings of intellectualism, the tendency to conservatism disappeared and the students not only overestimated the degree of correlation between the various pairs of variables, but were happy to make very high estimates.

Prior Theories and Estimates of Correlation.
Presumably the student subjects in the Jennings et

al. study described above had some theories which made them estimate high correlations between ambitiousness and intellectualism and so on. Theories such as these have been shown to exert strong influences on estimates of correlations between the sets of data that are of considerable practical importance. A series of widely quoted experiments by Chapman and Chapman (1969, 1971/1982) showed how people's intuitive, implicit, theories bias their estimates of the relation between signs on projective tests and the characteristics, symptoms, or syndromes, they are supposed to be correlated with. In one experiment, they asked practising clinicians what signs on the Draw-a-Person test (a projective test where the testee is simply asked to draw a person and the picture is used as a diagnostic instrument) were related to what characteristics. The clinicians tended to agree among themselves, for example, that drawings of people in which the eyes were emphasised were related to suspiciousness in the person doing the drawing. Next, a group of students were given drawings of various kinds, matched with supposedly true statements about the person who had drawn them. The pairing of the drawings and the statements were carefully arranged so that there was no correlation between, for instance, suspiciousness of the drawer and drawings of people with large or emphasised eyes. Despite this careful arrangement, the students tended to report that the correlation did exist, and even students offered large monetary rewards for accurate assessments made these errors. These illusory correlations presumably arose because people associate eyes and suspiciousness, without really realising that they do. In a further experiment using the Rorschach ink-blot, they began by asking clinicians what homosexuals typically see in some of the ink blots. Five signs were reported by the clinicians to be typical of homosexual men, including seeing in the ink blots buttocks or anuses, and seeing human figures of indeterminate sex. As with the experiment involving the Draw-a-Person test described above, Rorschach protocols were then given to students with descriptions of the people who had supposedly given the protocol, the pairing of the protocols and the descriptions carefully arranged so that there was no association between the homosexuality of the person and the sign of buttocks and anuses, or the sign of persons of indeterminate sex, in his protocol. Nonetheless, students reported that there was a

47

correlation between the sign and the symptom — presumably because they implicitly harboured the theory that these were the sorts of thing homosexuals would report seeing.

Sources of Error in Intuitive Estimates of Correlation.

While what has just been said is by no means a full review of the literature relevant to intuitive estimates of correlation (for more complete recent reviews, see Alloy & Tabachnik, 1984, and Crocker, 1981), enough has been said to support the conclusion that (a) people can detect marked correlation in data under some circumstances, and (b) that their detection of, and estimates of the size of, correlations, are far from good when judged against formal statistical measures. These conclusions are not surprising, given that the concept of correlation is not a simple one, and the data needed to make estimates of correlation between variables is necessarily extensive.

It is useful to try to analyse just where in the process of judgement the errors in intuitive estimates of correlation enter. Crocker (1981) identifies six steps in the estimation of correlation, and error may enter into any or all of them. They are: (1) Judging the relevance of the data to the correlation; (2) sampling the data, or judging how representative of the population is the sample of data to hand; (3) interpreting and coding the data as belonging to one or other category; (4) estimating the frequencies — often relying on memory — with which the data occurred in the various categories; (5) estimating whether a correlation exists and how strong it is; (6) deciding how to use the estimate of correlation for making judgements and predictions. There is good reason to suppose that error crops into each of these steps, and that the error is such as to favour conclusions consistent with the prejudices of the person concerned. We will consider each of the steps briefly, giving some evidence of errors found.

1. Judging the Relevance of Data. There is clear evidence that people regard as most relevant to judgements of covariation positive, confirming, cases. This strategy is bound to lead to error in many cases. It would lead to the conclusion that breathing air is correlated with (e.g.) lung cancer,

an obviously erroneous conclusion. Measures of correlation, such as the contingency coefficient whose significance is measured by the familiar chi-square test, take into account all four cells of a fourfold contingency table. For example, in the Ward and Jenkis (1965) study mentioned above, the students were asked to decide, given some data, whether cloud seeding was associated with rainfall. They found that the majority of the people involved adopted a strategy in which relative frequency of the 'seed - rain' combination (i.e. positive, confirming, cases) played an important part, and some of these also considered the 'no seed - no rain' combination. It was more unusual for them to consider the other combinations (seed - no rain and no seed - rain). Smedslund (1963) found that the nurses in his study also regarded as overwhelmingly important the cases where both the symptom and the disease were present, when estimating whether a symptom was diagnostic of a disease. Snyder and Swann (1978) in the second of a series of experiments, asked students to assess whether a person they were interviewing was an introvert. (Others were asked to assess whether the interviewee was an extravert.) They found that students trying to assess whether a person was an introvert tended to ask questions which would be appropriate if it were already known that the interviewee was an introvert, and students trying to assess whether a person was an extravert tended to ask questions which would be appropriate if it were already known that the person was an extravert. That is, they were seeking positive, confirming, cases. Similarly, Crocker (1982) presented students with data relevant to the correlation between practice on the day before a tennis match and the outcome of the tennis match. Some students were asked what information would be necessary to ascertain whether there was a 'relationship or connection between working out the day before and winning that match', others were asked the same question except that the word 'losing' was substituted for 'winning' and others were asked a question about the relationship which did not stress 'winning' or 'losing'. Over all three conditions, the students showed a strong bias to saying that 'practice - win' information (i.e. positive, confirming, instances) was the most relevant; what was interesting was that students asked the question regarding 'working out the day before and losing the match' tended far more frequently than students in the other two conditions to say 'practice - lose' information was relevant. This sort of information would be positive, confirming information for them, in view of the way the question was phrased.

Pyszczynski and Greenburg (1981) show that when people have positive instances confirming a readily available hypothesis, they simply do not seek further information at all. We know (c.f. the theory of correspondent inferences, Jones & Davis, 1965) that people make inferences about the characteristics of others based on the other's behaviour to the extent that the behaviour is not easily explicable in terms of situational factors. Pyszczynski and Greenburg showed that once behaviour is attributable to situational factors, people do not seek information which might lead to inferences about the personality of the participant, whereas they do seek such information if the participant's behaviour is not easily explained by situational factors. Specifically, they arranged for students to observe another student being asked to do someone a little favour involving very little trouble, or a big favour involving a lot of trouble. When the other agreed to the little favour or refused the big favour (behaviour easily explained by the situation), the observing students were less inclined to seek information about the kindness, mood, etc., of the other, than if the other refused to do a little favour or agreed to do a big one.

We can conclude, then, that when trying to detect, or assess the strength of, correlation, people are strongly inclined to follow the very suboptimum strategy of seeking positive, confirming, instances, where a proper assessment of correlation requires taking into account all four cells in a fourfold contingency table.

2. Sampling. It has been noted that people are simply not very good intuitive statisticians when it comes to sampling. Tversky and Kahneman's (1971/1982) demonstration that even psychologists, who have some familiarity with formal statistical theory, make poor intuitive sampling theorists, has already been referred to. So also have Pyszczynski and Greenburg's (1981) experiment, showing that when people have the information that seems to confirm their views, they just don't look for any more information. Similiarly, the propensity to attend to and pay disproportionate attention to cases which are vivid and 'representative' has also been

referred to above. Then we should note the tendency that people have to mix with others of similar background, social class, and opinions, to themselves, and hence the possibility of drawing random samples of behaviour and characteristics of other people is severely limited. Even social scientists who are making a profound effort to draw random samples of other people's behaviour and personal characteristics, find it impossible. Hence it is plain that people in general are likely to bring to any intuitive calculation they may make biased samples of the variables under consideration, and samples where size and representativeness are unsuited to the drawing of any firm conclusions.

3. and 4. Coding and Remembering the Data. In the section above on tendencies biasing general cognitive processes it was shown that (a) people adjust their very perceptions to align them with their schemas and prejudices; (b) people's inferences about other people based on their observations of the others' behaviour are similarly influenced by their existing schemas and prejudices; (c) memory is a very malleable thing, shaped by expectation and prejudice. It follows clearly that the data which is assembled, on which an estimate of correlation must be made, is bound to be affected very frequently by prejudice, working through coding and memory.

5. Using the Data to Estimate Correlation. Even when people are presented with data in a fourfold table, they do not always make good estimates of correlation. (e.g. Ward & Jenkins, 1965, referred to above). This observation is not surprising, considering how sophisticated a concept correlation is. When the data is haphazard and subject to the vagaries of bias by cognitive overload and prejudice, the estimates are likely to be even less congruent with formal statistical estimates of correlation.

6. Making the Estimate of Correlation. Tversky and Kahneman (1971/1982) found that psychologists at a conference on mathematical psychology had a poor intuitive appreciation of sampling theory. It is a common observation on the part of anyone who has had to teach statistics that the acquisition of an

appreciation of the meaning and implications of correlation coefficients is a painful and difficult process. The use of scattergrams, the interpretation of the square of the Pearson product-moment correlation coefficient as the proportion of variance in one variable <u>explained</u> <u>by</u> regression on the other, non-linearity of regression, the effects of unreliability of measures - these are only acquired by familiarity with correlation through use. It would indeed be surprising if people untutored in statistics had much appreciation of these concepts, or of the concept of significance, or of the sampling distribution of a coefficient, which are essential if one is to make proper use of an estimate of correlation. It is not surprising then that people fall back on their prejudices. It is a fortunate few who have the good luck to have their capacity for rational decision making immeasurably increased by learning some elementary statistics.

<u>A Difficulty with Research in this Area</u>
In the section on classical logic, it was pointed out that everday language does not always map clearly onto the language of the classical system of logic. The same applies to statistical logic. One particular difficulty, which has not been noticed by researchers, is the relation of a problem set in ordinary language to correlation. The problem is, when is correlation an appropriate formal model for what the subjects are asked to do?
We may explicate the question like this. Subjects may be asked a question like 'Decide from the data with which I present you whether (say) scientists are intelligent.' Data consisting of instances of intelligent scientists, intelligent non-scientists, non-intelligent scientists, and non-intelligent non-scientists, may then be presented. The experimenter may test the 'answer' of the subject by reference to a correlation calculated from a fourfold contingency table.
But the question is ambiguous. It can be interpreted as 'Are scientists more likely to be intelligent than non-scientists?' In that case, correlation is an appropriate model. It can also, however, be interpreted as 'If a person is a scientist, does that imply that he is intelligent?' This is a question of implication: in this case, positive confirming, and disconfirming instances are the <u>only</u> relevant data. It may be that subjects

interpret the question thus in many experiments when it is inappropriate to do so. In some experiments, however, the question can reasonably be interpreted in this way, and the experimenters are on dubious ground in using correlation as a normative model. Crocker (1982), for instance, gave her subjects this question: 'You want to find out if there is a relationship between working out the day before a match and winning that match'. It would not be unreasonable to 'translate' that into: 'Is it the case that "If you work out the day before, then you win?"' (i.e. if p then q.) The only data relevant (to that question) then becomes instances of working out and winning (i.e. p, therefore q). Reference to the section on logic above will remind the reader that not working out and not winning (not p, therefore not q) is not relevant, since (not p, therefore not q) is an <u>in</u>valid inference from 'If p, then q'.

Conclusions

It is too early, in terms of the life of research into the matter, to state more than very general conclusions and hypotheses regarding people's intuitive use of statistical theory and judgements. Research is ongoing and vigorous, and our view and knowledge of these matters are being refined.

The following conclusions seem justified:

Hypothesis:
> When making inferences which can be normatively modelled in terms of statistical sampling theory and measures of correlation, people usually perform very poorly compared with the formal statistical theory.

With the rider:
> Some reasons for poor intuitive performance in sampling and estimates of correlation are (a) the disproportionate emphasis on information which seems <u>representative</u>, which is readily <u>available</u>, and which is congruent with the theories or orientations of the person, such as the tendency to order events in terms of cause and effect; (b) the common tendencies to stick rigidly to initial estimates, to be conservative

when making data-based estimates of correlation and probability, and to be over-confident of estimates; (c) the tendency to code information or data in such a way as to make it congruent with expectation or prejudice, including the tendency to infer such characteristics of other people from their behaviour as conforms with the perceiver's expectations and prejudices; (d) the tendency for memory to be biased to conform with expectation and prejudice; (e) the tendency to give cases conforming to expectation and prejudice undue emphasis and attention.

DEFICIENCIES IN INTUITIVE LOGIC AND STATISTICS, AND PREJUDICE

If the reader has kept in mind the meaning of the term 'prejudice' some of the implications of what has been said above will be clear. This chapter will close with a few observations which will supplement those of the reader.

Prejudice, to quote the definition given earlier, is an opinion or belief held by anyone on any subject which, in the absence of or in contradiction to, adequate test or logically derived conclusions, or comparison with objective reality, is maintained as fact by the person espousing it, and may be acted on as though it were demonstrably true. What this chapter has shown is that people are not very easily able to derive logical conclusions or adequately - in logical and statistical terms - to test their opinions and beliefs. The facility we all have of coding the evidence of our senses to fit our prejudices, of adjusting our memories, of selecting the data we attend to, and so on, makes it plain that prejudice has a lot of scope for action. To quote Hazlitt's wonderful little essay, 'Prejudice is the child of ignorance . . .. The absence of proof, instead of suspending our judgment, only gives us an opportunity of making things according to our wishes and fancies' (1852/1970, pp. 83-84).

How easy we all find it to support our judgements and opinions! Scientists are no less prone to prejudice about matters they feel involved with than anyone else. Scientists find it very easy to find evidence to support their pet theories:

that is why ('psychologically') Popper lays such an emphasis on falsify ability as a criterion by which the 'scientificness' of hypotheses is judged.

Ethnic Stereotypes. Imagine a man from the country of Fordox who is greatly prejudiced in favour of Fordoxians, and against Bridgecamians. The following pseudo-argument seems very plausible, in view of what we know about people's use of logic:

> Some Bridgecamians are lazy.
> (All) lazy people sponge off the social security system.
> Therefore: Bridgecamians sponge off the social security system.

A few items on the mass media, which would catch our Fordoxian's eye, showing out-of-work Bridgecamians, would be sufficient evidence for both the major premiss and to confirm the conclusion, and our Fordoxian, having found evidence in favour of his conclusion, would not seek any more evidence. He would not appreciate that he had a biased and very small sample. His conviction that there was a clear correlation between being a Bridgecamian and being lazy would be increased by his having to hand positive, confirming, instances - lazy Bridgecamians. He would overestimate the correlation, and place great confidence in his overestimate. And he would not appreciate the limitations in the concept of correlation, which he was implicitly using. Hence his prejudice would feed on itself, and grow stronger thereby.

What to do
I have used nonsense names for groups in the above paragraph but it seems obvious that these processes are just what keeps ethnic and other prejudices going. What is to be done?
    Hazlitt supplies a part answer: suspend judgement. Dare to say, 'I don't know', except when you do. Examine your evidence. That is one of the great blessings of education - learning to examine evidence and ask about the basis of one's knowledge of something. A knowledge of logic and statistics is a very great advantage. The most elementary knowledge of these things immeasurably increases one's ability to make adequate judgements, and to

recognise when judgement should be suspended. Of course, very often one has to act on one's prejudices or judgements, because the circumstances do not allow us to collect sufficient evidence on all important matters. Indeed, just what constitutes <u>sufficient</u> evidence in any given case is often a debatable point: hence it is debatable when an opinion is a prejudice.

Greater use of logic and statistics is part of the answer. It strikes those of us with a liking for rationality as bitterly sad that people seem simply not to like making use of statistics. Meehl (1954) long ago showed that simple equations making use of psychometric and other easily obtainable and quantifiable data (age, marital status, etc.) were almost always as good as or better at predicting important behaviour than were judgements of interviewers, psychiatrists, clinical psychologists, and so on. The behaviour predicted ranged from future crimes of convicted criminals to flying proficiency of air force personnel. Yet to this day, there remains in the fields of social and behavioural science a wariness of - even a prejudice against - statistics. Like many very rewarding things, like Beethoven's late quartets and T. S. Eliot's poetry, logic and statistics are remote and difficult. Our prejudices are comforting, easy, and immediate.

A summary of the conclusions and principles educed in this chapter will be found in chapter 10.

Chapter Three

HISTORICAL PERSPECTIVES ON ETHNIC PREJUDICE:
'they are only black people'

It is instructive to look at the historical
development of race attitudes and prejudice,
particularly since such attitudes have become
institutionalized in various parts of the world. The
attitudes and prejudices of white people regarding
black people are best documented, and this is the
most frequently studied form of ethnic prejudice,
hence this chapter will concentrate on the growth of
prejudices against black people. Other histories,
equally enlightening, could be written about the
historical growth of other prejudices - anti-Jewish
prejudices, prejudices against Chinese in South East
Asia, prejudices against Asians in Britain, Catholic
and Protestant prejudices against one another, etc.
The prejudice of Whites against Blacks is emphasised
because it is prominent in Britain and the
United States (and there is the glaring example of
South Africa), and because it is well documented.
So a look in some detail at the growth of the
contact and development of Whites' attitudes and
prejudices about Blacks among English people (and
citizens of the USA soon after they ceased to be
simply English expatriates) will be undertaken. A
brief look at South Africa will follow, because of
the striking similarity in the natural history of
(Whites') race prejudice in that geographically
distant environment.

THE NEW WORLD

The Growth of the Slave Trade
I suppose the starting point is Columbus's landing
in the Bahamas late in 1472. The Arawaks, who were
native to the West Indian Islands (the name 'West
Indies' being a legacy of Columbus's inflexible
belief that he was near India and China), were

pacific and friendly, and gave him gold. Columbus took it, explored the Caribbean with their help, went back to Spain, and returned twice with gangs of unscrupulous adventurers to colonize the area. They encountered Caribs, a less pacific ethnic group of Indians, said to be cannibals - hence 'Caribbean'. The Spaniards quickly set about raping and pillaging, extracting tribute of gold from Indians, and establishing slavery. The Arawaks were extinct within a century and, as Spanish settlement in the Islands increased, and farms and gold mines were set up, slaves were imported from other islands. They died, of grief, of overwork, and of sicknesses like smallpox which the Europeans brought with them and to which they had no resistance. More and more islands were settled, and expeditions set off for the mainland of the Americas. The Spanish Empire in the Americas, born of the desire for loot, was quickly established. Cortes set off from Cuba for Mexico in 1519, and Pizarro for the gold of the Incas from Panama some years later. Treasure fleets fed the greed of the Spanish court, and Spanish settlement in the West Indian islands increased.

The Spaniards introduced many crops into the islands including sugar, which grew well, and was much in demand in Europe. But sugar needs labour as gold mines do, and labour was not available locally - there being few whites, and the local Indians exhibiting the distressing tendency to die rather than to work for their conquerors' enrichment. Black people of the West African coasts had been subject to enslavement by Europeans for some time. The Portuguese, whose ships had nosed their way down the African coast for years past, had established a trade in slaves, and black domestic slaves were not unknown in Portugal and Spain. In 1510 black slaves were sent to the Spanish West Indian island of Hispaniola, and subsequently licences were granted to private suppliers of black slaves to the West Indian Islands and to mainland America.

The Indians were not without their champions among the conquerors. In 1511 Fray Antonio de Montesinos caused the kind of offence to his Christian flock that some churchmen were to re-echo in many lands down the centuries, to David Livingstone in nineteenth century Africa and beyond, by suggesting that the Indians were human beings and had a right to be regarded as such, rather than as chattels - especially as some were Christian subjects of the Castillian King. No one seems to have spoken for the black Africans, who, when taken into European ownership, were not Christian, and not the subjects of any European King.

The slave trade grew, with trades in other commodities, and much unlicensed trade, or smuggling, was done in the Americas and West Indies by Europeans of varying nationalities. In the 1560's Hawkins anticipated the triangular trade that was to be such a money spinner for Liverpool, Bristol and London, when he traded black slaves in the West Indies, forcing the locals to trade when he was not granted the requisite licences. He made a lot of money, but the Spanish eventually caught him and drove him away after destroying most of his fleet. Spanish insistence on monopoly in the Americas and in the West Indies led to more and more smuggling and unlicensed trade, and to semi-official privateering expeditions like those of Drake in the later sixteenth century. The expeditions were at first largely motivated by desire for plunder, but later they became battles in the conflicts between the great European powers. In the early seventeenth century, Spain recognized she could not hog the whole of the New World for herself, and, tacitly at first, agreed to the exploitation of parts of the New World uninhabited by Spaniards, by the other European powers. In fact colonization by the English, Dutch, and French was slow at first, since there was plenty of money to be made by trade and piracy. Trading in slaves was very profitable, and the Dutch West India Company set up its own factories (i.e., slaving stations) on the West coast of Africa, and grabbed Portuguese factories. But colonization did increasingly take place by the English, French and Dutch in the New World. In England in particular there was a desire to emigrate, with religious intolerance and enclosure providing the push, and the hope of free land and wealth the pull. In English official circles it was felt that colonization was not only a source of useful commodities for Britain, but would also harm Spanish interests as an important bonus. St. Kitts was settled by Englishmen in 1624, Martinique and Guadaloupe by Frenchmen in 1635, and Virginia and New England by Englishmen in the early part of the century. England's colonies in the area increased apace. Tobacco and cotton were the important cash crops in the West Indies later, and rice was extensively grown in some areas of mainland America. Sugar became the dominant crop because of the insatiable demand for it in Europe, because sugar cane needs hot weather to grow (beet sugar came later), and because it could be processed and transported with relative ease. Tobacco was important on the American mainland, Virginia tobacco then - as now - being highly regarded. Cotton was important in the West Indies, these islands providing 70 per cent of British needs up to about 1790. The invention by Whitney of his famous cotton gin (a mechanical device for removing the seeds from the cotton) in 1793 provided slavery on the mainland of America with a fillip when some areas were becoming overstocked with slaves. The invention made cotton of the variety suited to mainland America much more profitable, and production increased tenfold between 1793 and 1810.

From our point of view the importance of these crops is that they were labour intensive. To yield good profits, large plantations were necessary, and a great deal of hard, heavy, boring work needed to be done. In the early years of English colonies in the New World, labour was by the hands of indentured servants. Men and women voluntarily signed indentures, or were transported for felonies as indented labourers by magistrates (some of whom accepted bribes to supply labour in this way) and, notoriously, by Judge Jeffreys. Cromwell 'barbadoed' - sent forcibly to Barbados - prisoners of war. Indented labourers led a hard life, and since their masters had complete rights to their work during the period of their indentures without having to pay wages, and since indentures could be bought and sold, they were virtually slaves for the time; but of course they were people, not property, and could not be used more cruelly than was common at the time; and they had their freedom to look forward to.

With the increase in numbers and size of commercial plantations, indented labour became increasingly inadequate to the need of the planters. Black slaves were the obvious answer. Not that pressing economic need was the only reason for turning to black slavery. New England had drifted into slavery, when a ship arrived with slaves in 1683, and slavery was accepted, and because it was convenient, became customary. The original white settlers of Barbados captured a ship with black slaves aboard on their way to the island, so Blacks and Whites settled the island together. But the economic convenience of the arrangement (to the planters, that is) ensured the rapid growth in the number of slaves. In Barbados in 1640 there were a few hundred slaves; by 1645 the number had grown to

6,000 - still very many fewer than the Whites. But white depopulation and the enormous importation of Blacks meant that eventually nearly fifty thousand Blacks inhabited the island to twelve thousand Whites. On Jamaica, the largest and most important sugar producing island in British possesion, in 1720 or so there were 74,000 Blacks to 7,500 Whites. In North Carolina 60 per cent of the population was black by the mid-eighteenth century, and in Virginia 40 per cent.

Trading in slaves was immensely profitable. Shares in slave trading ventures were widely held - when the predecessor to the Royal Africa Company became a slave trading concern in 1663 the Royal family were shareholders. Liverpool was the most important slaving port, followed by Bristol and London. The Industrial Revolution was financed in considerable measure through the profits of the slave trade. In the words of an actor exchanging words with members of an audience who took exception to his appearing on the stage drunk: 'I have not come here to be insulted by a set of wretches, of which every brick in your infernal town is cemented with an African's blood.' (Well, he was drunk! The words are quoted by the anonymous author of Liverpool and Slavery. 1884/1969). Ships left English ports, sometimes with shanghaied crew members, with cloth, arms, spirits and trinkets manufactured in Britain, for the African coast. On the coast permanent factories were established, that is, slaving stations, which were often strongly fortified. Either through the local factor (or middleman) - or direct from local chiefs and kings - men, women and children were bought in exchange for the British manufactured goods. These slaves were either captives in the wars of the kings, or simply kidnapped for profit. Originally the trade was concentrated around the Gulf of Guinea, but spread down to Angola and thence right around the Cape of Good Hope to Tanzania, whence slaves were walked in shackles from the centre of Africa. This spread was necessary because with 100,000 people being shipped to the New World every year in the eighteenth century, the population of potential slaves in West Africa became depleted.

Living Conditions of Black Slaves

Slaving captains had a decision to make: should they pack the slaves very tight, leading to a high average daily mortality, or loosely, with lower average mortality? (Tight meant that slaves were without room to turn over or sit up.) The first was more profitable if the crossing from Africa to the West Indies or America was quick, but as it put the mortality rate among the slaves up, it diminished profits on a slow crossing. Once the ship was under way, the slaves might be given exercise (with nets around the deck to prevent the frequent attempts at suicide, and cannons turned inwards in case of rebellion), or left to die in large numbers in their own excrement in the foul atmosphere of the hold. This middle passage might take three weeks or three months. In the slave colonies, the Blacks were sold, and rum and sugar bought for shipping back to Britain. This three part voyage, Britain to Africa, Africa to America or the West Indies, and then back to Britain, was the triangular trade.

Conditions aboard ship could only be terrible. We know a good deal about the slave trade and the lives of slaves from the many surviving documents of the time, and from the autobiographies of freed slaves. Unfortunately (but understandably), no biography by a West Indian plantation slave seems to have been written. The autobiographies we have are by slaves who were skilled craftsmen, body-servants, assistants to businessmen, etc. The interesting narrative of the life of Olaudah Equiano or Gustavus Vassa, the African, written by himself, is possibly the best known (now available in an edited version as _Equiano's Travels_, 1967). The ship in which Equiano was transported does not seem to be one of the worst, but his description of the conditions aboard are pretty harrowing: 'The closeness of the place and the heat of the climate. . . produced copious perspirations, so that the air soon became unfit for respiration from a variety of loathsome smells. . ..This situation was again aggravated by the galling of the chains . . . and by the filth of the necessary tubs. . ..' (1967, pp.28-29). The 'bloody flux', or dysentry, carried off many slaves, and successful suicides others; devices for force feeding were part of the equipment of all slave traders. Captain Conneau, who engaged in the slave trade during the early part of the nineteenth century - that is, after the supposed abolition of the slave trade - records that the slaves' fingernails were cut regularly on the middle passage, 'as in their nightly disputes when contesting for an inch more of room they generally vent their passion in scratching one another, the narrowness of their quarters seldom permitting a pugilistic settlement' (1977, p.83). What could be

62

more revealing than that they were even reduced to fighting over an inch of space! It was not possible for slavers to be humane in the circumstances of the trade.

Once sold in the New World, the slaves' troubles really began. The life of the slave seems to have been harder, in general, in the British colonies, and in mainland America, than in French, Spanish, and Portuguese colonies. In these colonies, some legal protection was given to the slaves - that is, they had a theoretical right to a trial before being savagely punished - and the separation of families was technically prohibited. Branding slaves was a common practice, though it became less common with the growth of humanitarian sentiment in the late eighteenth century. Whites lived in constant terror of slave revolts, outnumbered so greatly as they were throughout the West Indies and locally in many areas of mainland America. To keep slaves servile, and to extract work from them, punishments were savage. In the mainland colonies, castration, a punishment applicable only to slaves, and sometimes to free Blacks, was practised as late as 1758. In Jamaica, one foot of a runaway slave could be severed, and mutilation of other kinds could be practiced for other misdemeanours, and this maiming could be done simply on the master's order. In some colonies the law actually required masters to whip, brand, and mutilate persistent runaways. Frederick Douglass, writing of his life as a slave in Maryland in the nineteenth century recalls; 'I have seen him tie up a lame young woman, and whip her with heavy cowskin upon her naked shoulders, causing the warm red blood to drip. . .. Master would keep this lacerated young woman tied up in this horrid situation four or five hours at a time' (1845/1973, p.57). In her diary entry for 20th June, 1803, Lady Nugent, the young wife of the Lieutenant-Governor of Jamaica, records her distress at seeing 'the pole, on which was stuck the head of the black man who was executed a few days ago' (1966, p.165). In earlier days, Blacks who rebelled were often tortured to death, by having their hands cut off and then being burnt slowly until they died.

The lash was in constant use. The work of the slaves on the plantation was arduous, boring, and unremitting. Hours of work were long, and food was often in short supply. Owners of plantations insisted on profits being kept up, and with the relative decline in sugar prices after the early

1700's, and the decline in the fertility of the land
on which sugar was constantly grown, keeping up on
profits meant more and more work. Thirteen hours a
day, for six days a week, and for seven days a week
during the 'crop' (i.e. harvest), when the cane was
being cut and boiled into sugar, was not untypical
(see Craton and Walvin, 1970), and this at labour so
arduous it was considered that white people were
actually physically incapable of it. Overseers,
black and white, simply had to drive field-slaves
with whips.

Besides the casual cruelties in the field,
more formal whippings and punishments were given on
the plantation, for crimes - such as running away -
and misdemeanours, like laziness. Thomas
Thistlewood, a Lincolnshire man, worked as a
plantation overseer in Jamaica between 1750 and
1786. An entry in his (unpublished) diary records a
punishment for the 8th August 1754; '"Today Nero
would not work, but threatened to cut his own
throat. Had him stripped, whipped, gagged, and his
hands tied behind him, that the mosquitoes and sand
flies might torment him to some purpose"' (quoted by
Ward, 1979, p.9). This punishment is by no means an
isolated occurence.

Fear of Blacks
Slave owners were terrified of allowing to their
slaves religion or education, either of which might
contain the seeds of rebellion. Frederick
Douglass recalls his master's remarks when the
master discovered his wife teaching Douglass to
read: '"Learning would spoil the best nigger in the
world. Now," said he, "if you teach that nigger to
read, there would be no keeping him. It would
forever unfit him to be a slave"' (p.36). These
remarks embody typical sentiment. In Barbados in
early times it was actually illegal to teach slaves
to read. Missionaries, who pressed for the teaching
of Christianity to slaves, were regarded with the
utmost suspicion and hatred by Whites, though they
found it hard not to permit it in the face of
determined churchmen. Some churchmen were not too
keen, since in the words of one of them, '"when a
slave is once Christened, he conceits that he ought
to be on a level with his master, in all other
respects"' (quoted by Jordan, 1968, p.185). In
1680, some white planters in Barbados said '. . .
in order to their being made Christians it will be
necessary to teach them all English which gives them
an opportunity and facility of combining together

64

against their masters and of destroying them"'
(quoted by Jordan, 1968, p.185). But a century
later it was made mandatory in Barbados to teach
Christianity to slaves.

Planters had good reason to be terrified of
the massive populations of chattels upon which their
prosperity rested. Not that full scale slave revolts
were common. Jordan, (1968), reckons there were
fewer than a dozen before 1869 on the North American
mainland; and Craton (1982), chronicling resistance
among slaves in the British West Indian islands,
finds evidence of very few large scale revolts (i.e.
involving thousands of slaves). The small number of
revolts was due to the difficulty of organising
concerted revolution and achieving anything by them.
There were, however, cases of slaves killing their
masters, and there were continual rumours, founded
and unfounded, of disaffection and plotting.
Aptheker (1970) quotes an American Congressman,
speaking of the general fear of Blacks in Virginia
in 1811: '". . . some of us were shuddering for our
safety at home. I speak from facts when I say, that
the night bell never tolls for fire in Richmond,
that the mother does not hug the infant more closely
to her bosom"' (p.23). Thistlewood records in 1751
'"Much fear of the negroes revolting in this
island"' (quoted by Ward, 1979, p.10), and in 1760
there was a large scale uprising in Jamaica. In
1733, on a Danish island all the whites were killed
after a slave uprising. Lady Nugent's diary shows
how close apprehension always was to the surface.
She records a walk, in 1805, when the French fleet
was in the vicinity of Jamaica, when she saw a black
boatman, who 'gave us a sort of fierce look, that
struck us with a terror I could not shake off. . .
most of them (i.e. Blacks) are ready for every sort
of mischief' (1966, p.227).

Runaway slaves ('maroons', or 'wild negroes')
formed communities in remote parts of large
territories like Jamaica or Guyana. Military
expeditions against them were not successful, and
they had to be recognised as free people and
negotiated with. They were a source of anxiety as
an example to slaves and a source of occasional
attempts to organize disaffection among slaves. And
the uprising in the French colony of St. Domingo
(now Haiti) in 1791, when the slaves took the
'liberty, equality, and fraternity' of the French
Revolution as applying to them, and rose up against
their masters, is well known through Wordsworth's
sonnet in praise of Toussaint L'Ouverture, the 'most

unhappy man of men·. The story of that uprising
embodies all the bitterness of successful
revolutions (which, we are told, are not made on
tea). Chaos and massacre followed, then economic
ruin, the betrayal of men and of the ideals of the
revolution, and the reintroduction of black tyranny.
The Whites throughout the West Indies and America
trembled. Lady Nugent's 'blackies', waiting at
table, listened to talk of the rebellion: '. . .
what must it lead to!' she laments, before going to
bed 'with a thousand apprehensions' (1966, p.198).

Unease and Abolition

Throughout the eighteenth century the movement for
the abolition of the slave trade gained momentum.
The story is a long one, and cannmot even be
outlined here. Granville Sharp and William
Wilberforce in England campaigned vigorously against
slavery. The Quakers had stood out against it from
early on. The growth of humanitarian sentiment in
Britain and Europe was against it. English law was
ambivalent about the legality of slavery in England,
and though the famous case of James Somerset in 1722
did not, as is often supposed, find that slavery was
illegal in England, (see, e.g., Wilson, 1970) it did
settle that slavery was frowned upon. (James
Somerset was a black slave brought over to England
when his owner returned to visit England from his
West Indian plantation. When the owner wanted to
return to the West Indies, the slave refused to
accompany him, and the owner assaulted him, severely
injuring him. When the matter came to court, it
simply found, rather ambiguously, that even a slave
could not be taken out of Britain against his will).
Humanitarian sentiment was outraged by the case of
the slave ship Zong. Equiano brought reports to
Granville Sharp, that slaves had deliberately been
thrown overboard by the Master of the Zong when he
feared the ship was running short of water. Sharp
tried unsuccessfully to get a prosecution for
murder, and the court case that eventually resulted
was a result of action by the insurance company on
whom a claim for the dead slaves had been made. The
slave trade was abolished by Britain in 1808, and
other European nations followed. Slaves were
emancipated in 1834, with compensation to their
former owners, and again other European nations
followed. The abolition of the trade was
ineffectual however; Captain Conneau (1977) reports
that, since slave ships were in constant fear of
British cruisers after abolition, conditions abroad

actually became worse. Cuba and Brazil continued importing slaves until the latter part of the nineteenth century. In 1850, the number of slaves taken from Africa was something like 50,000, though the annual average declined thereafter (see Curtin, 1970). The last slave ship to be captured was taken off Cuba, in 1874.

Perspective   Before   we   leave   the   subject altogether, it may be instructive to get the treatment and conditions of slaves in perspective. Life for Europeans in the seventeenth and eighteenth centuries was unbelievably rough by our standards, for almost everyone (except, perhaps, the minute class of people who inherited substantial wealth). Diet was poor, the incidence of infant mortality very high, hours of work were very long, and punishments savage. Medicine was primitive; right up until the Crimean War, British soldiers on active service outside Europe were far more likely to die of disease than in battle. Crew mortality aboard slave ships in the eighteenth century was as high or higher than slave mortality, though the causes of death were very different: crew members died in great numbers of tropical diseases, like yellow fever, against which there was no inoculation.
    Consider, further, the following passages, which need no introduction. The first is from a report of a debate in Parliament, in 1815.

> Mr. Bennett, for leave to bring in a bill for the purpose of limiting the infliction of corporal punishment in the army. . . said that in the 10th regiment of Hussars between 4th January, 1813, and 4th January, 1814, no fewer than 62 persons had been flogged. . . He proposed that no man ought to receive more than 100 lashes when on foreign service . . . He limited the number to 100, because he had been informed, that no man in the navy ever received more than six or seven dozen lashes. Colonel Parker . . . [said] With respect to the number of lashes, it did not so much depend on the number as the manner in which they were administered, for there had been several instances in which men who had received 400 lashes had in two hours afterwards been found drunk in the streets. (Parliamentary Intelligence, 1815: a report of a debate in the House of Commons on military military punishments, from The Times, 22nd

June, 1815 - the edition printing Wellington's
first despatches from Waterloo.)

Neither in Wellington's army, were women (who
accompanied men on active service, as
non-combatants) exempt, though corporal punishment
was less severe and was unusual in their case.
Brett-James (1961) quotes a Scottish soldier saying:
'"He [Wellington] hung fifteen men in ae day there.
. . .And d-n me if he did'na once gar the Provost
Martial flog more than a dizen of the women . . .They
gat sax and thirty lashes apiece on the bare doup
. . ."' (p.165).

I had myself formerly boys [i.e. chimney
sweeps] as young as five and a half years, but
I did not like them; they were too weak. I
was afraid they might go off. It is no light
thing having a life lost in your service. They
go off just as quietly as you might fall
asleep in your chair, by the fire there. It
is just as if you had two or three glasses of
strong drink . . . I have known eight or nine
sweeps to lose their lives by the sooty
cancer. The parts (private) which it seizes,
are entirely eaten off. There is no cure for
it once it has begun.
The use of boys for climbing
seems to harden the women more than the men.
Only lately a woman who had put her child to
a sweep followed me and threatened to pull
my hair for speaking against having climbing
boys.
Machines will do the work well and are
not dear. (Children's Employment Commission,
1st Report, 1863, pp.298-300. Quoted from
Pike, 1967, pp.142-143.)

Moreover, it should be noted that slaves were
not, as some people might imagine, kept constantly
in shackles and under armed guard. Far from it.
Most slaves came to accept their position, or were
socialized into it from birth. Their ambitions were
concentrated on rising in the ranks of the slaves,
which meant getting off the labour gangs and
becoming a house servant, craftsman, a white
overseer's mistress (if a woman), or perhaps a
soldier. It was a black foreman who wielded the cart
whip in the fields. It was black slaves who were
likely to return the runaway to the owner. Blacks
were armed to fight against Blacks. On Sundays, out

of crop time, slaves attended markets in nearby
towns, and though they were supposed to carry
passes, this regulation, together with regulations
against allowing slaves to carry firearms, was
ignored except during times of exceptional alarm
about conspiracies and rebellion. Slaves on some
islands, notably Jamaica, were given plots of land
to cultivate for their own consumption and profit.
Towards the end of the eighteenth century, the West
India Regiments were formed, officered by Whites but
manned entirely by Blacks (still slaves, initially),
some of them straight from the slave ship. Lady
Nugent records for 26th March 1804; 'see the West
India Regiment out, and all new recruits. They made
a most savage appearance, having only just arrived
from Africa; all their names were written on cards,
tied round their necks!' (1966, p.199). These West
India Regiments gave good service, and such mutinies
as occured were little local barrack room affairs
brought about by local grievances. (The history of
the West India Regiments has been written up by
Buckley, 1979). The conditions of slaves were
thus more analagous to that of Blacks in present day
South Africa, than to a chain gang. Nonetheless, we
must not allow the pendulum to swing too far the
other way. Slaves were treated abominably.
Recalcitrant slaves were whipped and whipped and
whipped again. Stable family life was often
impossible, when an owner might separate a family
whenever he wished. Englishmen in England might
work long hours in dreadful conditions, but in the
West Indies it was only Blacks who laboured, and so
the comparison with Whites - relative deprivation -
was very galling. Field labour, which occupied most
slaves, was more arduous and went on for longer
hours than almost any labourer or industrial worker
in England had to endure. Whites were hanged and
flogged, but torture had been abolished in England
in the seventeenth century. Only Blacks were
tortured to death, had their severed heads stuck on
poles, were mutilated, and (occasionally) castrated.
With the growth of humanitarian sentiment, laws
against the wanton mutilation and murder of slaves
by owners began to be passed on various West Indian
islands, but the punishment for breaking these laws
was usually only a fine, and seldom enforced. No
wonder Whites were uneasy about the lot of black
slaves, and no wonder public opinion in Britain
turned so decisively against slavery.

Why Racism?

Having gone into the history of contact between white and black people this far, can we succinctly answer the question of why racism arose? The answer looks deceptively easy at first, then difficult, then easy again.

First, why were black people enslaved? Some suggestions have been made.

(a) Because they were not Christians. This is not the whole answer, because Christians of Western Europe were constantly coming into contact with other non-Christians whom they did not enslave. Persians are referred to in Hakluyt (1972) as 'wicked infidels' (p.43), in accounts of voyages.

(b) Because they were barbarous. Again, not the whole answer, since many other peoples were described as barbarous, savage, or in other unflattering terms, but they were not enslaved. We find, for instance, references in Hakluyt to the 'barbarous Russians' (p. 63), of whom is said 'Drink is their whole desire' (p. 129). Eskimoes are unflatteringly described (p. 191 et. seq.), as are Indians ('. . . worse than Jews', p. 259), and Tartars (p. 78).

(c) Because Blacks were traditionally slaves. This suggestion helps little. It is true that the Spanish and Portuguese enslaved Blacks first, and the English and others had this model to copy. But others had been made slaves – Russians and Tartars enslaved each other (Hakluyt, pp.79, 88). And even Englishmen were enslaved and cruelly treated by Turks (p.248-249), and by the Spanish – though they did receive somewhat superior treatment, qua slaves, than the Indian and black slaves in the latter case (see 'A discourse written by one Miles Philips, Englishman, put on shore in the West Indies by Mr. John Hawkins', 1568, in Hakluyt, 1972, p.132 et. seq.).

(d) Because the Bible recommends black slavery. Again, this explanation is inadequate. The story of Ham, even if it was accepted theologically, says nothing about colour (see Gen. 9, 10), merely that Ham and his descendants shall be 'servants'. Jordan (1968) indicates a Talmudic reference to the colour of Ham's descendants, which 16th and 17th Century theologians might have known about. In fact, the story of Ham was used as an explanation of the colour of Africans more often than of slavery, initially, and it was widely regarded as an inadequate explanation in the seventeenth century (see Jordan, pp.17-20). It is fairly obvious that the Biblical references to Ham and to bondmen were used as rationalizations once slavery began, not as motives for the initiation of the enslavement of Blacks. None of the above suggested answers is sufficient. The answer to the question posed seems to be that Africans were militarily weak and divided and they were discovered by Europeans just when it was becoming profitable to sell them into slavery. That they were non-Christians, barbarous, and had a history of enslavement, were helpful preconditions, but not in themselves sufficient to explain the germination and growth of enslavement of black people. Once they were slaves, rationalization had to be found to ease the cognitive dissonance so barbaric a practice caused. So the Bible was panned, and Locke invented the 'just war', to justify slavery as 'the state of War continued,' between a lawful Conqueror and a Captive' (Locke, 1741/1960, p.302). (A 'just war' included, apparently, any means by which slaves were acquired.) The bit about Ham may well have been a widely accepted shibboleth, though it appears in writing more often in the traits of anti-slavery writers, for the purpose of their refuting it, than of pro-slavery apologists. 'Black' was a traditional metaphor for 'bad' in the English language, but the use of the word in this way before slavery has been exaggerated in extent and importance. It helped to believe that Blacks were lower in innate intelligence than Whites, and so people did not believe it; Jefferson, who drafted the American Declaration of Independence which held liberty as an 'unalienable Right', agonized over this question, and the great philosopher Hume's (see 1898, p.258) prejudices on the subject admitted of no doubt. Then, as now, there was no absence of voices pointing to the sufficiency of the environmental explanation for the difference in attainment between Blacks and Whites, and then, as now, people who wanted to believe it did believe that Blacks were innately inferior in intelligence to Whites. Sherwood and Nataupsky (1968) have shown that the age and background of psychologists is a good predictor of whether they believe that black Americans are innately inferior to Whites. Confidence men know how easy it is to convince some people of anything that abets their economic advantage! Once slavery was established, and only black people were slaves, racism was inevitable, as we can now judge with hindsight. All slaves in America and the West Indies were black, so a free black became an anomaly, and a disturbing influence since runaways' lives were made easier by the presence of legitimately free Blacks. During the seventeenth and eighteenth centuries restrictions were placed on the right of masters to free slaves, and attempts were made to expel free Blacks from some colonies. Racist laws of all kinds began to appear, excluding Blacks from militia, prohibiting black men from sleeping with white women, forbidding Blacks to vote, and so on. And where at first the term 'Christian' was used for the (white) colonists and 'heathen' for Africans, black Christians were an anomaly. In early days in America, there was some fear (among Whites) that baptism of slaves might mean automatic manumission, but legislative bodies in various colonies stated specifically that baptised slaves did not become free thereby. So gradually the purely racial criterion took over, and these sets of terms became synonymous; 'Christian', 'English', 'free', and 'white', on the one hand (each term succeeding the others as the most commonly used); and 'heathen', 'slave', 'negro', and 'black' following the same pattern.

SOUTH AFRICA

It is amazing how similar the course of the rise of racism was in South Africa, though there was little contact between South Africa and the New World.
In 1486, Bartholomew Diaz, a Portuguese, 'discovered' the Cape, and Vasco da Gama landed there in 1497. The Dutch East India Company set up a small station in 1642 to supply fresh food to ships travelling between Holland and the East Indies. In 1658, a substantial number of slaves were landed for the first time from a captured Portuguese slaver (though there were about twelve Madagascan and Bengali slaves in the colony by that time); how similar to the first slaves in New York and Barbados! More slaves from a captured slaver arrived in 1659, but most were sent on to the East Indies. In 1662, an English slaver was captured and its cargo landed at the Cape. From 1691, slaves began to be imported in increasing numbers, to supply the needs of 'free burghers' (i.e. persons not in the employ of the Dutch East India Company who, in increasing numbers, were setting up frontier farms), since labour was not available locally. Again, at first racism was absent, and Christianity

was the important distinction; baptised slaves were entitled to freedom. Black free burghers (citizens) were to be found. Concubinage with non-Whites was accepted, and so was intermarriage, to such an extent that it is calculated that about seven per cent of the ancestors of present day Afrikaners were non-white (see Jordaan, 1974). But racism began to emerge, because of the large overlap of 'black', 'heathen' and 'slaves', and of 'white', 'Christian' and 'free'. Half-white slaves could claim freedom at the age of 25 in the early days of the Cape colony - a racial criterion. Early in the eighteenth century, an unpopular 'coloured' (mixed race) governor was vilified for his black ancestry; the colonists were seizing on anything to express their dislike of his tyrannical behaviour, but it is interesting that a racist jibe emerged. The church eventually accepted that baptism did not automatically lead to manumission, since churchmen feared that no slave would ever be baptised if manumission would automatically follow.

But racism took longer to gel in South Africa than in the New World, because there was a large indigenous population of free non-white people - the Hottentots (who were decimated by smallpox in the early eighteenth century), and the black Africans, with whom Whites came into contact during the eighteenth century. Simon, and subsequently his son Adriaan, van der Stel, men of mixed race, were made Governors of the Cape in the eighteenth century, which would scarcely have been conceivable in the New World. MacCrone (1937/1957) records an incident in which Whites in the militia refused to serve under a black corporal in 1788 though they agreed to serve <u>with</u> him, provided he was not given rank), which shows that racism was not quite solidified even then. Indeed even as late as the early days of the nineteenth century, interracial marriages at the Cape were normal, though most common among white men who were of the 'inferior order'. As late as 1781, a commando (military unit) is spoken of as consisting '92 Christians and 40 Hottentots' (MacCrone, 1937/1957, p. 124), showing that the religious distinction was still important. In a famous letter about the trek away from the Cape Colony after the emancipation of the slaves, Anna Steenkamp wrote '. . . it was not so much their freedom that drove us to such lengths, as their being placed on an equal footing with Christians, contrary to the laws of God and the natural distinctions of race and religion . . .'

(MacCrone, 1937/1957, p. 126). But by this time racism was an accepted norm: that is, racism was hardening. There were complaints when a man of mixed race was appointed by a Dutch Commissioner General (an official of the Batavian Republic, of which the Cape was briefly a colony) to a parish council in 1803. Racism was driven into the bedrock of the culture by the conflict between the white tribes and the black during the nineteenth century.

Thus in South Africa the same racist course was taken as in the New World. Starting non-racially, with the main distinction being religious, racist criteria began to be adopted coincidentally with the arrival of black slaves. The same agonizing over racially mixed parentage was gone through; the same agonizing over the status of Christian Blacks. But eventually the path of convenience was chosen, and skin colour became a caste sign.

CONCLUSION

We can see now that racism, the institutionalization of prejudices against black people in Anglo-Saxon culture, had its roots in economic exploitation (if this view is redolent of stale Marxism, it did not arise from Marxist theory, but was developed independently of it). Plantations could not be run without large amounts of very cheap labour. The plantations themselves, and the trade which supplied their labour needs, were enormously profitable. There was no alternative way for the slave traders, the plantation owners, or the other Whites in the West Indies, to make anything like such a decent living; and a great many working people - sailors, people involved in the making of ships and guns and cloth etc. - depended directly on the slave trade. Many, many others depended indirectly on it - the people who built fine houses in English towns and counties for the wealthy plantation owners and slave merchants, traders and workers who needed their custom, and so on. Yet there was this nagging unease about treating other humans worse than if they were animals. Hence, in order to rationalize their economic motives, racism emerged. It is much easier to treat people badly if one can convince oneself that morally, from a religious point of view, intellectually, and physically, they deserve, are capable of, and indeed want, nothing better. Hence the myths arose, that have grown into our culture, so that even now people learn them as though they were facts: Blacks are fit only for menial tasks and harsh conditions, because they are unChristian, they are physically strong but innately stupid, they are innately libidinous and not adapted to family life, they are innately brutal and hence must be treated brutally. But most of all, they are innately too stupid to benefit from or appreciate anything better than menial work and awful living conditions. And the unease always remained, fuelled by the abolitionists, to fuel in its turn the ugly rationalizations. Thomas Jefferson, the third American President, slave owner and express believer in freedom and equality, was always torn: 'Indeed, I tremble for my country when I reflect that God is just' - one of the most famous of his remarks, reveals his apprehensions. He was a slave owner, whose livelihood depended on slavery. When he considered the question of aboliton, he found the practical difficulties of the rapid emancipation of slaves overwhelming. Yet he passionately believed in the Declaration he had played so prominent a part in drafting: 'We hold these Truths to be self-evident, - that all men are created equal; that they are endowed by their Creator with certain unalienable Rights; that among these are Life, Liberty, and the Pursuit of Happiness' (from the Declaration of Independence, 1776). How could so intelligent, idealistic, yet practical, a man reconcile slavery with his conscience? By trying to convince himself - not entirely successfully - that black people were not quite up to the standard of Whites. Blacks might have memories as good as those of Whites, but 'in reason they are much inferior' (1954, p. 140). He recognises that Blacks in America have mostly to labour very long and hard, but, he says, they have before them the improving example and conversation of their masters, which should be education enough. Indians, he says, do nice carvings, but Blacks - 'never yet could I find that a black had uttered a thought above the level of plain narration; never see even an elementary trait of painting or sculpture. . .' (p.143). Would his view have changed if he had seen the magnificent carvings and metal figures traditional in East and West Africa? No! His rationalization would simply have altered, as can be judged by his extraordinary twisting of the pitiful lives most Blacks had to lead: 'Misery is often the parent of the most affecting touches in poetry. - Among the blacks is misery enough, God knows, but no poetry' (p.140). Yet he himself recognised, if only dimly, tht he was being inconsistent and hypocritical, and, despite much agonizing in many of his writings, he could not bring himself intellectually - whatever his actions - to an overtly racist position. His conclusion is hedged: 'I advance it <u>as a suspicion only</u> (my emphasis) that the blacks are inferior to the whites in endowments both of body and mind' (p.143). And he remained fiercely against miscegenation throughout his life.

Jefferson's personal agonizing illustrates the process clearly. Negative attitudes to, and prejudices against, Blacks embedded themselves in Anglo-Saxon culture in consequence of the necessity of reconciling the forcible subservience of Blacks with unsullied consciences. Hazlitt (1970, p.465: the essay was written in 1821) quotes a black person, who pointed out that once prejudices against black people are ensconced, anything can be done to them, with the justification 'Oh, they are only black people . . .'

Chapter Four

ARE THERE RACE DIFFERENCES?

At this stage it is probably worth considering a
basic question, and popular controversy. We cannot
ignore the huge literature on this subject, which is
one of the most controversial of subjects in
psychology. Alas, the controversy is not primarily
scientific: the passions it arouses and feeds are
moral and political ones.

There is some literature on general
personality differences between races and cultures
(e.g. Iwawaki, Eysenck, and Eysenck, 1977), but it
is not great, and arouses little interest outside
the coterie of cross-cultural psychologists. More
and more interest is being shown in the heritability
of personality characteristics other than
intelligence. Even here, a large number of studies
done are between white and black Americans (see,
e.g., Dreger and Miller, 1968).

As in the field of sex differences, but to an
even greater extent here, passions are aroused by,
and attention concentrated on, the question of race
differences in <u>intelligence</u>. This is no place to
review the extensive, even vast, literature on the
subject. Instead, a few salient points will be
charted, and the conclusions pointed to. Interested
readers will find excellent volumes on the subject
by Block and Dworkin (1977) and Loehlin, Lindzey,
and Spuhler (1975), though it must be said that work
has burgeoned in the area since these two books were
written.

There has been a groundswell of controversy
about race differences in intelligence ever since
the early decades of this century. The accepted
view among most psychologists for most of this
century has been that there is no average difference
in intelligence between different racial groups, and
that the differences in IQs which have been widely

reported are due to deficiencies in the tests. This prevailing dogma is part of the liberal, humanist, ideology to which the majority of psychologists have attested. There has always been a minority of psychologists who have vocally subscribed to a different conclusion. Prominent among these have been Garrett (e.g. 1962) and Shuey (1966). The groundswell was whipped into a storm by the publication, in 1969, of an article by A.R. Jensen called Environment, heredity and intelligence. It created the storm it did partly because it was clearly written and closely reasoned, partly perhaps because it was published in a respected journal of education (rather than one of academic psychology), and partly because it was very disparaging of the compensatory education programs in the United States which were not having the clear and immediate effect the more sanguine of their supporters had hoped for.

The controversy centres around two propositions. These are:

1. Different sets of people have different levels of intelligence. These sets are defined in racial terms (and, less frequently, in terms of socio-economic class, or sex).

2. The differences in intelligence between these sets of people is largely hereditary. This usually carries the implicit assumption that hereditary differences are continuing and ineradicable.

Jensen and H.J. Eysenck, the other prominent person who appeared to lend support to these views (e.g. Eysenck, 1975), came in for much personal abuse. Both have been accused by intemperate critics of being racist, yet the writings of both belie that accusation: or, at least, that they are crude racists. For instance, Jensen says (1969b) that in his paper he merely 'proposed simply that the hypothesis of genetic racial differences in mental abilities is a reasonable one deserving of further scientific investigation' (p. 211). Further, he says that 'I would be inclined to rate Caucasians on the whole somewhat below Orientals, at least those in the United States' (p. 240), so if he is a racist, he appears not to be a white supremacist! Further, he makes it plain in a later work (1972) that he realises that whatever the 'facts' of the matter are, he endorses 'equality of rights as a moral axiom: it does not follow from any set of scientific data' (p. 329).

One of the most influential writers on the other side has been Leon J. Kamin (e.g. 1977), who asserts that 'the prudent conclusion seems clear. There are no data sufficient for us to reject the hypothesis that differences in the way in which people answer questions asked by tests are determined by their palpably different life experiences' (p. 226). Thus he asserts that, as there is no reason to think a person's genotype influences his or her intelligence, there can be no question of genetically determined differences in parameters of intelligence between different racial groups.

SOME FINDINGS ON IQ DIFFERENCES

Let us take very brief note of a few of the differences in IQ that have been reported. Only an iota of what Kamin calls (1977, p. 228) 'the dreary and at times revolting literature on race differences' will be referred to. The literature is vast and is well reviewed elsewhere (e.g. Dreger & Miller, 1968; Loehlin et al., 1975; Lynn, 1978). As Loehlin et al. carefully acknowledge, the majority of studies have been comparisons between Americans of different ethnic or racial groups, especially black and white.

According to Jensen, the mean difference in IQ scores between black and white Americans is 15 points, or one standard deviation; referring to Shuey (1966), he asserts that with 'gross socio-economic level' (1969a, p. 81) controlled, the difference reduces to 11 points. Whether one accepts Jensen's precise figures or not, it is indeed the case that a great many studies show that black Americans score, on average, lower than white Americans on IQ tests. Puerto Ricans and American Indians also score lower, typically, than Whites.

The Porteus Maze Test is considered to be less culturally loaded than most other tests of intelligence. It has been extensively applied all over the world by Porteus and others. He first administered the test to a group of aboriginal Australians (Australids) in 1929, and his research among different groups of aboriginal Australians has continued. He reports varying levels of 'maze age' or 'test age' of adult Australids, from 8.22 for a group of women tested in the 1920s, to 14.90 for a group in whose area a (white) mission station had been established for many years. Test ages for other illiterate groups vary through between 11.72 and 10.78 for various Southern African Bantu speaking peoples, 9.42 for Bengalis, 8.86 for Negritos in Luzon, to 7.56 for Bushman (Khoisan) men in the Kalahari, where Porteus went in 1934 (see Porteus, 1950, 1965).

Vernon (1969) quotes results which indicate that the median IQ based on various tests in Jamaica is between 70 and 80, though the mean on the Porteus Maze Tests suggests it is somewhat higher. Rural samples tended to score below urban. His battery of tests shows a group of Canadian Eskimos and Canadian Indians also somewhat below white norms on a variety of tests, in matrices and the Porteus Maze Test.

Lynn (1978) quotes numbers of results indicating that measured IQs of large samples in Northern Europe and New Zealand and Australia (of Whites, in the latter cases), mostly using matrices, were all about 100. Southern European samples gave lower IQs, however.

Two fairly recent articles by Lynn (1977, 1979) have drawn attention to results which may surprise some. One (1977) indicates that extensive testing with the WPSI and the WISC show that Japanese (in Japan) have a mean IQ 'significantly higher than North American Caucasians by somewhere between approximately three and ten IQ points' (p. 70). According to Lynn, the mean of 106.6 on three Wechsler standardizations is the highest ever recorded for a national population. Surveys of IQ tests and scores on them show that a) intelligence levels in both Japan and in the USA are increasing, and have been doing so for many decades, and b) the disparity between Japanese and American IQs is nonetheless continually growing. (Lynn, 1982; Flynn, 1984b).

Lynn's other article (1979) shows that very extensive testing in the United Kingdom and Ireland has shown that different regions have significantly different mean IQs. In London and South-East England, the mean IQ is 102.1, in Yorkshire 101.1, whereas in Scotland, Wales and Ireland, the mean is below 100. In another paper he shows that similar regional differences exist in France (Lynn, 1980). Critics (e.g. Kirby, 1980) point out that there is enormous variation within each region, but the point that there are regional mean differences remains. Lynn suggests that these differences are at least partly due to migration from the regions to London over the past two hundred years or more, the high road taken by Johnson and Boswell from their different regions, being selective for intelligence, though we need not accept this explanation.

Sharma (1971) investigated the scores on intelligence tests of groups of Indian children in India, Indian children who had lived more than five years in Hertfordshire, (whom he terms 'early arrivals' - from India, that is), Indian children who had lived from one to two-and-a-half years in Hertfordshire ('recent arrivals'), and a group of native English children, matched as far as possible for social factors. He found that on the WISC all groups of Indian children had mean scores significantly below the English children (the mean for the 'recent arrivals' was 87.96 on the WISC while that of the English group was 107.88). On Raven's matrices, the 'early arrivals' mean was not significantly different from the English sample's mean, but the 'early arrivals' scored significantly below the 'recent arrivals' (their mean was 86.35).

It should be noted that the differences in IQ being talked about are really quite substantial. If we take IQs of 130 and above as being 'high' and of 70 and below as being 'low', then with a mean of 100 and S.D. of 15, given a normal distribution, the percentage of people with high IQs is the same as with low, namely 2.275 per cent. With a mean of 106, the percentage of high IQs about doubles to 5.48 per cent, and the percentage with low IQs drops to 0.8. With a mean of 89, the percentage of high IQs is only 0.3 per cent, while the percentage with low is 10.565 per cent.

Whence the IQ Differences?

It is plain from the very selective rehearsal of the evidence in the section above, that there are fairly large differences in IQ between different groups; that, excepting the Japanese, white people in northern Europe, the United States, and the 'old' British Commonwealth tend to score highest on IQ tests; and that, broadly speaking, the more different a group is from being white, and of north-west European culture, the lower is its mean IQ. A few comments are in order at this stage.

1. Though it is not obvious from the above, the vast majority of comparisons have been between black and white Americans. Inferences about 'race differences' in general are often made largely on the basis of comparing these groups: careful writers, like Loehlin et al. (1975) explicitly acknowledge this limitation. It is important, partly because it has been selected, and partly because black and white Americans are more similar

in culture than, say, white Americans and Bushmen are.

2. Cultural similarity is important, because intelligence tests, which operationally define IQ, are inevitably culture bound. Some tests and subtests are grossly and obviously so: for example, information and vocabulary items. Some are less obviously so: items involving pictures may involve difficulties in interpretation by members of simple societies which sophisticated testers scarcely realize: difficulties involving pictorial depth perception, for example, are now well researched (Miller, 1973), and must affect (to an unknown degree) responses to pictorial items. And even a test like the matrices or the Porteus Maze Test must be assisted by the easy familiarity with books, patterns and pencils, and tests, that urban Europeans and Americans have and most other people do not. Sharma's (1971) work, which shows that scores on the matrices increase with the length of stay of immigrant children in Britain, shows that culture affects scores on the matrices.

3. The lack of cultural similarity may well reflect itself rather subtly. From an early age, Americans and Europeans take tests on which speed and accuracy must be balanced, and indeed much classroom learning is based on tasks which have these characteristics, though not all these activities are formally tests. Other peoples do not: hence they do not approach the IQ tests with which they are presented with anything like the orientation of Whites. Vernon (1969) comments that lack of motivation seemed to characterize his rural Jamaican samples. Porteus, who writes of the Bushmen and Aboriginal Australians with great affection, comments (1965) that they appeared highly motivated and that they understood the task well: but were they really doing just what a White, practiced in tests and driven by evaluation apprehension, would want to do in a test?

4. It is plain that environment does affect intelligence test scores quite dramatically, even when gross and obvious environmental effects, - such as those between developed, technological, complex, societies, and those between underdeveloped, non-technological, and simple, societies - seem to be eliminated. The difference between IQs of black Americans in the North and the South of the United States - the mean has usually been found to be higher in the better environment of the North - is frequently referred to (e.g. Anastasi, 1958).

Recently, adoption and other studies have pointed to the same conclusion. Claeys (1973) found that the IQs of Flemish children in Belgium, who had been adopted into 'good' (i.e. caring, stimulating, and relatively wealthy) family homes, scored about 10 points above the mean expected on the basis of their biological parents' characteristics. Scarr and Weinberg (1976) investigated children adopted into families in Minnesota. They found that (a) children adopted in the first year of their lives scored significantly higher on IQ tests than children adopted later, and (b) the mean IQ of black children adopted by white families was 106, well above the local 'black' average of 90 and significantly above the 'white' mean IQ. (Nonetheless, the mean IQ of the adopted children was below the mean of their adoptive parents' natural children, the difference being about 6 points.) The increment in IQ of the adopted children must have been due to their environments: it is far greater than can be attributed to any selection bias in the sample (it has been suggested that only adoptive parents with bright adopted children would allow themselves to be studied), or to the fact that severely mentally handicapped children are not put out for adoption. Another strand of evidence is provided by Wilson (1983), in his report on the longitudinal study of nearly 500 pairs of twins (not adopted, note) in Kentucky. Using multiple regression techniques it was found that, while the most powerful predictors of children's IQs was their parents' education and social class, nonetheless measures of how much the home was 'geared' to fostering development, and how pleasant the atmosphere at home was, added significantly to the prediction of IQ. Yet another strand of evidence is provided by Sharma (1971), whose study showed that the scores of Indian children (immigrants) in Hertfordshire (England) on the WISC increased by a mean of ten points (a large and very significant difference) between the first test 20 months (on average) after arrival, and their second, 42 months after arrival: not a score that can be explained simply by familiarity with the test. As was said above, Indian children who had been in England over five years scored higher on both the WISC and the Matrices than similar children who had been in England less than two-and-a-half years. And the importance of culture is shown by the fact that a notable part of the difference between the WISC IQs of the early and recent arrivals, and between the first and second tests of the recent arrivals, is accounted for by bonus points awarded for speed. In other words, children going to school in England learn to work at speed, and judiciously to compromise accuracy with rapidity.

5. However, if tests are culture bound, it should be possible to devise a test on which non-Whites of a particular culture would score high, and white Europeans and Americans low. Few attempts have been made to do so, and none have been successful. Dubois (1939) devised what appears to be a psychometrically sound 'Draw-a-Horse' test for Pueblo Indian children on analogy with Goodenough's 'Draw-a-Man' test, and it is apparently the case that white American children score much lower than Pueblo Indian children on it, (Norman, 1963): published details are scant. A test much quoted recently is William's tweely and meaninglessly named Black Intelligence Test for Cultural Homogeneity or 'BITCH'. The test does not appear to be publicly available. However, Matarazzo and Wiens (1977) find no correlation at all between BITCH and any Wechsler measures with samples of black and white police applicants in Oregon, and in the absence of other validating data the validity of the BITCH as a test of intelligence is too dubious to allow of its use as such.

6. It is hard to accept the reported IQs of people in simple societies, just on common-sense grounds. The Porteus Maze Test gives adult male Bushmen a mean IQ of below 60. Assuming IQ to be symmetrically distributed, this mean implies that more than half male Bushmen are morons, imbeciles, and idiots (to use somewhat outdated terms). Anyone who has seen examples of Bushman art, and anyone who will think of the difficulties of living in a vast area which has very little surface water and where game is very sparse, must find that implausible.

7. No-one, least of all Jensen, who goes out of his way to emphasise these points for groups in the US, denies that differences between racial-ethnic groups account for a smaller proportion of the total variance in IQ scores than differences within these groups, and that all levels of IQ are represented in all racial-ethnic groups. Racial-ethnic group is not a good predictor of IQ.

ARE RACE DIFFERENCES IN IQ HEREDITARY?

The highly complex and technical question of heritability of IQ can only briefly be explicated here, and commented on in the next section. Plainly, before one can say that real differences in IQ are hereditary, one must first show not only (a) that there are race differences in IQ, but also (b) that differences in IQ in general are affected by heredity.

There are several indices of heritability. The one put forward by Jensen (see 1972, p. 297-8) depends on the simple proposition that the correlation between characteristics of sets of people, A and B, can be divided into two additive parts:

$$r_{AB} = r_{gAB}h^2 + r_{eAB}(1-h^2)$$

where

r_{AB} is the correlation between the two sets of people, A and B. Normally this will be the intra-class correlation in the circumstances dealt with here.

r_g is the genetic correlation between the sets A and B.

r_e is the correlation between the environments of A and B.

h^2 is the heritability, and $\{(h^2 + \text{environmental influences}) = 1\}$ Thus $\{\text{environmental influences} = (1 - h^2)\}$

Note that h^2 is what is sometimes termed broad heritability: it includes genetic effects due to genetic dominance and epistasis. This h^2_B is contrasted to h^2_N (narrow heritability), which does not include effects due to dominance and epistasis, and which is more appropriate if one wishes to specify how much of the characteristic is likely to be passed on from parents to children. Broad heritability is an estimate of the total amount of variance in scores which is attributable to genetic factors of any kind.

The formula above allows us to derive a number of other formulae for estimating h^2. In general, for instance, we can estimate h^2

given the correlations between any two groups of paired persons (AB and CD), provided that estimates of genetic and environmental correlations are available. This estimate is derived thus:

$$r_{AB} = r_{gAB}h^2 + r_{eAB}(1-h^2)$$

and

$$r_{CD} = r_{gCD}h^2 + r_{eCD}(1-h^2)$$

assuming $r_{gAB} > r_{gCD}$ (or we will get a negative result)

$$r_{AB} - r_{CD} = r_{gAB}h^2 + r_{eAB}(1-h^2)$$
$$- r_{gCD}h^2 - r_{eCD}(1-h^2)$$

$$r_{AB} - r_{CD} = h^2(r_{gAB} - r_{gCD})$$
$$+ (1-h^2)(r_{eAB} - r_{eCD})$$

hence

$$h^2 = \frac{r_{AB} - r_{CD} - (1-h^2)(r_{eAB} - r_{eCD})}{r_{gAB} - r_{gCD}}$$

Here one would have observed correlations, r_{AB} and r_{CD} between, say, pairs of natural siblings and pairs of children adopted into the same family, and one would make various assumptions allowing one to estimate the other unknowns. The critical importance of these assumptions for the estimate of h^2 is obvious.

Where monozygotic twins are brought up apart in different families, that is, where A and B are sets of identical twins brought up apart, the original formula

$$r_{AB} = r_{gAB}h^2 + r_{eAB}(1-h^2)$$

applies <u>provided two critical assumptions are made.</u> These assumptions are (a) that the genetic correlation between monozygotic twins is perfect — i.e. in this case, $r_{gAB} = 1$, and (b) the correlation between environments is zero, i.e. in this case, $r_{eAB} = 0$. Then

$$r_{AB} = 1h^2 + 0(1-h^2) = h^2$$

Where we have set of monozygotic and dizygotic twins, each set brought up together, three assumptions make it possible to estimate h^2. If we refer to monozygotic twins as MZ and dizygotic twins as DZ, then the assumptions are

(a) $r_{gMZ} = 1$;

(b) $r_{eMZ} = r_{eDZ} = 1$;

(c) that we can put a number to r_{gDZ}.

Hence

$$r_{MZ} - r_{DZ} = (1)h^2 + 1(1-h^2) - r_{gDZ}(h^2) \\ - 1(1-h^2)$$

$$r_{MZ} - r_{DZ} = h^2 - r_{gDZ}h^2$$

$$r_{MZ} - r_{DZ} = h^2(1-r_{gDZ})$$

$$h^2 = \frac{r_{MZ} - r_{DZ}}{1 - r_{gDZ}}$$

Again, the critical importance of these assumptions is obvious.

There are a great number of heritability estimates around, based on various methods. The most direct method of estimating heritability, as appears from the above, is to find pairs of monozygotic twins whose environments can plausibly be said to be uncorrelated: in practice, twins who were separated early in life and brought up in different homes. There appear to have been only four studies of the intelligence of such twins, of which the largest was done by Sir Cyril Burt, who claimed to have found 53 such pairs. In all, 122 such pairs have been reported by the four studies, and the intraclass correlation for all 122 pairs was calculated by Jensen (1972, p. 315) at +0.82. Corrected for attenuation this figure rises to +0.86, and hence this figure can be taken as an estimate of h^2. It now appears that 'beyond reasonable doubt, Burt was guilty of deception', and in particular, that 'he produced spurious data on MZ twins' (Hearnshaw, 1979, p. 259); Hearnshaw's book is a very careful and balanced biography. Jensen himself (1974) seems to have abandoned reliance on Burt's figures. However, the correlations for the 79 pairs of separated monozygotic twins reported by the three other studies do not differ markedly from Burt's, and the conclusion regarding h^2 is scarcely affected.

Jensen also makes a number of estimates of for intelligence from the correlations of the IQs of monozygotic and dizygotic twins (1972, p. 300), based on a number of reported studies. A common estimate of h^2 (the genetic correlation between dizygotic twins) is 0.55. On that assumption, estimates of h^2 from these studies vary from 0.47 to 0.91.

Last, Munsinger (1978) presents weighted mean correlations based on an exhaustive review of studies done comparing the correlations between the IQs of adoptive parents and their adoptive children brought up in their families (AP-AC), biological parents and their children who were brought up by adopting parents (BP-AC), and biological parents and their own children brought up by themselves (BP-BC). These correlations, averaged over all the studies, are +0.14 (AP-AC), +0.43 (BP-AC) and +0.48 (BP-BC). All are significant. The last two are not significantly different from each other, and the BP-AC correlation of +0.43 was significantly higher than the AP-AC correlation of +0.14. Munsinger concludes that hereditary factors are shown to play an important part in measured intelligence. After examining a number of recent adoption studies, Scarr and Carter-Saltzman (1982, p. 862) conclude that they would support any estimate of between 0.4 and 0.7, but not one as high as 0.8.

Some Comments on Heritability Indices

A number of points about heritability indices need to be emphasised. These comments will be made in numbered form, followed by some comments on the idea of heritability. These points need emphasising, because heritability indices, heritability, and genetic differences are so often misunderstood.

1. Heritability indices. Several indices of
heritability have been proposed, and these are not
perfectly related, even when based on the same data
(see, e.g. Jensen, 1972, p. 297). Lies, damned lies
and statistics! A warning against deifying a
particular number.

2. Assumption of heritability. Jensen's h^2,
the index referred to here, is based on the
assumption (see above) that there is a
heritability component in the correlation (of
intelligence scores here) between relatives. This
assumption may be very reasonable, based on the
pattern of correlations between relatives and our
knowledge of genetic factors: but it is an
assumption, and there may be other ways of
conceiving the relationships between the figures
involved.

3. The limitations of correlation. h^2 is
based on a measure of correlation, and suffers from
the limitations and shortcomings that correlations
have. How carefully a correlation must be used, and
how sharply must one eye be constantly focussed on
its limitations and the dangers of generalizing on
the basis of a correlation! Correlation
coefficients may be looked on as a measure of the
variance that is common to two measures. Now, if
every-one in a population had the same genes (not
possible in practice, of course) but different
environments, there would be no variance in genetic
measures, hence h^2 would be zero. This
extreme and hypothetical case illustrates the
important point: h^2 is not perfectly
isomorphic to 'genetic basis'. Kamin (1975) makes
use of this point to suggest that since adoptive
parents and their children are in general selected,
and their IQs presumably have a smaller variance
(within adoptive parents and within their biological
children) than a randomly selected group of parents
and children would have, you would expect that
correlations involving these scores to be depressed.
(It seems unlikely, though, given the magnitude of
the differences between the correlations averaged
over many studies, that restrictions of variance
could account for the whole of the differences.)

4. <u>Heritability estimates apply to populations</u>.
h^2 and other indices are characteristics of
<u>populations</u> not of <u>individuals</u>. To say of
h^2, 'h^2 = .8', does not imply that '80
per cent of Joe Bloggs's intelligence was
inherited'. At most, h^2 can provide us with a
probability statement about Joe Bloggs.

5. <u>Heritability indices are STATISTICS</u>. A
heritability index is a <u>statistic</u>. A
statistic is a measure relating to a sample. It is
worked out on sample measurements, and is
generalizable to the population of which the sample
is a subset. There is no statistical basis for
generalizing heritability from one population to
another – say white Americans to black Americans, or
white Britons to aboriginal Australians. On the
other hand, one may suppose, on other grounds, that
heritabilities are not likely to differ much between
human groups.

6. <u>Assumptions underlying h^2</u>. The
assumptions in deriving and applying a formula like
that for h^2 need to be carefully examined and
noted, because they affect the conclusions one can
draw from it. Some of these will be detailed.
        (i) Jensen (1972, p. 229) acknowledges that
h^2 is affected by any variance due to
interaction between environment and genotype: that
is, some genotypes might respond particularly well
or badly to certain types of environment. This
source of variance could be important: it is
conceivable, for example, that extraverts more
nearly reach their full potential IQ in environments
where there is personal stimulation and severe
discipline and bustle, but that the intelligence of
introverts is best served by bookish environments
and an absence of punitive circumstances. Jinks and
Fulker (1970) estimate that only 8% of the total
variance can be accounted for by
genotype-environment interaction, (they also
indicate, by the way, that low IQs are more affected
by environments than high), but their method of
analysis (based on the correlations between the
means and differences of monozygotic twins brought
up together and apart) would only bring out
interactions of a particularly simple type. The
kind of interaction speculated on above would not be

90

revealed.

(ii) As well as genotype-environment interaction, there is the question of genotype-environment correlation. For example, if, in a hypothetical society, all children with red hair were locked in dark rooms until adulthood, then the genes bringing about red hair would be predictive of very low IQs for their bearers in that society. h^2 would be inflated since monozygotic twins separated at birth would have similar IQs, if they had red hair. But the correlation would be 'caused' by a genotype-environment correlation. This example is not so fanciful: in South Africa the type of environment you have is very predictable on the basis of your genetically determined skin colour. And it seems likely, intuitively, that in ordinary circumstances genotypically intelligent people enrich their personal environments (by, for example, seeking out books, computers, etc.), and these two factors can't really be separated.

(iii) In deriving the assertion that h^2 can be estimated as equal to the correlation between the IQs of monozygotic twins brought up apart, it was assumed that the true correlation between the environments of each set of twins was zero. This assumption is unlikely to be valid. In practice, twins are not separated and placed in different homes chosen randomly. They are likely to end up in homes which are fairly similar to one another, with regards to social class, the intelligence of the parent-surrogates, etc. Juel-Nielsen (1965), who conducted one of the studies on separated monozygotic twins, in Denmark, comments: 'As all the twins were brought up in Denmark, the geographical distance between the childhood homes was on the whole small, and owing to the relatively uniform social, educational, and cultural structure of the country, great diversities of environment are not to be expected' (p. 97). In countries such as Britain and the USA, separated twins are likely to live either with relatives, or to be placed in homes carefully selected by adoption agencies, etc. It seems likely, a priori, that there will be a positive correlation between the environments of separated twins.

(iv) When estimating h^2 from comparisons of monozygotic and dizygotic twins' IQ scores, it is necessary to assign a number to r_{gDZ}, the genetic correlation between dizygotic twins. This number is a guesstimate. It is usually set at 0.55, but changing it to 0.60 renders several of Jensen's estimates of h^2, based on different IQ tests with different samples, ridiculous by raising h^2 above 1.00 (see Jensen, 1972, p. 300).

Conclusion on heritability indices. It must be plain from the above that the limitations and qualifications of heritability indices need an educated appreciation if they are to be referred to. It is too easy to put number, say, 0.8, to h^2, and then allow a lot of uncertain inferences from that spuriously precise statistic.

Some Comments on Heritability
Turning now to the concept of heritability, a number of points need emphasising. To some degree the statistics and the concept are probably isomorphic, and hence some comments that have been made regarding h^2 apply also to heritability.

1. Heritability is relative. Heritability depends on the relative contribution of heredity and environment. Hence when the contribution of the environment changes, heritability changes. If we consider, say, Western Europe and North Africa, then the heritability of tuberculosis is probably low, because a large proportion of the difference between rates of TB is accountable for by environmental differences: that is, the environment in North Africa is conducive to tuberculosis (because the people are poor), whereas the environment is not conducive to tuberculosis in Western Europe (because people are relatively wealthy and medical services are good). Within Europe, or within Algeria (say), the heritability of TB is probably higher, since the environment of each region is relatively more uniform with regard to the number of TB bacilli to which a person is likely to be exposed (low in the case of Europe and higher in the case of Algeria). The implication for IQ is that even if the heritability of IQ is high in Western culture now, some modification in, say, education methods, may increase the relative contribution of environmental factors or the environment-genotype interaction contribution, in future, and thus reduce the measured degree of heritability.

2. 'Genetic' contribution may differ with age. It is only now coming to be realized that the contribution of genetic factors to intelligence may not be uniform for all ages. Scarr and Weinberg (1979) found that for families with both natural children and children who were adopted when less than one year old, the IQ correlations between natural sibs was 0.37 (N = 75), and between adopted and natural sibs it was 0.30 (N = 134), and between adopted and adopted sibs it was 0.49 (N=21). These correlations are, it will be noted, remarkably high. Correlations with parents in the case of natural children in the families were of the order of about 0.49, and with adoptive parents (the same people) in the case of the adopted children, the correlations were of the order of 0.37. These investigations were carried out with young children. The same investigators (Scarr & Weinberg, 1978) later looked at children and their adoptive and natural parents: the mean age of the children in this later study was now 18.5 years. Here the pattern was completely different. While the biologically adopted sibs still had significantly correlated IQ scores (0.35, N = 120 families), the unrelated sibs had IQ scores which were totally uncorrelated (-.03, N=104 families). The difference is significant. A study of unrelated sibs reared together in Denmark (Teasdale & Owen, 1984), which also looked at IQs assessed when the sibs were young adults, also found their IQs to be uncorrelated (the correlation was 0.02, N = 24 pairs). Similarly, Scarr and Weinberg found correlations with the midparent (i.e. the mean of the two parents or adoptive parents) of 0.52 in the case of natural children and of 0.14 in the case of adopted children. This difference, again, is significant. These are not isolated results (see Scarr & Carter-Saltzman, 1982). It appears, then, that the caretakers and home environment assert themselves over the genetic factors when children are young, but as children grow up, their genes as it were take over control of IQ more and more. Further evidence comes from the massive longitudinal twin study conducted in Louisville, in Kentucky (Wilson, 1983). Over more than 25 years, 494 pairs of twins and their families (brought up together) have been studied longitudinally. What has been found is that intellectual development seems actually to occur in spurts, and that these spurts tended to occur more nearly at the same time in pairs of monozygotic twins than in pairs of

dizygotic twins, and in pairs of dizygotic twins than in ordinary siblings: the spurts seem to be genetically programmed. Further, looking at the correlation at various ages between 3 months and 15 years, what emerges is that the correlation between monozygotic twins and dizygotic twins starts off very similar, but while the IQs of monozygotic twins becomes increasingly similar with age, (0.88 at 15 years), the IQs of dizygotic twins become progressively less and less similar, until by the age of 15, correlations between the IQs of pairs of dizygotic twins is about the same as correlations between twins and their ordinary siblings (about 0.5). These differences are far too great to be explained by the differences between environment for monoygotic and dizygotic pairs of twins. Again, the conclusion is that genetic factors assert themselves increasingly as children grow older. Hence the heritability of IQ appears to increase with age.

3. **'Heritable' is not the same as 'innate'**. To emphasise one strand of what has just been said, even if heritability is high, that does not imply that we may as well accept that differences in IQ are innate, and that there is nothing that can be done. If it is desired to change IQs, saying the heritability is high does not imply that environmental intervention is foredoomed. It implies nothing at all about environmental intervention: compensatory education may or may not work, but that is not directly to do with the heritability of IQ.

4. **'Genetic' does not mean 'unalterable'**. Intelligence may be affected directly by genetically controlled constitutional factors. Even so, it may prove easy to modify. There may be some simple dietary trace element, for example, which acts in some genotypes to modify intelligence. And if this were so, it would obviously be simple to modify intelligence by controlling diet. Analagously, it is known that cretinism - a condition resulting in low intelligence - is brought about by a hypoactive thyroid, and the administration of the appropriate medication early in life provides a remedy.

5. **There may be strong environment-genotype interactions**. This last point gives force to the

speculaton that different environments may have profoundly different effects on different genotypes. Heredity and environment may not be so separate after all!

6. There may be strong genotype-environment correlations. Interest in the covariation between genotype and environment is growing as the probable importance of this covariation comes to be recognised. In our society bright parents pass on 'bright' genes to their chidren, and less bright parents less 'bright' genes: but of course the environment provided by the former is likely to be more conducive to the cultivation of intelligence: that is, one would expect to find books, a bias towards informative television programs, conversation, etc. more in that environment. This is a passive genotype-environment correlation. Scarr and McCartney (1983) suggest we distinguish two other types of genotype-environment correlation that may be important for intellectul development. One of the other types is an evocative kind: that is, bright children may act in such a way - by showing an interest in intellectual things, for example - as to render it more likely that their parents, etc. will put books, computers, etc. their way. The third type is the active kind: bright children may seek out bright friends, go to the library in their spare time, save pocket money for a home computer, and so on. It was noted above that Scarr and Weinberg (1978) have found that by late adolescence, the similarity in intelligence between adopted children and their unadopted sibs is zero, and that between adopted children and their adoptive parents is much lower than between natural children and their parents. While the children are young, the resemblances are much more striking. These facts are consistent with the supposition that as children grow older, their genotypes assert themselves, and they both evoke different responses from other people in their environment, and actively seek out environments which suit them. That is, they in effect create a genotype-environment correlation. Heredity and environment may not be so separate after all!

7. Genes may affect intelligence only indirectly. Point 3 lends force also to the idea that heritability may operate indirectly: that is, a

genotype might predict low or high intelligence, but this prediction might be modified by different environmental circumstances. The example of South Africa has already been cited; here the genes bringing about dark skin and tightly curled hair also predict an impoverished, in a material sense, environment. Under other political circumstances, genes might not predict IQ, or at least not as strongly.

8. **Within groups variance is not the same as between groups variance.** Even if it is shown that differences within groups are heritable, differences between groups might be less so or not at all. The TB example above is relevant. Of course, if within groups differences are heritable, it makes it intuitively more feasible to suppose that between groups differences are too. But it is an _inference_, not a _proof_.

CONCLUSIONS: ARE THERE RACIAL-ETHNIC DIFFERENCES? SO WHAT?

We have come a long way around to see the conclusion that lay at our feet. Enough was said about IQ tests to make it doubtful that they are sufficiently adequate measures of intelligence, when applied cross-culturally, for us to accept results bearing a number attached to 'IQ' as very meaningful. (Tests of other psychological differences either make no pretence of cross-cultural validity or are of little interest in discussions of this kind.) The difficulties lie partly in the practical difficulties in the technology of testing, and partly in the very nature of the concept of intelligence and how it is to be conceived of and defined. Differences in IQ between white Anglo-Saxons and Bushmen, and between white Anglo-Saxons and Japanese, are as likely to reflect various artifacts and cultural differences as differences in innate intelligence. When IQ tests are given to black Americans these problems are minimized, though not by any means extinguished, and this raises the question of race: plainly black Americans have a very different gene pool from aboriginal Australians, Bushmen, and so on, and even black West Africans and (the very different) black South Africans. White Europeans sometimes associate these groups, and even Asians, as all being 'black':

but any conclusions drawn about the genetic factors among black Americans cannot be generalized to other 'black' groups. Race is not a precise concept, and there is no clear agreement as to how many races mankind can be divided into and where they begin and end. Enough has also been said about heritability and its associated indices to make us cautious about drawing omnibus conclusions about genetic bases for intelligence on the evidence that we have.

So what may we conclude about IQ differences? To the present author the conclusion that many others have reached about the heritability of IQ appears correct. That is, that, <u>provided we bear in mind what we mean</u>, the evidence seems strongly to support the view that IQ differences are heritable to a degree: whether we are prepared to put a figure of .8 on it is another matter. (We must also bear in mind that environment affects intelligence level as well: a 'good' environment raises intelligence markedly.) On the other hand, there is no convincing evidence of race or ethnic differences of innate intelligence; indeed, our tests are inadequate to find such a difference if it does exist. We must therefore endorse the conclusion of the UNESCO statement of 1952, signed by a large number of geneticists, anthropologists, medical men, zoologists, etc. (see Montagu, 1963, p. 182): 'Available scientific knowledge provides no basis for believing that the groups of mankind differ in their innate capacity for intellectual and emotional development'. That is, we must remain agnostic on the subject. Any other conclusion is a prejudice.

A detailed discussion of the issue was forced on us by the publicity the issue has received and is receiving, and by its emotive nature. Why is intelligence so emotive an issue? So emotive is it that I suspect that third world governments would devote many more resources to, say, nutrition, if it were shown that it raised the intelligence of their populations, than if it simply raised physical health and well-being, and prevented a number of deaths. Intelligence is important in the modern world: it does correlate — to an extent which can be exaggerated - with the attaining of good things, like money and pleasant surroundings, in modern industrial societies. (So does amount of education, which is affected much more than IQ is by environmental factors.) Now, whether the IQ-good things correlation will rise or fall in future is unknown. Flynn (1984) shows that the correlation does not seem to have altered very much over the last fifty years. It may be that as the electronic age makes work more complicated, the intelligent will be even more advantaged. It may be that the opportunities for people with little skill will become minimal as computer controlled robots take over their jobs, while opportunites for talented and educated people, who design computers and robots, will become more and more advantageous. The unintelligent could end up on the scrap heap. Or, it may be that in the eletronic age computer controlled robots will bring plenty for all in terms of material goods and in terms of opportunities to self-actualize. In that case, IQ will be of less importance in the future than it is now, in determining how much of the good things of life a person gets. Whether that occurs or not, the distribution of the good things depends on moral and political processes, and there is every hope (or fear, if one is of the opposite persuasion) that rewards will be more equally shared in future than they have been in the past.

So whence the heat? Jensen has often been accused of being a racist, but, as has been said, his writings overtly belie this accusation. He says again and again that even he is not absolutely convinced of race differences in intelligence (though his tone makes it clear where his feelings lead him), that differences in intelligence do not have anything to do with the rights of people, and that all racial-ethnic groups have all levels of intelligence in them. But he did set out to be provocative in his original paper (as he agrees, see 1969b, p. 209); and the tone of his writing, and the apparent but spurious accuracy of his figure for h^2, have given comfort to persons with racial prejudices. Jensen does not say, 'Blacks are stupid, so let us stamp on them', but some people may have thought this inference justified from his work. Overtly racist organizations have certainly made use of the publicised work of Professor Jensen and others of similar views. For example, Martin Webster, an official of the overtly racist British organization the National Front, wrote in 1973 ' "The most important factor in the build-up of self confidence among 'racists' and the collapse of morale among muti-racialists was the publication in 1969 by Professor Arthur Jensen in the Harvard Educational Review" ' (quoted by Walker, 1978, p. 169). Discussion of heritability and associated research is fine in universities. To publicise tentative and qualified conclusions to a world which will oversimplify them can be mischievous. The essential oil of science is calm and rational consideration of substantive issues. Behaviour appropriate to politicians and advertisers of commercial gimmicks demeans scientific debate.

Chapter Five

PSYCHOLOGICAL EXPLANATIONS OF ETHNIC PREJUDICES:
THE F SCALE

I have tried to show how prejudice
against non-white people became part of Western
culture. No doubt ethnic prejudices in other
cultures are equally susceptible to historical
illumination, as is the wide-spread anti-Semitism in
Western cultures. On a personal level most
prejudice is explicable as ordinary learning,
acquired in the course of socialization in the
ordinary way, much as religious dogmas and other
supposed facts are acquired; how many of us can
present evidence for such simple beliefs as that
deficiency of vitamins in the diet is detrimental to
health, or that brushing our teeth promotes dental
health? However, since the strength of people's
prejudices differ in different people socialized in
the same culture, this cultural/historical
explanation is clearly insufficient; so is any
explanation of ethnic prejudice in terms of economic
advantage of members of one group. And these kinds
of explanations have nothing to say about prejudices
other than those concerning ethnic groups. A
psychological explanation must be more molecular in
nature.
One psychological explanation is in terms of
displaced aggression and the frustration-aggression
hypothesis. The frustration-aggression hypothesis
has dropped from prominence in psychology: it
postulated that frustration resulted in aggression,
(and that aggression always resulted from
frustration, even though that part is not relevant
here). A piece of evidence often quoted in its
support is Hovland and Sear's (1940) analysis of
lynchings in the Southern states of the USA, between
1882 and 1930. They plotted a regression line for
the price of cotton - the most important economic
factor in the rural areas - against time. Naturally,

with inflation, the price increased steadily; they found that when the price increased to a greater extent than predicted by the regression equation, then the number of lynchings decreased, but when the price of cotton was lower than predicted, the number of lynchings went up. Mintz (1946) reanalysed the data and reduced the correlation between the economic index and the number of lynchings per year, but the relation was still significant. If this evidence is to be accepted as supporting the theory, then it must be accepted that economic stagnation is tantamount to frustration, and that lynching is a good index of aggressive feelings. The first of these two assumptions is very dubious. Even if it were not so, the theory is very incomplete, even as a theory of ethnic attitudes.

The frustration-aggression theory is sometimes said to involve scapegoating. But that use of the term distorts the original metaphorical use of the 'scapegoat'. The scapegoat was a goat chosen by lot to bear the sins and transgressions of the Children of Israel, which were ritually placed on its head, and the animal was subsequently driven into uninhabited wilderness, taking the people's iniquities with it (Leviticus 16, 21 and 22). There is no suggestion that it was to be harmed (other than by being released). Hence the metaphor fits the theory underlying The Authoritarian Personality better: one aspect of that theory, to which we now turn, is that prejudiced people project their own shortcomings on to others, who then bear the prejudiced person's sins; these persons are now the scapegoat, whom the prejudiced person consciously would like to drive away.

In this section we will be dealing principally with ethnic prejudice, bearing in mind that prejudice against members of a group, the maintenance of a high social distance between the person and members of an ethnic outgroup, holding a negative attitude to members of the ethnic outgroup, are assumed to be functionally equivalent. Evidence for this assertion was presented above.

Germany After World War II

McGranahan (1946) and McGranahan & Janowitz (1946) studied the attitudes and personalities of German youths immediately after the Second World War and compared them to the attitudes and personalities of American youths and a group of Germam girls deliberately educated in an anti-Nazi atmosphere. Differences between the samples and a possible bias on the part of the investigators attenuate the value of the findings somewhat, but by no means invalidate the study. They found that German youths counted as the worst crimes, crimes against the state, whereas American youths stressed crimes against the person. German youths felt that they were superior to Italians, Poles, Russians and Frenchmen, but not to Englishmen and Americans. They were in favour of newspaper censorship, because of the supposed gullibility of the masses. They felt that Germany needed a strong leader. Historical figures most frequently named as the greatest men in history were all powerful figures - Roosevelt, Bismarck, and Frederick the Great. The girls with anti-Nazi home backgrounds are said to have been more willing to say they didn't know who was the greatest man in history, and were more likely to know who Heinrich Heine was - which brings home the possible differences in education between the two groups. McGranahan and Janowitz were of the opinion that the German youths were basically still totalitarian youths in search of leadership. 'They echo what they consider to be the official view of their current masters' (p.5). Their acceptance of 'democratic' views simply illustrates their 'implicit and uncritical acceptance of authority' (p.5). (Research conducted by Lederer in 1979, published in 1982, shows that German youths have dramatically changed: they are now very much less authority oriented and ethnocentric than the German youths of 1945, and are less, if anything, authority oriented and ethnocentric than American youths - who have also changed since 1945.)

Working Class Anti-Semite

Another study to look at is Robb's, an excellent piece of research which was carried out between 1947 and 1949 in Bethnal Green, in the East End of London. Bethnal Green was chosen as a traditionally close-knit, crowded, working-class suburb, in which the British Union of Fascists had a considerable following before the War, and in which meetings of Fascist parties were again attracting support during the time of the study. It had a noticeable population of Jews. A large proportion of the men were employed in small furniture factories, some owned by Jews. Unemployment, which had dreadful moral and material consequences, was quite high in the area before the War.

As an outsider – he is a New Zealander – Robb found he could ask questions a native Briton would not easily have been able to. (At least one informant contacted New Zealand House to check that he was a New Zealand student, as he claimed.) He spent some time in the area getting to know the subculture and its argot, before embarking on a series of interviews with a random sample of men in the area. Interviews lasted half an hour, usually on the interviewee's doorstep, and were often followed by a Rorschach test! They were usually about housing initially, a topic everyone was concerned with at the time, and branched out to more general topics fairly naturally. He gave his interviewees a score of 1 for anti-Semitism if they made a prejudiced statement about Jews early on in the interview. A score of 2 was given if the question 'Are there any types of people you would keep out of these new towns altogether?' elicited an anti-Semitic reply. 3 was given if the first anti-Semitic remark was given only after further probing; 4 for mentions of anti-Semitic sentiments with real prompting; and 5 for a total absence of anti-Semitic remarks during the interview.

Of the total sample of 103 (excluding refusals), 9 were rated 1 ('extreme anti-Semites'), and 18 were rated 5 ('tolerant'). He found the usual positive correlation between anti-Semitism and age, and found positive correlations of anti-Semitism with ratings of pessimism, and with feelings of inability to control the person's environment and fate. There was no relation between anti-Semitism and employment by Jewish 'guvnors', having Jewish workmates, living in a predominantly Jewish area, or belonging to a trade union. Extreme anti-Semites who were not in positions of authority were submissive, but 'always unadmitted rebellion smoulders beneath the surface' (p.147). They were notably submissive to their parents, rigid in their notions of right and wrong, and unsociable; they felt hard done by, with regard, for instance, to housing, though their past lives did not seem to have been more affected by anxiety creating situations – like unemployment – than those of the tolerant men. They felt cut off from society and its leaders, and that the environment, despite their own stalwart efforts, was too powerful for them. They were pessimistic and cynical, and harked back to a roseate past, which they felt to be in contrast to the present, and they were sure the future would be even worse. The typical stereotype of the Jew held by the extreme anti-Semites entailed political and enonomic power and extreme clannishness. One man averred that 'War was inevitable from the moment Hitler threw the first Jew out of Germany' (p.120). In contrast, the characteristics that stick out about the men in his tolerant group are their cheerfulness and self-confidence.

The interesting thing about Robb's study is the similarity of his results and conclusions to those of Adorno and his colleagues, despite the very different populations they were working with, and despite the fact that Robb must have done much of his work in ignorance of the detail of the theory of the authoritarian personality.

THE AUTHORITARIAN PERSONALITY

The above studies are all mentioned because, as will be seen, they come to conclusions fairly similar to those of Adorno, Frenkel-Brunswik, Levinson, and Sanford (1950/1964), though their work was done independently of the authoritarian personality study (McGranahan's 1946 study is referred to only in a footnote by Adorno et al.), in very different circumstances, and on different populations (German youth, and British working-class men) from those studied by Adorno et al. In spite of these differences their conclusions are precursive and supportive of those of Adorno and the others.

As has been said, the Adorno study was begun at the instigation of the American Jewish Committee, who, for obvious reasons, were particularly concerned during the early 1940's about anti-Semitism. The investigation, had, as a preliminary, to identify white non-Jews who were anti-Semitic, and so set about constructing a scale to measure anti-Semitism. They devised a Likert-type scale, consisting of items which related to Jews. Examples are

'Jews seem to prefer the most luxurious, extravagant, and sensual way of living'

and

'Anyone who employs many people should be careful not to hire a large percentage of Jews'.

Having constructed their anti-Semitism scale, Adorno et al. considered the nature of anti-Semitism further, and it became clear that people who were anti-Jew did not evince only anti-Jewish attitudes, but negative attitudes towards members of other outgroups as well. The unitary nature of attitudes to ethnic minorities has often been noticed. Bagley, Verma, Mallick and Young (1979) found that measures of attitudes to Blacks and to Asians correlated very highly among high school pupils in England. Adorno et al. formed the hypothesis that anti-Semitism was part of a more general tendency to hold negative attitudes to outgroups in general (and positive attitudes to members of the ingroup). On checking the literature, they found support for the hypothesis, and went on to develop their E (for 'ethnocentrism') scale. This was also a Likert-type scale, originally comprising three subscales. The subscales (with examples of items measuring them) were

(a) Negro subscale. 'Negro musicians are sometimes as good as white musicians at swing music and jazz, but it would be a mistake to have mixed negro-white bands' (1964, p. 105). 'Manual labor and manual jobs seem to fit the negro mentality and ability better than more skilled or responsible work' (p. 105).

(b) Minority subscale. 'The many faults, and the general inability to get along, of the Oklahomans ("Okies") who have recently flooded California prove that we ought to send them back where they came from as soon as conditions permit' (p. 106). (During the 1930's and 1940's, soil erosion forced the migration of many - white, native American - small farmers from Oklahoma to California). 'We are spending too much money for the pampering of criminals and the insane, and for the education of inherently incapable people' (p. 106).

(c) Patriotism subscale. 'Patriotism and loyalty are the first and most important requirement of a good citizen' (p. 108). 'There will always be wars, because, for one thing there will always be races who try to grab more than their share' (p. 108).

These subscales, and the whole scale, were shown to be reliable (the Spearman-Brown corrected split-half reliability coefficient was .91) and to correlate highly (+.80) with the A-S scale. This correlation is sufficiently high for the authors to infer that the A-S and the E scales were measuring essentially the same thing, and modified versions of the E scale were constructed including items from the A-S scale. A form of E scale was developed for use in Britain by Warr, Faust, and Harrison (1967).

From the E scale, the authors went on to develop a measure of political and economic conservatism - the PEC scale. Preliminary studies, and a consideration of the Conservative values (that is, values espoused by persons right-of-centre in political terms) led them to expect that the PEC scale should correlate highly with the E scale. In fact, correlations were only moderate, around .50. Although clearly significant, the correlation is not sufficiently high to make one think the two scales were measuring something essentially identical. Examination of the relationship led to the conclusion that low scores on the PEC scale ('liberalism') almost invariably went with low E scores, but high PEC scores ('conservatism') did not necessarily go with high E scores. Hence no further consideration was given by the authors to the PEC scale.

They went on to consider ethnocentric ideology further. One reason was that they wanted to develop a scale which would measure ethnocentrism without mentioning minority groups - since the open admission of ethnocentrism might be baulked at by some respondents. But they were beginning to think that ethnocentrism was an expression of a deeper personality pattern, which personality pattern might be expressed in attitudes and opinions and values with wider referents than members of outgroups. Interviews with individuals scoring high on the E and A-S scales confirmed this impression. Hence they went on to develop the F scale, ('F' for 'Fascism'), which is most frequently referred to as a measure of authoritarianism in personality, but variously as a measure of 'implicit anti-democratic trends', and of 'pre-fascist ideology'. The latter two terms stem from the idea that persons of this personality type would probably explicitly embrace fascist ideology if it were socially acceptable to do so.

They hypothesised that there were nine underlying dimensions of authoritarianism in personality. These, with brief explanations of their meaning and some items supposed to measure them, are given below. Some items were intended to measure more than one dimension.

(a) Conventionalism. 'Obedience and respect for authority are the most important virtues children can learn.'

(b) Authoritarian Submission. 'Every person should have faith in some supernatural power whose decision he obeys without question.'

(c) Authoritarian Aggression. 'An insult to our honour should always be punished.'

(d) Anti-intraception. (a dislike of the subjective and 'weak'). 'Nowadays more and more people are prying into matters that should remain personal and private.'

(e) Superstition and Stereotypy. 'Some day it will probably be shown that astrology can explain a lot of things.'

(f) Power and 'Toughness'. (Concentration on strength and dominance relations). 'People can be divided into two distinct classes, the weak and the strong.'

(g) Destructiveness and Cynicism. 'Human nature being what it is, there will always be war and conflict.'

(h) Projectivity. 'The wild sex lives of the old Greeks and Romans was tame compared to some of the goings-on in this country, even in places where people might least expect it.'

(i) Sex. (an undue concern with sexual behaviour, especially of other people). 'Homosexuals are hardly better than criminals, and ought to be severely punished.'

The scale was administered to a variety of groups, such as college students, adult students of extension classes, patients in psychiatric clinics, prison inmates, members of service clubs, and so on, and scores on the A-S, E, and PEC scales were also obtained. It was presented as a survey of public opinion. Note (it will be important later) that all

107

the items were worded in such a way that agreeing gives the respondent a high score: there are no 'reversed' items, such that disagreeing would raise the respondent's score and agreeing diminish it. Respondents were asked to rate their degree of disagreement-agreement on a seven point scale, -3 to +3, in the usual Likert-type way. Since the scores are on an interval scale, it is possible to add a constant to each one without altering the meaning of the scores, and a constant of 4 was added, to get rid of negative numbers. Thus 1, in the transformed scores, represents 'strongly disagree', 4 is 'neutral', and 7 is 'strongly agree'. If the reader will think about it for a moment, it will be obvious that the actual numbers used don't matter, provided they go up in equal intervals. We could just as well transform the scores to 10, 20, 30, 40, 50, 60, and 70 if that were convenient. At any rate, the F scale proved very reliable (average reliability being .90, which is quite high for a split-half reliability coefficient). The authors indicate that, corrected for attenuation due to the unreliability of the scales, the correlation between the E and F scales would be in the order of .9 (see Adorno et al., 1964, p. 264), which is very high - high enough for the scales to be used interchangeably. Of course a correlation quite as high as this may not be obtained now, thirty years later. Correlations with the A-S and PEC scales average about .5. The mean item score on the various F scales for various groups was in the range 3.50 - 3.96 (4, it will be remembered is neutral, and 3 meant 'slight opposition, disagreement').

Having constructed the scales, the authors conducted extensive interviews with 80 people, 40 men and 40 women, some of whom scored very high on the E scale, and some of whom scored very low. They also used a variety of other techniques for exploring the personalities of high and low scorers. One such technique was the TAT (a set of pictures, about which the person is asked to tell a story: as the pictures are deliberately made vague and undetailed, the story a person tells is largely dependent on his or her personality). They included in their TAT some pictures which could elicit stories concerning Jews, black Americans, and other minority ethnic groups. Another was to ask 'projective questions', such as, 'We all have impulses and desires which are at times hard to control but which we try to keep in check. What desires do you often have difficulty in controlling?' and 'What do you consider the worst crime a person could commit?'

Their very extensive research led them to conclude that they had identified a personality type, which arises as a result of certain child rearing practices, and which constitutes an explanation for ethnic prejudice. In their own words: 'The most crucial result of the present study, as it seems to the authors, is the demonstrating of close correspondence in the type of approach and outlook which a subject is likely to have in a great variety of areas . . .. Thus a basically hierarchical, authoritarian, exploitive parent child relationship is apt to carry over into a power oriented, exploitively dependent attitude towards one's sex partner and one's God and may well culminate in a political philosophy and a social outlook which has no room for anything but a desperate clinging to what appears to be strong and a disdainful rejection of whatever is relegated to the bottom' (p. 971).

The following paragraphs summarize the traits and background which Adorno and his colleagues conclude are characteristic of 'highs' or authoritarians, and constitute a statement of the authoritarian personality theory.

Authoritarianism viewed by Adorno et al.

Authoritarians report experiencing harsh, rigid, threatening home environments and discipline as children, which leads to repression of impulses objectionable to the parents, who are status conscious and conventional in outlook. The repressed (and therefore, unconscious) impulses result in the projection of the impulses onto outgroups, which impulses are consciously condemned.

Their preoccupation with surface conformity makes them give conforming, unadventurous answers to all problems posed. Their personality is largely role-playing. They submit to their parents out of fear, and (repressed) hostility to their parents results, which in turn (by reaction formation) results in outward glorification of the parents. The hostility is displaced. Later, other authorities take the place of the parents, resulting in conformity to the authority and its rules, with underlying hostility and destructiveness, which destructiveness can be released under certain circumstances, leading to the violence of, say, Nazi-ism. The anti-weakness attitude typical of the authoritarian is explained less satisfactorily. The father of the child is domineering, leaving a tendency to passivity as a legacy in adulthood, with a compensating striving for the independence, and a conscious goal of emulating the strong, stern father. There is imperfect identification with the mother, hence no adoption of gentler values is possible. They tend to conceive sex roles as dichotomous, that is, they think that men should do the things conventionally assigned to men in our society (fighting, working, seducing), and women should do the women things (submitting, cooking, weakly resisting seduction). Authoritarian men repress any 'feminine' impulses, women their 'masculine' ones. Men have greater opportunity for overt expression of reactions against inner weakness, hence women tend to exhibit greater covert defences. Authoritarians are unwilling to admit to themselves that covert defences exist - there is less communication with the unconscious in the prejudiced than in the unprejudiced person. Projection is the mechanism used against the internal fear, weakness, sex impulses, passivity, and so on. Due largely to the poor experience with their first love relationship (i.e. with their parents) they tend to withhold love from their sex partners, and to isolate sex from the rest of personality. Status plays a part in sex relationships, achieved conventionally through seduction and 'sexual prowess'. The surface admiration and underlying hostility to women is handled by a dichotomous view of women - women are seen as either 'good' or 'bad'. They have superficial relationships with others, liking conventional persons and people of high status. Hostility is projected onto others. Fear of failure leads to a dichotomous conception of 'strong' and 'weak'. The world is feared dangerous and threatening, and the utility of other people is perceived as their ability to survive and get ahead in the Edgar Rice Burroughs jungle we live in. On the surface, they stress the positive and desirable aspects of their personalities - their 'will-power', energy, decisiveness, and thrust; this surface ideal of themselves is a defence against the underlying tendencies of their personalities which are opposite to the surface ideal traits. They regard themselves as conventional and describe themselves in a 'moralistic' tone; any deviation from conformity that they recognize in themselves are ascribed to external forces over which the individual has no control, or are thought beyond explanation. There is little perceived continuity between childhood and adulthood, since socio-psychological explanation of themselves tends to be avoided; hence spontaneous references to childhood are few. They are reluctant to admit that they fall short of their ego-ideal. They exhibit the anal syndrome ('rigid-moralistic'). They are dependent without affect - and turn to the Bible for support, not as an internalized system of ethics.

They seethe with diffuse, undirected, aggression. Unable to admit of ambivalence to their parents, they reject all ambivalence and dichotomous thinking results, leading to the good-bad, strong-weak conceptions mentioned above. Repression of the 'hate' part (of the love-hate feeling towards the powerful) 'leads to socially dangerous forms of displacement aggression' (Adorno et al., 1964, p. 451).

The authors hypothesize that a 'normal Oedipal situation' is more typical of low scorers. The superego is never satisfactorily internalized. Id tendencies are repressed. They have weak egos generally, but may show strength in certain aspects of their egos - when pursuing success, for example.

They tend to distort reality, and exhibit a distorted evaluation of other people and themselves. Because their own impulses are repressed, they protest too much about moral misbehaviour in others. They have rigid cognitive structure, taking over rules and values in rigid and dogmatic form. Intolerance of ambiguity leads to an acceptance of 'psuedo-science' and superstition and a negative attitude to science in its pure form, which is always tentative and subject to qualification. They shun introspection and insight into the workings of society and psychological mechanisms (intraception). In bowing to authority, they are suggestible and gullible.

It will be seen that prejudice is explained thus: The authoritarians have many impulses, desires, feelings, traits, ideas, and so on which, because of the rigid and harsh socialization they underwent as children, are unacceptable to themselves. These impulses etc. are repressed, and projected onto members of outgroups, who are then denigrated for supposedly having these impulses, traits, etc. Minority groups are typically chosen because they are weak and unable to retaliate for this denigration.

CRITICISMS OF THE AUTHORITARIAN PERSONALITY STUDY

So important was <u>The Authoritarian Personality</u> that a few years after it was published an entire book devoted to its criticism was published (Christie and Jahoda, 1954): a high compliment indeed for a piece of research. And both between 1950 and 1954, and between 1954 and now, a vast amount of research - the word 'vast' is used advisedly - has been published, inspired directly by that work.

Reliance on Psychoanalysis

One of the first things one notices in looking at the summary of the theory presented above is the apparent relevance of psychoanalytic theory. Freudian 'mechanisms' are referred to, notably repression, projection, reaction formation, and various other Freudian terms abound, such as the id, ego, and superego, the Oedipal situation (which, in Freudian theory, is essential to the formation of a strong superego) and the 'anal syndrome'. Psychoanalysis has little credence as a scientific theory, but the reliance of their theory on psychoanalytic postulates is more apparent than real. Rather, Adorno and the others couched their ideas in psychoanalytic terms, making use of the form more than the substance of psychoanalysis. 'Superego', for instance, is a person's conscience together with his conception of his ideal self: calling it the superego does not make the theory essentially dependent on Freudian ideas, neither does the absence of evidence for their hypothesis that the 'normal' Oedipal situation is more characteristic of low scorers (non-authoritarians) than high scorers (authoritarians) have the effect of seriously weakening their important findings, or of invalidating the F scale as a measure of authoritarianism. The Freudian mechanisms that are important to their theory are repression and projection. Now the first of these has little empirical support, and in a review of research on repression, Holmes (1974) concludes that there is no evidence for it. But he adopts an unrealistic criterion for it, excluding material apparently repressed under hypnosis, and other evidence which many psychologists would accept. At any rate, he accepts that suppression takes place, if not quite in the way Freud envisaged it. And there is evidence that people can purposely inhibit anxiety. One such piece of evidence is supplied by Epstein and Fenz (1965), who showed that experienced (as opposed to inexperienced) parachutists felt maximum fear the night before the jump, and thereafter inhibited their fear so that it was at a very low level at the time of exit from the aeroplane. Moreover, for what it is worth, a moment's introspection will convince most readers that there are unpleasant thoughts they have been avoiding thinking about in their lives: don't most of us shun those pages of the newspapers which carry large adverts for Oxfam showing starving children? One does not have to suppose that these repressed thoughts are rendered utterly unavailable to consciousness, as Freud does.

Repression is a fairly important part of Adorno et al.'s theory, but even more important is projection. For projection there is much empirical support, which has been summarized by Holmes (1968). His review indicates that, contrary to what Freud suggested, projection takes place where conscious (not unconscious) impulses are concerned, and that projection serves to justify the impulse where it is unacceptable. Thus men students led to believe that they had homosexual impulses projected these impulses onto other men, as a means of convincing themselves they were not abnormal; and children who were afraid rated pictures of men as frightening. Thus projection of imperfectly repressed (and therefore conscious) impulses is quite credible, and this crucial part of the theory of prejudice contained in The Authoritarian Personality is good.

The Subject Sample
One of the chief criticisms levelled at the authoritarian personality study is that the subjects studied were in the main youngish, white, American, better than average in educational attainment; many belonged to institutions whose members could be expected to be more politically and socially conscious than average, and hence to have more integrated opinions and attitudes than most other poeple. There were some subjects with very different characteristics - inmates of a prison supplied one small set - but the sample was unrepresentative and biased in the former direction. Now they themselves found, and this finding has been confirmed very frequently since, that there is quite a marked correlation between the scores on the E and F scales on the one hand, and education and similar factors relating to social class on the other (for example, Weller, 1964; Rubenowitz, 1963 - this

research was done in Sweden; Beswick and Hills, 1972, in Australia; and Stankov, 1977, in Yugoslavia). That is, less educated people are apparently more ethnocentric or prejudiced, and more authoritarian. But, the measure of authoritarianism (i.e., the F scale) is less closely related to prejudice as measured by the E scale) among less educated people (Weller, 1964). The implication of all this is that Adorno and others probably overestimated the extent to which authoritarianism forms a coherent cluster of attitudes, traits, dispositions and so on, in populations other than that from which their dominant sample was drawn. They also overestimated the relationship between authoritarianism and ethnic prejudice in the general population.

Authoritarianism and Prejudice

The authors of The Authoritarian Personality were interested, for reasons which have been explained, in prejudice and negative attitudes regarding members of ethnic outgroups. They did not examine prejudices favourable to ethnic outgroups, nor yet prejudices regarding objects other than ethnic outgroups, and these failures have not gone unnoticed.

It was noticed, by the authors of The Authoritarian Personality and by others, that while high scorers on the F scale seemed to form a relatively homogeneous group, the 'lows', or tolerant, or unprejudiced, persons were much more diverse. Adorno in The Authoritarian Personality classified the 'lows' into types, one of which we called the 'rigid low' scorer, a 'syndrome' (sic) in which 'the absence of prejudice is derived from some general external, ideological pattern' (p. 771). Frenkel-Brunswik (1948) observed one girl whose results on tests, were similar to those of 'prejudiced' children, though she in fact indicated positive feelings for minority groups. Frenkel-Brunswik observes that this girl's background was a dogmatically, rigidly, liberal one. Taft (1958) observed that persons scoring on the extremes of a social distance scale were very similar to one another in scores on the Rosenzweig Picture Frustration test and the Bernreuter Inventory, though both differed from those scoring at an intermediate level. In particular, though the tolerant group was higher than both other groups on scores (in the Bernreuter) of social ability and self sufficiency, both were higher than the intermediate group on a score of dominance, and (in the Rosenzweig test) on needs to defend the ego, and on the number of scores more than one SD from the mean. And Haimowotz and Haimowitz (1950), found many similarities between persons scoring very high and very low on a social distance questionnaire, and observed that those who scored lowest on social distance towards minority ethnic groups scored (not surprisingly) highest on social distance towards the Ku Klux Klan, Nazis and Fascists.

It appears, then, that though the F scale taps a form of dogmatic belief in unproven opinions, because of the bias in it (towards measuring 'potential Fascism' - rightest authoritarianism) it tends to miss those persons whom, despite their disposition to judge matters in terms of their own preconceptions (partly in response to needs for ego-defence and dominance perhaps) do not hold preconceptions against minority groups.

Not surprisingly attempts got under way to measure 'authoritarianism' in a way which was not contaminated with the political and ideological bias of the F scale. The term authoritarianism of the left (left in the political spectrum) was used, but using authoritarianism in that way introduces ambiguity. Rokeach, whose work on this problem culminated in a book on The Open and Closed Mind (1960) used the more general phrase 'dogmatism'. For a variety of reasons, which need not detain us here, the D (for 'dogmatism') and 'Opinionation' scales seem not to be good measures of dogmatism.

If dogmatism is to be measured, it must first be defined. The essential points that characterize the definitions of 'dogma' and 'dogmatic' in the shorter Oxford Dictionary are that there is an assertion of an opinion which is 'a priori' or 'not tested', and that this assertion is 'arrogant' or 'positive'. The affinity with the definition of prejudice is apparent. Examination will reveal that dogmatism and prejudice are more closely related still. To hold a conviction or belief domatically is to assert that this belief or conviction (dogma) is correct and any other belief or conviction pertaining to the subject is wrong. Hence if a person holds a contradictory belief or conviction it follows logically from the premiss that the dogma is correct, that such a person is wrong; if he is wrong he must be misguided or wicked (or both). Cognitions regarding such misguided or wicked people will tend to consistency, and hence prejudice against them may result, particularly if emotional involvement leads to strong negative feelings about them. Hence dogmatism implies prejudice. Ethnic prejudice is in part a system of dogmas having reference to members of groups which are defined in terms of ethnic criteria; similarly, feelings about people having opinions consonant or contradictory is in part ethnocentrism relating to groups defined in terms of their opinions on certain questions.

Rokeach tried to measure intolerance of persons holding views different from the respondent's with his Opinionation scale. His scales are heavily biased towards politics and political subjects, and while he attempts to broaden the basis of the F scale (which he and others have maintained measured authoritarianism of the political right) he broadened it merely to include both the political left and the right: his opinionation scales altogether miss dogmatic centrists and the politically uninterested and naive. In any case, it should be noted that the terms 'left' and 'right' have all but lost their meaning in the political context. What is needed then is a scale which will measure the extent to which untestable opinions in an area in which the respondent is interested are asserted in a 'positive', 'arrogant' and 'assertive' manner.

The present author (Bethlehem, 1969) attempted to provide such scales by having statements of opinion scaled for dogmatism by the method of successive categories. The statements related to four different areas of interest – social values, economic values, political values and religious values. Examples, first of a dogmatic, then of an undogmatic statement, from the dogmatism scale designed to measure dogmatism in the economic sphere, are 'Money can buy anything', and 'Economic factors can rightly be said to have some bearing on a country's politics'. A measure is available (the Allport-Vernon scale of values, as revised for use in Britain by Richardson) to assess the relative importance of these values in different people. It seemed unlikely on the face of it that people would hold dogmatic opinions on matters which did not really interest them, so the scales dealing with different areas of interest were intended for persons whose scores on the scale of values were high for relevant value. In fact, as expected, persons for whom the questions were personally relevant (i.e., who had scored high on the corresponding value in the Scale of Values) did tend to score higher on the relevant dogmatism scale than did persons to whom the area was not relevant. Moreover, an empirical relation with prejudice was shown: dogmatic people were shown to stereotype (i.e., have prejudices about) persons belonging to groups defined in terms relevant to their dominant value, but not others. Thus, people with high social values (that is, people who valuehelping the unfortunate) have prejudices relating to 'prejudiced people' and 'people who do voluntary service overseas', but not about ethnic groups like 'West Indians' or 'Pakistani immigrants'.

Response Bias
It has been pointed out that all the questions in the E and F scales are worded so that a positive (agreeing) answer adds to the respondent's score: there are no items written so that disagreeing is indicative of authoritarianism. The authors did try to write some such items, but they were discarded in the item analysis.

Response biases have long been recognized in psychological testing. A response bias refers to any tendency to emit a type or class of response independent of the content of the question. Where this tendency is due to a a desire (perhaps unconscious) to project a certain image, for instance to answer questions in a way which reflects well on the respondent, the bias is referred to as a 'response set'. Where it is due to a habit, such as (where judgement of whether one light is dimmer than another is being made) the tendency just to say 'dimmer', 'dimmer', 'dimmer' through boredom, it is referred to as response style. The response bias which has most concerned psychologists in the F scale is an acquiescence response bias - a tendency to agree with items without fully considering their content; it is not clear whether this bias is a 'set' or 'style', but that doesn't really matter.

What is important is the possibility that was entertained that acquiescence response bias was so strong, and accounted for so great a proportion of the variance of F scale scores, that the F scale was not a valid measure of anything but the tendency to say 'Yes' to silly questions. If F scale scores are heavily contaminated with response bias, what needs doing to make the F scale valid? In fact, academics disagreed violently about whether the F scale was heavily contaminated by response bias. Rorer, in an article wittily entitled 'The great response style myth' (1965) states that response bias 'appears to account neither for substantive findings nor for the double agreement findings obtained with authoritarianism scales' (p.354); while Peabody (1966) reckoned that 'response bias . . . is a major factor in authoritarianism scales' (p.11). Who shall decide when doctors disagree? The answer is, of course, you and me. My own conclusions are that there is a tendency for persons who are in doubt to answer a question in a consistent way, usually by acquiescing. The tendency to acquiesce is increased by two major factors: the uncertainty of the respondent, and the opinions of others. The F scale, E scale, and A-S scale each contain many items which are ambiguous or of uncertain answer, particularly to undergraduates in their first year at university or college, and the authoritative way in which the items were phrased helps to create the impression that the statement is endorsed by solid bodies of wise, authoritative persons. Hence acquiescence is to be expected. There may also be personality factors which increase acquiescence.

What evidence have we for the analysis in the preceding paragraph? Let us briefly consider the steps in the paragraph one at a time:

Uncertainty on the part of a person and ambiguity in a situation lead to acquiescence. Cronbach (1950) and Peabody (1966) have been at pains to stress that it is in conditions of uncertainty that response bias can be expected to occur. Outside the context of questionnaires, studies relating to this matter usually appear under the heading 'conformity'. It has been shown that the more difficult and ambiguous a situation, the more subjects defer to an acquiescence to the opinions of a confident associate or majority. For example, London and Lim (1964) varied the difficulty of assessing whether a stated conclusion followed logically from premises given: the more difficult it was to decide whether the conclusion did in fact logically follow, the more the subjects conformed with majority opinion. On the other hand there is a considerable body of evidence to suggest that scales dealing with the personal characteristics and feelings of the respondent are virtually immune from response bias. Several investigators have sought, and failed to find, evidence of response bias in several different personality inventories (e.g., Chapman & Campbell, 1959; Christie, Havel, & Seidenberg, 1958; Eysenck, 1962; Eysenck &

Eysenck, 1964; Green & Stacey, 1966; Rorer, 1965; Rorer & Goldberg, 1965). These inventories have items which are personally relevant to the respondent, for the most part asking specific questions about him- or herself, his or her personal behaviour and attitudes. Thus, they are not ambiguous for the respondent, and further, the respondent is the only one who is in a positon to know the answer, and so need fear no contradiction. Further indirect evidence is to be found in the fairly numerous studies which show that persons whom one would expect to have no opinion or weak opinions on a subject are the most acquiescent. Christie et al. (1958) report that their undergraduate sample were much more acquiescent than Washington Lobbyists and graduate students, and attributed this to the confusion of undergraduates coming into contact with the liberalizing environment of the campus for the first time. Weller's (1964) is one of a number of studies indicating a negative relation between F scale and intelligence/education/social class. He goes on to demonstrate that in the lower classes, F does not relate so strongly to prejudice, which seems to indicate that less educated or intelligent people are simply acquiescing, since they probably have no strong opinions of their own about such matters as astrology and the spread of disease. Again, the present author (Bethlehem, 1969) used a 20-item version of the F scale in an English college, with 10 of the items reversed. The reversed items were the ones which had proved most adequate in previous research and in terms of the logical requirements put forward earlier. It was found that students doing honours degrees - the more sophisticated of the students - showed acquiescent response bias (i.e., 14 or more agreeing responses - see 'Measuring response bias' below) significantly less frequently than students not reading for honours degrees. Himmelweit and Swift (1971) found that schoolboys of lower ability (at a secondary modern school) were more acquiescent than boys of higher ability (at a grammar school), but only on quesionnaire items which did not relate to their own experience. More direct evidence is provided by Hankey (1962, 1965) who found a negative relation between item length and difficulty (measured by respondents' confidence in their answers), a negative relation between confidence and acquiescence, and a positive relation between item difficulty and acquiescence. McBride and Moran (1967) scaled the items and some of the reversals of the F, A-S and Dogmatism scales for ambiguity. They report a positive correlation between the amount of double agreement on a statement and its reversal (see below) and the mean ambiguity of the item and its reversal, for items of all three scales.

Why acquiescence rather than negativism? This is not the place to enter into a theoretical discussion of the issues of conformity. Suffice it to observe that people do conform, by which is broadly meant according, verbally or behaviourally, with the opinions of other people. Conformity is most marked to the opinions of wise, respected people. Now, the more resoundingly authoritative a statement sounds (provided the respondent is uncertain about the answer) the more likely he or she is to agree (Couch & Kenniston, 1960), since by 'authoritatively' is meant 'endorsed by many wise, respected people'. It is clear, prima facie, that the F, A-S, and E, scales contain items of authoritative cast, and their reversals are often equally authoritative. Consequently, being uncertain, respondents agree to both, and the more concerned they are with making themselves agreeable to others the more likely they are to agree to both: hence McBride and Moran's findings that the Marlowe-Crowne Social Desirability scale correlates with number of double agreements.

The F scale and similar scales contain items which are ambiguous or to which the answer is uncertain.
The evidence provided by Hanley (op.cit.) provides a direct and clear demonstration of the positive relation between item length and difficulty, and difficulty and acquiescence. McBride and Moran (op.cit.) also provide clear evidence that the items in the F scale are ambiguous. What is responsible for the tendency to acquiesce is not the ambiguity of the item in itself, but the uncertainty of the respondent: i.e., the important factor is the item 'difficulty', in Hanley's terms. The more ambiguous an item, the more likely it is that the respondent will be uncertain. But terms will often cause uncertainty in some subjects and not in others. The essential point, though, is, as Adorno et al. explicitly state (p.241-242), they tried to formulate items which were neither so 'wild' that virtually no-one would agree with them, nor so clearly true or false that respondents could respond

on this objective, rational basis; i.e., the answers were factually uncertain.

Personality factors may account for some part of the variance in acquiescence. More than one author has suggested that Adorno et al., by a lucky fluke, hit upon an ideal method of increasing the power of the F scale by scoring all the items in the same way. Authoritarians are acquiescent; they defer; and the more they say 'yes' when in doubt, the more authoritarian they show themselves to be. Operationally, this argument is quite circular, but it does have some justification, in that measures of authoritarianism have been shown to correlate with measures of acquiescence such as, e.g. the Bass Social Acquiescence Scale (Zuckerman & Eisen, 1962; see also McGee, 1962a, 1962b, 1962c, below), as has Rokeach's Dogmatism scale (Lichtenstein, Quinn, & Hover, 1961). There is also evidence that persuasability is a factor common to different situations (see, e.g., Hovland & Janis, 1959) and that persuasability and conformity relate to the F and Dogmatism scales (Hovland et al., op. cit.; McGee, 1962b; Zuckerman & Eisen, 1962; Vidulich & Kaiman, 1961). Marlowe and Crowne (1961) have shown a relation between their measure of the need for approval (the Marlowe-Crowne Social Desirability Scale, or M-C SDS) and a tendency to acquiesce in a behavioural situation. McBride and Moran (1967) have shown a relation between the M-C SDS and acquiescence on the F and Dogmatism scales. On the other hand, acquiescence is not perfectly correlated with the F scale - Christie et al. (1958) quote some examples of subjects who are acquiescent but not authoritarian, and others who are authoritarian but not acquiescent.

In summary: The basis of acquiescence response set.
There is thus considerable support for the view that the F scale, the Dogmatism scale, and similar scales do contain items which give rise to uncertainty, are authoritatively stated, and that, combined with other factors (personality and intelligence and knowledge or ignorance of the respondent), this ambiguity tends to elicit an acquiescence response bias in many subjects. Rorer's (1965) conclusion that this response bias is a 'myth' seems to be based on the failure of response styles to correlate

across all tests, and on the assertion that 'there is no reason to believe that respondents are guessing when they respond to objective personality, attitude or interest inventory items'. Both points have been dealt with above. Measures of response set do tend to correlate across pencil-and-paper tests, but not across behavioural tests - results that may be due to faults in the measures rather in the hypothesis. Secondly, there is every reason to believe that subjects do 'guess' when they respond to attitude inventory items of the F and Dogmatism scale type, though not when responding to more personal items: indeed, confronted with questions about the sex lives of ancient Greeks, or about astrology it is hard to know how any one but an ancient Greek historian or a real clairvoyant could do anything else.

Controlling Response Bias in the F Scale

The only practical way of controlling response bias is to use 'reversed' items ('reversals'). That is, to re-word half the items in such a way that a disagreeing answer increases the authoritarianism score. The trick is to find adequate reversals. Adorno and his colleagues failed. Many later attempts failed too.

Endorsements of both the original and reversed items were a very high proportion of responses, and double-rejection of items was not uncommon; correlations between the scores on nonreversed and reversed portions of the scale were often zero or negative, or at least very low (e.g., inter alia Bass, 1966; Jackson, Messick & Solley, 1957; Couch & Kenniston, 1960; Leavitt, Hax & Roche, 1955; Jackson & Messick, 1957; Peabody, 1961; Christie et al., 1958; and reviews by Rorer, 1965, and Peabody, 1966). At first, this was taken as indicating that response bias accounted for a major proportion of the variance on the F scale.

Then it began to be noticed that it is really quite consistent to reject, for example, both the statements 'The businessman and manufacturer are much more important to society than the artist and professor' and 'The artist and professor are much more important to society than the businessman and manufacturer' (Bass, 1955). An examination of reversed items began, and it was revealed that many of the reversals used were quite different from one another, and that they had fairly apparent shortcomings. Moreover Mogar (1960) found that the various reversal F scales did not correlate positively among themselves.

One of the shortcomings, as noted by Christie et al. (1958) was that though a reversal might be logically 'opposite' to a statement on the F scale, it might not reverse the (hypothetical) dimension - conventionalism, authoritarian submission, etc. - which it was meant by Adorno et al. to tap. Another factor which must tend to reduce correlations is that answering a reversed item must sometimes involve use of double negatives. This may be difficult, particularly for less intelligent respondents, whose answers may not reflect their intentions.

There is a more serious consideration Rundquist (1967) reviews in some early work (1932) of R. B. Smith on what he calls the 'form of an item'. Smith found a high degree of inconsistency between 'acceptable' and 'unacceptable' items, the one supposedly a reversal of the other. (e.g., an 'acceptable' item is 'It is easy to be cheerful at home'; its 'reversal' is 'It is hard to be cheerful at home'). Bass (1955) deliberately set out to make each reversed item 'as opposite as the author could make it' (p.617) and scaled the degree to which F scale items and his reversed items were opposite, and other authors seem to have had something of the same view in mind. Samelson (1964) thinking in terms of conventional scaling theory, talks of this as 'displacing the neutral point' and of the need for 'symmetrically reversed' items, and in his 1967 article on this subject he and his co-author present evidence for this view. He scaled items and two of their reversals for the degree to which his judges thought a person making the original statement and another person asserting the reversed item would be in disagreement. They found that the greater the degree of disagreement thus measured, between an item and its reversal, the smaller the incidence of double agreements.

Broadly, what all these objections are circling around is the question of the logical relation between the non-reversed and the reversed item. In order logically to demand that respondents who accept one must reject another, and vice versa, one must have a reversed item that is the contradictory of the non-reversed item: 'extreme' reversals are most commonly contraries (or sometimes sub-contraries), and here it is perfectly consistent to reject (or accept) both. (For explanations of these logical terms, see note 1, at the end of this chapter). For example, here are two pairs of contraries followed by a pair of what are probably subcontraries: all reversals are drawn from Bass (1955), and are stated after the original item:

'Every person should have complete faith in some supernatural power whose decisions he obeys without question' and 'No person should have complete faith in some supernatural power whose decisions he obeys without question.'

'Familiarity breeds contempt' and 'Familiarity does not breed contempt.'

'The wild sex life of the Old Greeks and Romans was tame compared to some of the goings on in this country, even in places where people might least expect it' and 'Some of the goings on in this country, even where people might least expect it, are tame compared to the wild sex life of the Greeks and Romans.'

On the other hand, the following two pairs of items are plainly contradictories, and Peabody (1961; the items are actually quoted in Peabody, 1966, p. 19) found that these pairs received the highest content consistent responses of all the pairs of items he quotes:

'No sane, normal, decent person could ever think of hurting a close friend or relative' and 'Even a normal, decent person will sometimes think of things that might hurt a close friend or relative.'

'Obedience and respect for authority are the most important virtues children should learn' and 'There are other virtues children should learn at least as important as obedience and respect for authority.'

This logical analysis cannot account for all the apparent inconsistency in responses to the reversed items, or even all that part which is not due to response bias, partly because of the limitations of classical logic. It is not possible to rephrase all statements in an unambiguous form, and classical logic cannot deal with ambiguities in meaning. Similarly, where statements are in the form of a subject and predicate joined by a copula, classical logic deals in distributed and undistributed subjects and predicates (either 'all' or 'some and perhaps all'); it cannot deal with everyday words and phrases like 'most' or 'perhaps' or 'it is highly unlikely that'. Hence, it is not possible to know in all cases what logical relation a statement and its reversal have, and different interpretations and rephrasings might yield statements having different relations. Nonetheless some statements are unambiguous and subject to logical analysis, and examining these shows the importance of the point. Some statements and their reversals are irrelevant, hence double endorsements and rejections are quite consistent (e.g., 'Nowadays when so many different kinds of people move around and mix together so much, a person has to protect himself especially carefully against catching an infection or disease from them' and 'Nowadays people move often and meet all sorts of people; only a foolish person would worry about catching an infection or disease from them' (Peabody, 1961).

Reversals which do take account of the points raised in the preceding paragraphs do elicit fairly content consistent responses. Whereas work making use of poor reversals such as that of Leavitt et al. (1965), Bass (1955), Jackson and Messick (1957), and Peabody, (1961), shows a good deal of supposed inconsistency, the more adequate reversals of Christie et al. (1958) show much less: in twelve out of twelve diverse samples, correlations between reversed and non-reversed scales were all such as to indicate content consistent responses.

Measuring response bias. Given that the probability of answering 'yes' to a question is 0.5, one can work out the probability of a person giving a given number of 'yes' responses to a series of questions by chance. It is easy to show that (using the binomial expansion, or the normal curve approximation to it) that, with 20 questions, the probability of a person answering 'yes' (or 'no') to 14 or more of them is less than 0.05. If we have an F scale with an equal number of reversed and non-reversed items, then (provided the reversals are adequate) we would expect that if a person is answering in a content consistent way, then the probability of the person answering 'yes' to any item is, on average, 0.5. Hence, it is possible to say when a person's responses seem to be influenced by response bias: i.e., when he or she gives 14 or more yes responses.

The response bias myth. It seems plain then, that acquiescence response bias is a factor in F scales; but that it is possible to control for it, and, despite alarms and excursions arising from investigations using defective reversed items, there is no reason so far to question the validity of the theory of the usefulness of the F scale. Let us look at some further evidence concerning the validity of the F scale and its limitations.

THE F SCALE IN USE.

F and ethnic prejudice
If the F scale does not measure ethnic prejudice, it is clearly of little value. Adorno and the others provided pretty clear evidence that it did. There is much evidence that the relationship has persisted. Ray (1980a) refers to correlations between a balanced (for acquiescence) F scale and measures of negative attitudes to Blacks and Aboriginal Australians with random white samples in Los Angeles and Sydney, of 0.44 and 0.32. Data collected in 1964 on a sample of 1,975 adults in the USA show that a 5-item version of the F scale (not controlled for acquiescence) is a significant predictor of anti-black, anti-Catholic, anti-immigrant, and anti-Semitic attitudes (Middleton, 1976). Orpen (1970) conducted a study in South Africa with first year students at a university whose ethos is generally supportive of apartheid, and whose members are predominantly Calvinist in religion. He obtained very high scores on the F and E scales (the item mean on the F scale was 4.88, whereas in a British student group, it will be recalled, the item mean was 3.22), and, even controlling for response set, there was a significant correlation between F and E: the E scale, it will be remembered, is a pretty direct measure of ethnic prejudice. In 1956 Pettigrew (1958) found among both Afrikaans and English speaking Whites (Afrikaans speaking white people in South Africa are generally more anti-black in attitude than English speaking Whites, as the research of MacCrone (1935/1957), Lever (1968) and Rogers and Frantz (1962) testifies: this

observation applies to means, of course, and the overlap between the groups is great) that the correlation between the F scale and a measure of anti-Black attitude was greater than +0.5. The relationship in South Africa persists: Ray (1980) reports a correlation between a measure of anti-black prejudice and a balanced version of the F scale of 0.59, in a white non-student, South African sample. Heaven and Nieuwoudt (1981) report mean scores on the F scale for samples from two Afrikaans universities which reanalysis shows to be significantly higher than the F scale scores of an English language South African university. These results are similar to those reported by Colman and Lambley (1970), Lambley (1974), and Mynhardt (1980), in South Africa. In Britain, Warr <u>et al</u>. (1967) found that with a non- student sample, their version of the E scale, which is predominantly a measure of ethnic prejudice, correlated +0.52 with the F scale. And Kohn (1974) using a version of the F scale with half the items reversed, found correlation of .84 with the Warr <u>et al</u>. E scale, with a student sample. Hoogvelt (1970) found significantly higher scores on an ad hoc modified F scale for people writing to a Wolverhampton newspaper in 1968 in favour of Enoch Powell's (hostile and pessimistic) views on immigration and race relations than among persons writing to express a contrary view. (Enoch Powell is a well-known English politician, whose anti-immigrant views received much publicity in 1968.) F is a good predictor of ethnic prejudice and negative ethnic attitudes, then, and not only among North American students.

F and political and social attitudes
In the original study, the F scale correlated with a measure of politico-economic conservatism. Because of the meaning of conservatism in our culture, this correlation is to be expected, but only among people where conservatism is part of a conforming ideology, or where it is a deliberately chosen political stance. The relation should not be expected among traditionally socialist families in Britain. Kohn (1974) found the following mean item scores for members of different student political societies at Reading University (the differences are significant) on his F scale: Socialist Society, 1.82; Labour, 2.72; Liberal, 2.76; Conservative, 3.93. Rubenowitz (1963) investigated a sample in Sweden including a group of railway employees, 242 military conscripts, and 172 university students,

and found that high F scorers tended to belong to conservative political parties. The C (for 'Conservatism') scale measures the related characteristics of religious dogmatism, right-wing political views, preference for conventional art and design, punitiveness, negative feelings about pleasure, and negative attitudes to minority ethnic groups. It was first published by Wilson and Patterson in 1968, and extensive use has been made of it since. Its interest lies in its (unsurprising, considering its content) relation to the F scale. Kohn (1974) found a correlation of 0.81 between the C scale and his version of the F scale, with British undergraduates. Crano (cited by Wilson, 1973) found a correlation of 0.68, with American undergraduates. Mynhardt (1980) reports that Afrikaans speaking students scored higher on both F and on C than comparable English speaking students in South Africa; the correlation (0.46) between F and C was significant for the English speaking students (but not for the Afrikaans speaking students, for reasons which remain unexplained). Ray (1982) reports a correlation between F and favouring the death penalty, in a (white) South African sample. Mann (1973) investigated attitudes to the punishment of soldiers who killed non-combatants while on active service, and asked whether the respondents themselves would kill non-combatants if they were in the army. (The investigation was done while the massacre at My Lai was in the headlines. The world has little remembered that incident: Lieutenant William Calley and a patrol of American soldiers murdered a number of women and children, and the social climate of the time was such that a number of people were upset, and Calley was arrested.) Mann found that in his Australian non-student sample, high F scorers were more likely than low to favour letting Calley off rather than punishing him, and more high Fs said that they would shoot civilians if ordered than lows. French and Ernest (1956), using American Air Force personnel, and Henley, Dixon, and Cartmell (1977) among RAF officers and among a separate civilian sample, found high positive correlations between F scales and scales measuring acceptance of and liking for things military and military ideology. And Kerpelman (1968) found that supporters of Barry Goldwater, a very conservative presidential candidate in the 1964 US election, scored higher on F than supporters of his opponent Johnson. Beswick and Hills (1972) found among a large Australian sample, considering those with more than 12 years education, there was a clear tendency for high F scorers to be politically conservative. The F scale does predict political and social attitudes then, as expected.

F and religion

Kohn (1974) is among those who have found (in a sample of Reading University students) that religious people (i.e., Christians) score higher on F than non-religious people.

F and prestige

Siegel (1954) is one of those who found supporting evidence for the contention that high scorers on F are desirous of prestige. He found that among girl students at an American college there was a correlation between desire to live in high status but less comfortable residences and scores on the F scale. Rubenowtiz (1963) also found a relation between the F scale and desire for prestige.

F and authoritarian aggression and authoritarian submission

Mann's (1973) work has already been mentioned, and is evidence of the relationship between F and authoritarian submission and authoritarian aggression. Elms and Milgram (1966) report that men who conformed to an experimenter's instruction to give severe electric shocks to another person in Milgram's famous experiments (see Milgram, 1974) scored higher on the F scale than men who refused to conform in that situation. (The difference seemed not to be due to acquiescence response bias in the F scale used; but the usual differences in education level of the two sets of men were found: high F, conformity, and low education, all went together.) Epstein (1965) found that American students scoring high on the F scale were more willing to give shocks to a victim in a learning situation than lows particularly where the victim was of low status: this study provides weak evidence for the relationship. Mitchell and Byrne (1973) found that high F students in the USA recommended stiffer punishment for a hypothetical student stealing an exam paper, particularly where the culprit had attitudes dissimilar to themselves.

F and conformity

There is some evidence that persons scoring high on the F scale conform more in experimental situations. One such piece of evidence is presented by Smith (1964), who used American college students, and found the effect where there was one dissenter from the majority view, who was a Chinese. Vaughan and White (1966), using an acquiescence free version of the F scale among New Zealand students, found a positive correlation between the F scale and conformity in two experimental situations. Nadler (1959) found a positive correlation between frequency of yielding on an Asch type task and the F scale, with American students. The weight of the evidence supports the hypothesis of a positive relationship between the F scale and conformity.

F and person perception

It is expected that high scorers, because they want to be conventional, (i.e., typical members of the ingroup), and think of themselves as good people, and because they tend to stereotype people as either good or bad, will judge most other people as being more similar to themselves than low scorers. Rubenowitz (1963) confirmed this hypothesis with his Swedish sample. Granberg's (1972) result is not expected, however: he found American students high on F assumed greater similarity between themselves and other American students than low scoring students, but they also assumed greater similarity between themselves and Chinese Communist students - scarcely good conventional members of the ingroup! As expected also, there is evidence that high F scorers think that a person with an undesirable trait will have other undesirable traits, and that one desirable trait entails others, as opposed to low scorers who are expected to see people as more of a mixture; evidence from work with American college students confirm this expectation (Steiner, 1954; Steiner & Johnson, 1963; Anderson, 1968).

SOCIALIZATION AND AUTHORITARIANISM.

The evidence above is supportive of the authoritarian personality theory. Perhaps it should be noted that it is all based on the use of the F scale. There is some evidence for the genetic theory of prejudice put forward by Adorno and his colleagues. They present evidence based on the recollections of their interviewees of their own childhood, and this evidence has been questioned. However there is some further supporting evidence, though the two pieces of evidence here do not refer directly to the F scale. Harris, Gough, and Martin (1950) found 25 children who displayed ethnic prejudice, and 25 who did not. They found that, in contrast to the relatively unprejudiced children's mothers, the mothers of prejudiced children endorsed questionnaire items indicative of authoritarian child rearing practices (e.g., 'I am strict and firm with my child'), and items indicating rigid standards (e.g., 'My child is expected to be neat and tidy in the house'). Weatherley (1963) found a correlation between a measure of maternal punitiveness and children's anti-Semitism. In a study of personal constructs, Bagley, Verma, Mallick and Young (1979) compared a group of prejudiced with a group of unprejudiced English university students. They found that, compared with unprejudiced students, the prejudiced students saw their fathers (and other authority figures) as more distant, and as hard, cold and dominating. Thomas (1975) examined the responses of Brisbane (Australia) mothers with children between four and six years old. They filled out the C scale (see above) and he also interviewed them extensively about their child rearing practices. High conservative mothers practiced the authoritarian modes of child rearing expected on the basis of the authoritarian personality theory: that is, they were non-permissive with regard to masturbation and nudity, they demanded obedience and orderliness, they differentiated sharply between the roles of boys and girls and so on. A weakness of the studies by Weatherley and Thomas is that neither controlled strongly for social class - it is known that both prejudice and authoritarian child rearing practices are commoner in working class than in middle class families. Further, none of the studies mentioned could differentiate between the effects on prejudice and negative attitudes of punitive child rearing practices, and direct teaching of prejudices by the parents. Still, they do provide some corroboration of Adorno et al.'s theory of the development of the authoritarian personality.

COMPLICATIONS

It is plain that authoritarianism is not the sole factor predictive of ethnic prejudice. Pettigrew, in his study carried out in South Africa in 1956 (1958), found that white students born in Africa exhibited stronger anti-Black attitudes than their fellow students at the same university who were born overseas, but were no higher on F; and in the Southern states of the USA (i.e., former slave states) Whites' scores on the F scale were no higher in regions with large black populations than in those with small, but their anti-Black attitudes were stronger. Examining data collected from 1,975 adults all over the USA in 1964, Middleton (1976) finds that, while persons in the Southern states did have slightly and significantly higher F scores than in other states, they had very markedly higher anti-Black attitudes; the difference in attitudes was too great to be accounted for by difference in F scores. Ray (1980a,b) finds with random samples of adults in Johannesburg, South Africa, Sydney, Australia, and Los Angeles, California, that anti-Black attitudes were higher in Johannesburg and Sydney than in Los Angeles (very similar scales were used), scores on the F scale were not significantly different. Weller (1964) in the USA divided his subjects into four social classes: I - managerial and professional; II - clerical and craftsmen; III - operative, domestics, social workers, and labourers; IV - farmers. He found through partial correlations that in classes I and II personality factors (including F) played a greater part in determining E (his measure of prejudice) than among classes III and IV; among the latter, non-personality factors like age, education, place of upbringing, religion, played a greater part than they do in higher classes. Weima (1964) found that among Dutch Protestant samples the F scale correlated more highly with anti-Catholic attitudes in well educated than in less well educated groups (and, though Weima does not say so, the difference is highly significant).

What these results strongly suggest is that cultural factors play a part in determining ethnic prejudice. (Cultural factors no doubt also play a part in determining authoritarianism. Gainer and Bass's results, 1959, show a significantly lower variance on F scale scores among students in Louisiana - in the 'deep South' - who were high on E and F, than among Kansas or Maryland students.) The point sounds like a truism, but it will be repeated below. What needs, perhaps, to be stressed once more, is that over and over again, through a long period, it has been shown that scores on the F scale predict negative ethnic attitudes (see the section above on F and ethnic prejudice). In different milieux mean levels of ethnic prejudice are different, but the variation around these means is explained by the same variables - namely, notably, authoritarianism, and a combination of the mutually intercorrelated factors of class, education, and intelligence.

CONCLUSIONS REGARDING THE F SCALE

The F scale has survived more than three decades, and is still useful today. The personality theory behind the F scale, set out above, has been reasonably well tested and finds much direct support. Direct tests on various hypotheses comprising the theory have been done in many cultures, including Sweden, Great Britain, and South Africa. Indirect evidence for the theory has been presented by Robb, who, working in a different culture with very different respondents from Adorno et al. (East London working class men as opposed to the predominantly middle class sample of Adorno et al.) came to very similar conclusions regarding the personality of the prejudiced person. So, though in less detail, did McGranahan (1946), and McGranahan and Janowitz (1946). And evidence that Calvinist conformists in South Africa (McCrone, 1937/1957; Lever, 1968; Mynhardt, 1980), are more anti-Black in attitude provides further indirect support. The latter also found the expected kinds of differences between children showing characteristically high and those showing relatively low social distance scores, on judgement of how bad a transgression it is 'if a boy or girl your age asked one of his parents about sex', '. . . made a noise while in the church service', and so on. It is clear then, that scores on the F scale can be contaminated with acquiescence response bias, but that it is possible to detect and to control this bias. Hence, given to fairly sophisticated people, socialized in Western European culture as found in Britain, the USA, white South Africa, etc., it measures a somewhat hazy but recognizable factor called 'authoritarianism' which is imperfectly but quite strongly correlated with racial prejudice, certain political and social attitudes, certain tendencies, and, perhaps, a disposition to overt fascism. It is important to include 'imperfectly', because no one suggests that an authoritarian personality is the only factor behind prejudice or fascism, so that implied criticisms of the F scale made when people find that high F scores are not the only factor in prejudice (e.g., Paige, 1970) are quite misplaced. Conventionality in prejudiced cultures, for example, is an important factor underlying prejudice, as has long been known.

Authoritarianism is not necessarily a complex ideology, but is a network of more-or-less related attitudes and tendencies ('syndrome' Adorno and his colleagues called it, revealing their feelings on the matter). Criticisms of the F scale for failing to measure a coherent and complex ideology are entirely misplaced. There is a relation, perhaps a curvilinear one or one which breaks down at the extreme ends, between the authoritarian component of F scales, and sophistication (some compound of intelligence, education and experience). At lower levels of sophistication as Weller (1964) for one shows, and where cultural factors play an important part in determining prejudice, the F scale is a somewhat less strong predictor of prejudice, other factors accounting for a greater proportion of the variance. It seems, prima facie, probable that at very high levels of sophistication dispassionate analysis of the items and the facts relating to them may destroy the basis on which the F scale measures authoritarianism (or do I have too great a faith in the intellect of intellectuals?)

The theory and hypotheses are set down in summary form in the last chapter.

NOTE 1

The logical relations which are important in this context are these:

<u>Contradiction</u>. Statements p and q are <u>contradictory</u> provided that if p is true, q is false, and if p is false, q is true. They cannot both be true or both be false. Together they include the whole universe of discourse. Examples of pairs of contradictory statements in classical

logical form are: 'All dogs are mammals' and 'Some dogs are not mammals'; and 'No dogs are mammals' and 'Some dogs are mammals'.

Contrariety. Statement p is contrary to statement q provided that p's truth implies q's falsity. They can both be false, but they cannot both be true. e.g. 'All snakes are poisonous' and 'No snakes are poisonous'.

Subcontrariety. Statement p is subcontrary to q provided that p's falsity implies q's truth, and q's falsity implies p's truth. They cannot both be false, but they can both be true. e.g. 'Some animals are mammals' and 'Some animals are not mammals'.

The important difference between contradiction on the one hand, and contrariety and subcontrariety on the other, is that contradictories exhaust the universe of discourse. To be logical, if one affirms one of two contradictory statements, one must deny the other, and if one denies one of two contradictory statements, one must affirm the other. This consideration does not apply to contraries or to subcontraries.

Chapter 6

PRINCIPLES OF ETHNIC PREJUDICE

Let us now try to formulate some principles of ethnic prejudice. These probably apply, <u>mutatis mutandis</u>, to prejudices about objects other than ethnic groups. Note that these principles are hypotheses or incipient <u>laws</u>. Their formal function in the scientific scheme of things is to explain and predict prejudiced behaviour and thinking; less formally, they have the human function of summarizing and clarifying our knowledge, and making it easier to remember.

PRINCIPLE I
There are two interacting types of prejudice: one is based on personality structure and needs, and the other is based on misinformation - some of it culturally based - and the need to keep cognitive load light.

Much of the evidence for this principle has been given already above. There is considerable evidence for the theory outlined above, of the type of personality described as 'authoritarian', and the relation (among middle-class Western peoples at least) of this personality type to ethnic prejudice. It is not quite clear at this stage whether more general prejudices are accountable for in a similar sort of way, but it seems likely that they are, in view of the indications that there are 'rigid lows' on the F scale, and that dogmatism does relate to prejudice (Bethlehem. 1969) as one would expect. It is clear, as has been said above, that authoritarianism is not the only factor in ethnic prejudice, still less in other prejudices. Everyone is prejudiced, since we all voice and act on opinions which we have not properly tested: life is too short to test all our opinions, even if we accept weakish tests. Indeed our very perceptions may sometimes be prejudices: the well known Ames demonstration shows that input we ordinarily accept as implying one thing can mean something very different. Artists have of course known this for years. Visitors to art galleries may well have seen examples of 'peep-shows': there is a famous one, by the seventeenth century Dutch artist van Hoogstraten in the National Gallery in London. These are basically wooden boxes with small holes in the sides through which the opposite wall may be viewed with one eye: on the opposite wall, an interior scene is painted, the perspective so cleverly done that until the secret is revealed the viewer supposes that he or she is seeing a three dimensional model, rather than a painting on a flat surface. Perceptions serve the same kind of function as cognitions – they code or organize data into meaningful chunks, because we cannot deal individually with the mass of potential information provided by individual sensations. Ethnic prejudices are useful in keeping cognitive load light, and are the subject of misinformation.

It has been shown how prejudice against black people became almost a part of Western culture. The part played by cultural factors in accounting for prejudice was mentioned (under 'Complications') at the end of the previous chapter. Some further points will be briefly made. This cultural aspect is highlighted in some milieux such as present-day South Africa, where those most committed to the culture (the Afrikaans speaking Whites) are most prejudiced (e.g. MacCrone, 1937/1957; Lever, Mynhardt, 1980). There is the complication that they are also the most likely to be authoritarian. Rogers and Frantz (1962) found in Zimbabwe (then Southern Rhodesia) that among white immigrants, the longer they had been in Southern Rhodesia, the more anti-black their attitudes, suggesting that the longer term immigrants had become acculturated to the dominant Southern Rhodesian (white) attitudes. Middleton (1976), in his analysis of the 1964 survey data referred to in the last chapter, shows that compared with other regions in the USA, in the old Confederate state (i.e. areas of traditional anti-black attitudes), anti-black attitudes are elevated above anti-Semitic and anti-Catholic attitudes, and to a greater extent than can be accounted for by the difference in F scale scores alone. Elkin and Panning (1975) showed that the

137

more strongly a person identified with their neighbourhood (the data was obtained in London), the closer the person's attitude toward minority ethnic groups was to the neighbourhood mean. Bagley, a sociologist, and his co-workers (Bagley, 1973; Bagley & Verma, 1979; Bagley, Verma, Mallick, & Young, 1979) report that in Dutch society prejudice and discrimination are frowned upon — though the proportion in the Netherlands population of 'coloured' immigrants from former Dutch colonies is about the same as the proportion in the British population of 'coloured' immigrants to Britain from former British colonies. His empirical work with questionnaires and with discrimination tests (comparing, for instance, the number of black applicants with the number of similarly qualified white applicants who are refused accommodation and jobs) show that in the Netherlands the level of prejudice and discrimination against non-white people is much lower than it is in Britain. The Netherlands did not have the heavy involvement in the slave trade that Britain had. Nonetheless, in the Netherlands, as elsewhere, it is older people, and people of lower socio-economic status and less education, who are relatively prejudiced. Ethnic prejudice, then, is in some part explained by cultural differences, since different cultures provide differing norms of (mis-) information about members of outgroups.

Further evidence of how the inability to deal with all the information available to us affects people's judgements and opinions, making us less rational than we might be, was provided in the chapter on the influence of prejudice on reasoning and judgement. We are not all expert logicians and statisticians, and hence we do not always make optimum — or any — use of the sampling data, and correlational data, etc., which is potentially available. This inability partly explains two commonly observed characteristics. One is the way people may in some sense 'know' that most Asians (in Britain) are poor, that most Jews are reasonably honest, that most Whites are not rabid racists, but nonetheless talk and act as if Asians are all wealthy, Jews are all untrustworthy, or that Whites are all racists. The other thing that is partly explained is the cognitive let-out device of admitting exceptions: 'Blacks are treacherous', but (putting aside the generalization) 'My black servants are very loyal'. Dickens (in Hard Times) implied a sneer at Mr. Gradgrind when, after the elderly Mr. Bounderby had proposed to his daughter, he acquainted himself with the statistics of the success of marriages between older men and young women. But then Dickens was not a scientist! And yet, even psychologists seem by and large to prefer clinical to statistical prediction!

Yet a further illustration of how the need to keep cognitive load light might feed prejudices is provided by Taylor, Fiske, Etcoff, and Ruderman (1978). They tape recorded conversations, attributing some voices to Blacks and some to Whites in one experiment, and in other experiments some voices were men's and some were women's. Several versions of the same conversation - carefully rehearsed - were taped, and the tapes cleverly spliced so that points made by Whites (or men) in some versions were made by Blacks (or women) in others. They found that when listeners were afterwards asked who had said what, their mistakes tended significantly to be in attributing something one white had said to another white, and one black's conversational points to another black; one man's conversational points to another man, and one woman's to another woman. What appears to occur is that listeners cannot remember all the individuals, so they reduce the load on memory by coding in this way: 'A _black_ said that', or 'A _woman_ said that'.

A corollary of the main proposition is that unconventional persons in our culture are less likely to be ethnically prejudiced than conventional ones. This proposition follows from the authoritarian personality theory (conventionality is one facet of the authoritarian personality) and also from the proposition that some prejudice is attributable to cultural norms: an unconventional person by definition is one who does not accept all the norms and conventions of a culture.

Direct evidence for the corollary is provided by Pettigrew (1958) who found that in the Southern USA church-goers were more prejudiced - church attendance being indicative of conventionality. Kohn (1974) also found a difference on his F scale between conventionally religious British students and students not conventionally religious, those professing conventional religion scoring higher. Now, some people have been surprised at the correlation consistently found between degree of Christianity (as measured by church affiliation, self-reported belief, etc.) and prejudice -

particularly as some churchmen have always been prominent in the struggle against racism - Dr. Livingstone and Father (as he was in South Africa) Huddleston are simply two that spring to mind, as men of religion who suffered for their outspokenness against racial prejudice in Southern Africa. There are further complications in the pattern of the relation of religion and prejudice. In Britain, and in Holland it appears that people who claim affiliation to a large Christian religious group - particularly, in England, the Church of Englnd - but attend infrequently at church and/or donate little to their church, tend to be prejudiced (Bagley, 1970; Bagley et al., 1979). On the other hand, certain sects are notably non-racist: cadets of the Salvation Army in Britain and committed members of the Re-Reformed Church in Holland (Bagley, 1970; Wilson & Bagley, 1973). Allport and Ross (1967) investigated this problem and developed a scale measuring the degree to which Christianity was accepted as a personal moral system as compared to being accepted as the right or conventional thing to do. They found that the more a person accepted Christianity as an internal, personal, moral system, the less likely he or she was to be racist. Weima (1964) found that his scale of extrinsic religious values (the degree to which Christianity is valued for its institutional conventional structure) correlated very highly with the F scale in a Dutch sample. The empirical relation of Christianity to prejudice, then, seems to hold because they are both related to conventionality. Christians who are religious for reasons other than a comfortable conventionality (i.e., who feel real personal commitment) tend not to be prejudiced.

PRINCIPLE II

When groups are in competition or conflict, or members of one group fear those of another, or sometimes when a person simply recognises that he or she belongs to one particular group as opposed to another, discrimination in favour of the ingroup and unfavourable attitudes to members of the outgroup become norms in each.

About a decade ago, Henri Tajfel began to perform a number of experiments, with collaborators, on minimal group situations. These experiments have now given rise to a theory sufficiently well developed to make it worth devoting some attention to in this work. The experiments demonstrated that when people were divided quite arbitrarily into groups, they tended to choose outcomes maximizing the relative gain of a member of their own group relative to another group, over outcomes maximizing the joint gain of members of each group, or the equalizing of the outcomes of members of each group. These results, which have frequently been replicated, were surprising to some, because the groups formed were groups in name only (the members had no interaction with each other or with members of other groups in or out of the laboratory), were temporary - lasting for the duration of the experiment only, and people were assigned to one group or another on the basis of arbitrary, unimportant, and nearly meaningless criteria. The experiments were not performed in the service of any theory, but rather in consequence of a general feeling that the 'group' should be brought into greater prominence in social psychology: in scientific terms, that implies casting hypotheses in terms of groups rather than in terms of individuals.

The following experiment is typical. Tajfel, Billig, Bundy, and Flament (1971) divided comprehensive school boys, 14 or 15 years old, into four groups on the basis of their estimates of the numbers of dots flashed briefly onto a screen. The groups were termed the 'better accuracy' group (i.e. those whose judgements were supposedly accurate relative to members of the other groups), the 'worse accuracy' group, and the 'overestimators' and the 'underestimators': in fact, boys were assigned to groups without regard to their performance on the task. Following that, they were invited to choose a column in a matrix assigning a small sum of money to a member of the ingroup (not to themselves) and a different sum to a member of the outgroup (see table 2), these sums being determined by the chosen column. This table is similar to ma_rices used in various experiments. Of course, an infinite number of such matrices can be constructed, and many different matrices have been used, as well as different procedures.

In all groups in the experiment by Tajfel et al., whether they were labelled 'better' (accuracy) or 'worse' (presumably a label with connotations of value) or simply 'over-' and 'under-estimators', there was a significant tendency

Table 2: Matrix similar to those used in experimental studies of ingroup bias. Maximum fairness is obtained by choosing columns 7 or 8; columns 8-14 represent increasing relative gain (and increasing own gain, or profit) to the ingroup member, and columns 7-1 represent increasing relative (and absolute) loss to the ingroup member.

Amount to be given to	COLUMN													
	1	2	3	4	5	6	7	8	9	10	11	12	13	14
Ingroup member:	3	4	5	6	7	8	9	10	11	12	13	14	15	16
Outgroup member:	16	15	14	13	12	11	10	9	8	7	6	5	4	3

to favour relative gain for the ingroup member over the other outcomes. In fact the tendency was not extreme, the mean of choices being about at the level of column 9 in table 2 - that is, one column above the maximum fairness, and that is generally the order of magnitude of the obtained effect. But it is plain that there was a tendency for relative gain to influence choices. A second experiment reported in the same paper corroborated the result, as have a great many experiments since. Brewer and Silver (1978), for instance, found that American women students divided into groups in a somewhat similar manner to that described above, tended to maximize relative gain for the ingroup when the reward structure was competitive and when the rewards received by ingroup members were totally independent of the rewards of the outgroup. Even when the rewards to ingroup and outgroup were explicitly made dependent on the joint gain (i.e., the sum of the amounts obtained by ingroup and outgroup) students did not choose the outcomes maximizing joint gain where there was a superficially _relative_ difference. These results are a close parallel to the results with experimental games played between individuals. Other experiments have shown that ingroup bias occurs when the groups are comprised of 7-11 year old children (e.g. Vaughan, Tajfel, & Williams, 1981), 14-16 year old children (Hewstone, Fincham, & Jaspers, 1981), as well as adults of both sexes; and when what is distributed or allocated is small amounts of money, (Vaughan _et al._, 1981), plastic chips (Locksley, Ortiz, & Hepburn, 1980), or ratings on desirable characteristics (Locksley _et al._, 1980).

Interest in groups had never been absent from social psychology. Of the two books on _Social Psychology_ published in 1908 - the year the term first appeared in book titles - Ross's was primarily sociological in orientation, and McDougall's psychological. Both proved sterile ultimately, despite the great interest they tapped, but both reflect traditions which have always been alive in social psychological thought. On the one hand, there is McDougall's emphasis on the individual person: ' . . . social psychology has to show how, given the native propensities and capacities of the individual human mind, all complex mental life of societies is shaped by them and in turn reacts upon the course of their development and operation in the individual' (this quotation is in fact from the seventh edition, p. 18). On the other hand, Ross (1908, p. 1) asserts that 'Social psychology, as the writer conceives it, studies the psychic planes and currents that come into existence among men in consequence of their association.' The latter tradition within psychology has been kept up, much of it under the banner of 'group dynamics'.

Perhaps the most famous of studies of intergroup relations are studies done by Muzafer Sherif (who is equally well known for his seminal studies on attitudes and on social influence), and his collaborators. These are too well known to require extensive recounting here, and they are clearly summarized by Sherif himself (e.g. 1967). Very briefly, three experiments were performed, the first in 1949, and the results are usually considered together. Boys of 11 or 12 years old were taken to holiday camps by adults (who were experimenters). They were split into two groups. Quite soon, pressures to conformity within each group were observed, and hostility to members of the outgroups developed. Insults between members of different groups were commonplace. Prejudices against members of the outgroup developed. The only way the experimenters could find of reducing the hostility and prejudice between groups was to introduce a series of situations where co-operation between the groups was necessary to achieve some goal desired by both of them: as, for example, to push-start a lorry which was to fetch food for them at a picnic. These results are valuable, in that they were experimentally produced and led to semi-formal conclusions. But they should surprise no-one who attended a school divided into 'houses', where, after random allocation to one or another house, many pupils develop a fanatical loyalty to their house and its interests. Robert Graves remarks, in recounting his experiences during the Great War, that British soldiers were motivated through those terrible years in the trenches primarily by <u>regimental</u> pride; patriotism was 'too remote a sentiment' (Graves, 1960, p. 157). Nothing would induce all the members of the British army to wear the same uniform, and with good reason!

To return for a moment to the question of the effect of competition on intergroup attitudes: it has often been noticed that economic competition between groups seems to be at the base of a lot of prejudice and hostility. It is notable that in South Africa it is the white working class, who would face the most immediate competition for jobs and status if the <u>apartheid</u> system were to break down, who are among the strongest supporters of the system. In the USA, it has often been noticed, members of some ethnic groups - e.g., Jews - are less anti-black than most. Cummings (1980) investigated attitudes to contact with Blacks, to civil rights legislation, and to black protest, among various ethnic groups in the USA. He found that, while it was indeed true that Jews, French and Irish Catholics, protestants of British descent, and persons of Scandinavian descent, were more 'tolerant' than protestants of Irish descent, Italian Americans, and Americans of East European descent, this difference was not evident where members of the different groups mentioned occupied the same niche. Jews in jobs where there was potential competition with Blacks (e.g., manual jobs in the construction and motor vehicle manufacturing industries) were not consistently more tolerant than, say, Italian Americans; and Italian Americans in professional and high managerial positions were not more intolerant than Jews in those positions.

For historical and cultural reasons Jews are under-represented in working class jobs where competition with Blacks is likely. This economic competition does seem to predict negative attitudes - an observation consonant with the conclusions of the chapter on historical perspectives.

Tajfel (e.g. 1978) has outlined a very loose theory relating to social groups ('Social Identity Theory'). It is not clear or testable at this stage, but shows signs of being developed that way. At the moment it may be regarded as a valuable prolegomena to a scientific theory. It will be briefly outlined.

A group, for the purposes of this theory, is a set of people who feel themselves to belong to the same group, or are felt by others so to belong. No operational definition of the concept has so far been attempted, and the difficulties are evident. Are Jews a group? If yes, does that include exogamous and non-religious Jews? Are the black people in South Africa a group? The answers to these questions must obviously be 'yes and no', which is in itself little help to prediction. It is postulated that people strive for a satisfactory self-image, and a person voluntarily stays a member of a group only as long as being a member enhances his or her self-image. It is also, even more vaguely, postulated that people do in fact understand and predict the 'social environment' in terms of 'groups', and these groups allow people to compare their ingroups with a variety of outgroups. In some circumstances people behave as a member of a group, and in these circumstances members of one group will act fairly uniformly to members of another group. Social movements arise for or against change when members feel they are marginal, or when members of superior groups feel the elevated position of their group threatened and/or when members of a lower group cease to accept the legitimacy of their lot or the immutability of the social system.

The very general nature of this theory does not need to be further stressed. Its importance for social psychology in general lies in the way it points for formulating testable hypotheses and more careful definitions of its terms. Where the subject of prejudice is concerned, its importance is in focussing attention on the way in which people fall into groups, these groups then develop hostility to other groups, and prejudices against members of the outgroup seem to develop naturally from there. It has been shown by Sherif (see 1967) and his co-workers that members of the ingroup judge the performance of members of their own group better than that of members of the outgroup, even when there is no objective difference. And Tajfel and Wilkes (1963) have shown that differences between lengths of lines are exaggerated when the lines are said to belong to two separate groups. Hence it appears that where people are divided into groups, prejudices against members of the outgroup will develop, and distortions in judgements and perceptions will occur which will support these prejudices.

The fundamental problems are to ascertain the circumstances which will predict and explain the formation of groups and the identification of people with groups. At present we have nothing beyond a few vague and intuitive ideas. We can discuss only along historical lines why some groups remain separate (e.g. Basques, Walloons, Palestinians, Afrikaners), while others assimilate and merge with each other (Normans with Vikings with Angles with Saxons, for instance). The only reasonably satisfactory explanation that can be offered for identification is in terms of the relation of authoritarianism to ethnocentrism. A start has perhaps been made in the investigation of identification, by Genesee, Tucker, and Lambert (1978). Defining 'identification' operationally as perceived similarity to self measured on a rating scale, it was found with English-speaking Canadian school children that those who attended French medium schools identified in this sense less with English Canadians and more with other groups than children in dual medium or English medium schools, although there were signs that identification with English Canadians increased as a function of age. Studies of Asian immigrants in Britain (Mercer, Mercer, & Mears, 1979), and of immigrants in Australia (Taft, 1966) suggest that the language a person chooses to use is a good indicant of how closely a person identifies with a group: for English speaking immigrants in Australia, frequency of use of Australianisms (such as bonzer, and to winge - i.e., very good and to moan the Australian term has since come into more general use) is a measure of acculturation and identification with Australia. Mac Greil (1977) asked Dubliners from a list of groups (e.g. Dubliners, Southern Irish, etc.) the one that 'best describes the way you usually think of yourself', and to note whether they were a 'strong' or an 'average' Dubliner, Southern Irish person, etc.: he found that persons who rated themselves 'strong' members of a group expressed greater social distance to outgroups. On the other hand, Brewer, in a very important paper (1979), has begun to delineate circumstances which are conducive to making people act as members of a small ingroup against members of an outgroup in laboratory situations. It may tentatively be hypothesised, following Brewer, that the following factors serve to increase discrimination in favour of members of an ingroup: (a) real or imagined personal similarity between members of a group; (b) sharing of a common fate between members of a group; (c) prominence of the basis of division into groups. Even more tentatively, more recent research has indicated that the following factors were to diminish discrimination in favour of the ingroup: (a) where penalties, rather than rewards or points, must be distributed (Hewstone et al., 1981); (b) where other members of the ingroup fail to discriminate in favour of ingroup members, or members of the outgroup fail to discriminate (Locksley et al., 1980); (c) where there is no element of competition at all - where ratings of in- and outgroup members are done in different dimensions (Mummendey & Schreiber, 1983).

Two disparate points can now be made. One is that the effect of actual or anticipated competition with an outgroup does not seem clear at this stage; and the other is that reward for one member of an ingroup does seem to function as reward for others. Empathy may be an important factor in relations between members of a group, and one may speculate that the callousness sometimes displayed to members of outgroups is partially explicable by a lack of empathy with their suffering.

PRINCIPLE III
> The less information we have about a
> person, the more likely we are to respond
> to him or her in terms of stereotypes or
> the prevailing social norms.

In a way, this is almost self evident. If we know little about someone, what can we do but respond in terms of some stereotype or norm? Yet that begs an important question: Why not either not respond at all, or wait until we've found out something about the person? Sometimes, of course, neither of these two courses is open to us. When it is, the authoritarian personality theory holds that authoritarians are unable to stand uncertainty, and will make judgements without evidence rather than admit to themselves they are ignorant; in fact there is little evidence for this assertion, since measures of 'intolerance of ambiguity' which are clearly valid are lacking.

But the proposition does seem to accord with common experience. Weak evidence is provided by Secord's (1959) experiment which showed that no matter how 'white' a face looked, if it was said to be the face of a black man (in America, 'black' included anyone with black ancestry), prejudiced Whites attributed its owner with traits assigned to Blacks in general. All studies in which people respond to pictures of others, or to members of named groups (Bemba, Mexicans, Yorkshiremen and -women) or to their voices or accents, also provide weak evidence in favour. Again, Banton (1959) found that of 15 respondents in a series of interviews concerning attitudes to 'coloured' immigrants conducted in different areas in England and Scotland, 14 replied 'No' to the question 'Have you had any experiences which have influenced you for or against coloured people?'

If the reader will recall the chapter on the influence of prejudice on reasoning and judgement, it will be remembered that people are very much influenced by information which appears to relate to specifics, even when this information is of little real value. Conversely, when specific information is not available, it must be more general factors that affect judgement. Hepburn and Locksley (1983) have provided some fairly direct evidence on the point. They presented students with a questionnaire asking, for instance, what proportion of Blacks are athletic and what proportion of Whites are athletic, and what proportion of overweight people are impulsive and what proportion of people of normal weight are impulsive. These measures relate to widely held implicit theories of personality, of which stereotypes are a subset. They found that students' judgements of how athletic a black or a white was, or how impulsive an overweight or a person of normal weight was, were more heavily influenced when the person was simply identified as a black, an overweight person, etc., than when the person was identified as a black, an overweight person, etc., with the addition of some further information. This finding held even when the additonal information applied was irrelevant to athleticism or impulsiveness. What is more, the students showed no awareness of the degree to which their judgements had been affected by their implicit personality theories! Quattrone and Jones's (1980) result qualifies the conclusion that individuating information gets rid of the effect of stereotyping. Using students at two different rivalrous American universities, they found that individuating information about the behaviour of a member of the outgroup had less effect on judgements about the typical behaviour of the outgroup when subjects had strong prejudices about the outgroup. Individuating information, it seems, has most effect in reducing stereotype based judgements where weak prejudices are held, and less effect where strong prejudices are held. This last study provides reasonably strong evidence for the proposition, though none of the quoted studies have shown that people are responded to differently on the basis of stereotypes in the flesh: however, this assumption seems safe enough. In my experience, white South Africans who would certainly say the most ferocious things about Blacks in general, have shown great gentility and affection towards individual black people. Triandis and Vassiliou (1967) show that Americans who have had experience of contact with Greeks, and Greeks who have met with Americans, do have somewhat different stereotypes of Greeks and Americans than those without experience of contact. Other studies (reviewed by Amir, 1969), show that under some circumstances contact reduces unfavourable prejudices.

It seems clear then that responses to people in terms of categories are made, and that responses are, or would be, modified by having more information about persons responded about.

PRINCIPLE IV

The socially accepted attitudes to and stereotypes of various ethnic groups are widely known to members of a society, and have widespread effects on behaviour.

There is widespread evidence that people in any given culture know and accept cultural norms to do with attitudes to members of their own and other ethnic groups. By way of illustration, Strongman and Woosley (1967) showed that English students from places north of Staffordshire and those from southern England held partly similar stereotypes of Yorkshiremen as industrious, reliable chaps, (Northerners held additional, also very favourable, traits to characterize Yorkshiremen as well). Similarly Cheyne (1970) showed that both English and Scottish subjects rated Scottish people (identified by their accents) as more friendly than English (the Scots subjects rated Scots men as higher on traits like generosity as well); English and Scots subjects rated Englishmen as more ambitious, intelligent, self-confident, and so on - a result which may have been affected by their thinking of the Scots as of lower class and status than the English. These norms are, of course, the basis of the culturally founded prejudice mentioned above. Buchanan (1951) reports a survey done on large samples in nine different countries (Britain, France, Germany, Italy, Netherlands, Norway, Mexico, and the United States) in 1948, in which respondents were asked to select adjectives from a list which they thought descriptive of various peoples (people described will be called target groups). They were explicity given the option of saying they did not know or that the target group was impossible to characterize. One would have thought that more sophisticated respondents would make most use of this latter ('Don't Know') type of response, but in fact it was the less sophisticated respondents who made most use of it. In opinion polls this finding is almost universal. Hence people do seem to be fairly confident of their characterizations. What is striking is that there is wide agreement among people in a given country about what adjectives apply to various ethnic and national groups. Thus, for instance, 81 per cent of the French sample, and 61 per cent of the Dutch sample chose 'practical' as characteristics of Americans. The picture of the Russians was most consistent from country to country (hardworking, cruel, backward, domineering, and brave), and that of the Americans almost as consistent (progressive, practical, generous, and intelligent). The cold war was icing over at the time, giving rise to super-stereotypes of the major publicised posturers. The British, incidentally, were described by the German, Dutch and American samples as intelligent, self-controlled, and conceited. For each group, there was a high degree of agreement about which adjectives characterized their own group, and these adjectives were invariably favourable. Ziegler, King, King, and Ziegler (1972) found agreement among tribal groups in Ethiopia about members of other Ethiopian groups. Similarly, Bakare (1977) found agreement among Nigerian students of the Hausa, Yoruba, and Ibo tribes about the characteristics of the Hausa, Ibo, and Yoruba: all agreed that Hausas are 'kind', for example, that Yorubas are 'progressive', and that Ibos are 'industrious' and 'boastful'. Mitchell (1956) found that one factor in social distance between members of tribal groups in Zambia was the widely disseminated reputation each group had - the Bemba and Ngoni as men of military prowess, for instance. Bethlehem and Kingsley (1976) asked Zambian students to mark those adjectives on a list which applied to members of various ethnic (tribal) groups. The adjectives had previously been scaled for 'likableness', on a 0 to 6 scale. Thus 'kind' had a scale value of 5.12, 'seriousness' a neutral scale value (3.43), and 'quarrelsome' a very low scale value (0.88). This is a fairly straight measure of prejudice. It was found that members of certain ethnic groups (or tribes) were generally regarded by all or most others in a favourable light (positive prejudice), whereas members of other groups were the targets of the negative prejudices of all or most other groups. These differences were attributable to nationally prevailing stereotypes.

Further evidence is provided by the experiment of Taylor et al., (1978). They recorded rehearsed conversations between men and women, cleverly splicing them so that some listeners heard men taking some parts and making some points, and some heard women taking those same parts and making those same points. Despite the fact that what men and women said, and the way in which they said it, was identical, when different groups of listeners who had heard different versions rated the participants, stereotypes of men and women asserted themselves: men were rated on average as more influential, less sensitive, and less warm, than women - despite the fact that the only available evidence was the same, on average, for both sexes.

A very sad aspect of the widespread nature of the dominant ethnic attitude is the apparent influence it has on children of minority and less dominant ethnic groups. A common finding in doll and picture studies with children is that black children, when asked to choose the 'doll that looks like you' or to show some preference for black or white dolls or pictures, (such as 'show me the doll that is a nice doll' or 'who do you like best?'), even black children often choose the white doll or picture; or at least, while white children tend almost universally to choose Whites, the non-Whites do not show a consistent preference for their own ethnic group. This finding has been reported in the United States (e.g., Clark & Clark, 1958 - the study was done in 1940-41); in New Zealand (Vaughan, 1964; here 'black' refers to Maoris); in South Africa (Press, Burt, & Barling, 1979); and in Britain (e.g., Pushkin, in Pushkin & Veness, 1973; and Milner, 1973: the children in Milner's study were white, or of Asian parentage, or of West Indian parentage); and with Mexican-American (rather than black) children in the USA (Weiland & Coughlin, 1979); Tajfel, Nemeth, Jahoda, Campbell, & Johnson (1970) and Tajfel, Jahoda, Nemeth, Rim, & Johnson (1972) show that Scots children do not show such ethnocentric responses (where 'Scottish' is concerned) as, say, English, Dutch and the Austrian children do, and the latter investigation shows Israeli children of Oriental ancestry exhibit less prejudice in favour of Orientals than Israeli children of European origin show in favour of Europeans. Scots and Orientals, in these cases, are not oppressed minorities, but they are in a sense somewhat poor relations in their countries, and the dominant attitudes, subtly expressed in the cultures though they are, do permeate the children's thinking. Studies indicating an absence of ethnocentrism among minority group children may not cause too much heartache - quite the reverse, in fact, if one regards ethnocentrism with disfavour - but it is a trifle sad to have non-white children exhibiting preferences for white dolls, and more positive attitudes towards Whites than to Blacks. 'Say it loud, I'm black and I'm proud' may have some point. In fact, it is very difficult to compare different doll studies since different questions are asked, and different dolls, pictures, etc. are used. It is encouraging to note four points:

1. Some of the apparent choices of white dolls by '_black_' children seem to have been sensible responses to the questions asked by the experimenters. Clark and Clark's (1958) results indicate that 'Negro' children of light skin colour (anyone suspected of any black ancestry is regarded as a 'Negro' in the United States) were far more likely to choose the white doll in response to 'Give me the doll that looks like you', than to medium or

dark children. (The figures for light, medium and dark children's choices of the white doll were 80%, 26%, and 19%). Milner (1973) reports a similar trend in Britain. It seems likely that this type of response may not wholly reflect 'racial misidentification': it may be simply a straightforward, reasonable response to the request, into which experimenters have read too much. Greenwald and Oppenheim (1968) reduced the amount of apparent misidentification by using a light brown doll in addition to a white and a black one, and showed that misidentification is not entirely absent among white children.

2. It seems that the race of the experimenter sometimes affects the degree of preference for white dolls and the extent of apparent racial misidentification of non-white children. Indeed, it would be surprising if this were not so, as it is known that the race of the tester affects black American children's scores on IQ tests (see Dreger & Miller, 1968). Most experimenters on doll choice of black children have used white experimenters - though the Clarks are black.

3. Black people are regaining status and self-esteem. The common attitude to black people is shifting. Hraba and Grant (1970) repeated the Clark and Clark study in Lincoln, Nebraska, (Clark and Clark had done their study in Massachusetts and in Arkansas) after an interval of nearly 30 years, and found a marked difference in results: significantly more of their children chose the black doll as the one they would like to play with, the nice doll, the doll of 'the nice colour'. Jahoda, Thompson, and Bhatt (1972) found little misidentification and outgroup preference among their Asian children in Glasgow: they comment that Glasgow children are very tolerant of ethnic differences.

4. Vaughan's (1964) and Clark and Clark's (1958) results indicate that preference for white dolls and figures reaches a peak at a certain age (about 5 years in the Clark and Clark study, and later among Vaughan's white and Maori children), and thereafter declines somewhat.

Nor is the existence of stereotypes confined to ethnic groups. Vine (1974) found wide agreement among psychology students at Bristol University about what sort of handwriting went with extraversion and what sort with neuroticism - though there was no validity in these judgements (that is, they did not relate to the scores of the writers on the Eysenck Personality Inventory).

Perhaps we should just remind ourselves that stereotypes may have a 'kernel of truth': that is, Britons may really be intelligent, self-controlled, and conceited! - there must be cultural differences in expressive behaviour. But within any group there are wide individual differences. It seems obvious that, true or not, stereotypes are propagated by the mass media in modern society: hence the widespread nature of the stereotypes of the news-worthy Americans and Russians. George Orwell (1962) made an informal content analysis of boys' weeklies - Champion, Hotspur, Magnet, etc. - in 1939. These magazines were widely read at that time. In them, he found foreigners were largely stereotyped, Arabs and Chinese invariably being represented as sinister and treacherous, Scandinavians as kind-hearted, and so on.

Perhaps one should also say at this point that it is unlikely that anyone believes any adjective or trait to be characteristic of all members of a particular ethnic group, or that all members of one group would assign a particular trait to another. Investigations show that people make qualifications when given the chance, and are fairly consistent about their attributions of traits, even where prejudices are strong (e.g., Mann, 1967, whose investigation was done on students in South Africa). Nonetheless stereotypes are widespread, in the sense that a large percentage of respondents are usually willing to attribute certain traits and characteristics to a large percentage of members of certain target groups. Another point is that American students, at any rate, show less tendency to stereotype nowadays than was formerly the case (see Brigham, 1971), and it seems likely that the tendency is less marked among persons other than students as well.

PRINCIPLE V

Prejudices can be self-fulfilling: belief that a person has certain characteristics or attitudes may itself lead to 'evidence' for that belief.

The importance of this principle is becoming more apparent as evidence relating to it accrues. It has long been recognised that people can find evidence for what they want to believe. All the evidence in the chapter on the effect of prejudice on reasoning and judgement is evidence for this principle.

But what has become more apparent recently is that people can very easily elicit the behaviour they expect from others. Of course, it has always been known in a general sort of way that that is so. Penologists have frequently pointed out that brutal prison conditions must result in brutish behaviour on the part of the inmates. If a person is afraid of another (say because he thinks all Blacks are dangerous), then he may act aggressively towards the other; the other might respond with aggressiveness, and the first person finds his prejudice is confirmed. But the same thing can happen more subtly.

Snyder and Swann (1978) asked students to interview others, and the interviews were recorded. Half the interviewers were asked to assess whether the interviewee was an extravert; and the other half were asked to assess whether the interviewee was an introvert. Tapes of the responses of the interviewees only - not the questions asked by the interviewers - were subsequently played to a group of raters, who knew nothing about the first half of the experiment. The interesting finding was, that the raters rated those interviewees who were being assessed in the interview to see whether they were extraverted as more extraverted, confident, poised, and energetic, than those whose interviewers were assessing them to see if they were introverted. It appears then, that the kind of questions asked and the assumptions of the interviewers led to the interviewees actually behaving differently in that situation. Again, Snyder, Tanke, and Berscheid (1977) tape recorded the telephone conversations of men and women students in a laboratory. The men were given (bogus) photographs of the girl they were talking to; half of the photographs were of very attractive girls, and half of girls who were not very attractive. Subsequently, the tape recordings of the girls' part of the conversation only were played to another group of people, who knew nothing of the first part of the experiment. These people rated the girls whom the conversation partners had thought attractive as more sociable, poised, sexually warm, and outgoing, than the girls thought by the conversation partners to be unattractive. These traits have all been shown to be expected by male students to correlate with attractiveness. The supposedly attractive girls were also judged as having been more animated, more confident, and to have enjoyed the conversation more and liked their partner more, than the supposedly unattractive girls. That is, the expectations of the male conversation partner actually affected the behaviour of the girls themselves.

Prejudices can be self-fulfilling both by affecting the cognitive processes of the prejudiced person, and by acting through the prejudiced person's behaviour actually to affect the behaviour of people with whom the prejudiced person comes into contact.

PRINCIPLE VI
> The category of people about which prejudice centres differs from one group to another.

This statement is virtually a truism. We all know that in Lilliput the important category about which prejudice centred was a political one, whether a person was a Big-Endian or not, whereas in Eatonswill (only Dickens could invent a name as expressive as that: it is in The Pickwick Papers) the important category was a different political one - Blues and Buffs. In Northern Ireland, religious denomination is the important category, in South Africa it is race, in Zambia an important category is tribal origin, and Hazlitt (1852/1970) wrote an essay in 1821 inveighing against class prejudice in England.

Formal evidence for this proposition is provided by Bethlehem and Kingsley (1976), who showed that in Zambia tribe affected social distance and prejudice, whereas such a category is clearly irrelevant elsewhere (unless one extends the meaning of the term 'tribe' to cover larger ethnic groups). Class affected social distance in Zambia, and affected social distance scores of a sample of American middle class children more than race did (Epstein & Komorita, 1965). Brigham (1971) reviews evidence showing that prejudice against black Americans by Whites is often predicated on the assumption that Blacks are members of the lower socio-economic classes, and Feldman and Hilterman (1975) provide further evidence that this assumption underlies some white-black prejudice; explicitly upper class Blacks are not stereotyped in the same way as Blacks in general. Even in South Africa, the social distance of white students was lower to ethnic outgroup members of upper or middle class than to outgroup members of lower class: and this result applied to both white and non-white outgroups (Heaven & Bezuidenhout, 1978). Cheyne's (1970) study suggests that similar considerations may apply to English stereotypes of Scotsmen. Triandis, Davis, and Takezawa (1965) report that in Greece social distance is determined primarily by religion, followed by race and occupation; in Germany and Japan occupation was the most important factor, and nationality was an important factor in Japan, but not elsewhere. In the USA, race is a very important factor, though class also plays a significant part, as Triandis, Loh, and Levin (1966) also showed. Triandis and Davis (1965) and Goldstein and Davis (1972) found that some American students respond to others primarily on the basis of the other's race, and other students are more influenced by the other's beliefs - but both types of students tend to be influenced primarily by race where intimate behaviour is concerned. And clearly, within any category of people there are other individual differences too. One is the personal beliefs of each person: one person may be religious, another not; one may be nationalistic, another not. Taylor and Guimond (1979) showed, for instance, that French Canadian students who were inclined to Quebec separatism showed a greater social distance towards English speaking Canadians than did French Canadians who were not separatists: as one would expect.

Rokeach (1960) suggested that prejudice in America was determined, not by the race of the target, but by the beliefs imputed to members of other racial groups: that is, that there would be no prejudice by Whites against Blacks holding the same beliefs as themselves. (He did qualify this opinion by saying he was referring only to prejudice not consequent on cultural factors, but sought to eliminate that kind of prejudice, operationally). He tested this hypothesis by asking people to rate others whose race and beliefs were varied on a scale where 1 meant 'I can't see myself being friends with such a person' and 9 meant 'I can very easily see myself being friends with such a person'. He found that beliefs affected these ratings for both Northerners and Southerners, even the latter preferring as friends Blacks who have acceptable beliefs to Whites who are atheist or communists. Now Triandis (e.g., 1967) has found different factors on the traditional social distance scale. Among these are formal social acceptance ('I would admire the ideas of'), friendship acceptance, and social distance ('I would allow into my neighbourhood', 'I would accept as close kin by marriage'). These factors are not unrelated, however, the traditional social distance scale still scales in Guttman's sense (e.g., Triandis, Loh, & Levin, 1966). Triandis and Davis (1965) report, surprisingly enough, that a person's ideas determine whether respondents would 'admire the ideas of' that person to a greater extent than his own, whether they would be friends with the person, or whether they would allow the person to move into their neighbourhood. What results in the USA (Triandis and Davis, 1965; Goldstein and Davis, 1972) and in South Africa (Orpen & Pors, 1972) indicate is that for the more intimate behaviour race is the more important variable in determining social distance, and beliefs gain importance as one deals with less intimate behaviours. However, much as the typical white South African or typical white Southerner admires the ideas of a black man, the latter would not be permitted to approach the white's sister or luncheon table. Also some people are more influenced by the beliefs of the target than others: Smith, Williams, and Willis (1967) show that, where friendship is concerned, persons in a more racist culture (white students in Louisiana) tend to approximate the former type more closely than persons from a less racist culture (students in Wisconsin and Missouri).

All that has been said about 'belief and prejudice' is really in the nature of a digression, since when we are dealing with friendship acceptance and 'admiring the ideas of' there is no reason to suppose prejudice is strongly implicated. It seems eminently reasonable and defensible in the light of previous experience to assert that one would not admire the ideas of or get on with a person of very different ideas or opinions from oneself on important subjects. The only evidence known to me supporting the contention that people categorize others on the basis of their beliefs, and that these categories serve as bases of prejudice, is my own work showing that dogmatic people tend to stereotype categories of people when and only when the categories relate to the ideas the dogmatic person is ego-involved with.

Hence, in different cultures and among different peoples there are various ways of categorizing people as a basic for prejudice. Among these bases are race, religion, class, sex, nationality, and opinion.

PRINCIPLE VII
Prejudices are at least in part a reflection of norms. Consequently they remain relatively stable as long as norms remain stable, and suffer change when norms, e.g., those governing relations between members of different groups, undergo change.

There is some evidence (Bourhis, Giles & Tajfel, 1973) that, with the increase in Welsh assertive nationalism, Welsh people are seeing themselves in more favourable terms vis-a-vis the English than formerly.

In the mid-1950s Mitchell (1957) conducted a study of social distance between members of different tribes in Zambia (then Northern Rhodesia). Nearly 20 years later Bethlehem and Kingsley (1976) performed a similar study with a similar sample. In the intervening period, Zambia had become an independent democratic country. A comparison between Mitchell's study and our own showed that members of the largest ethnic group or tribe had formerly been the most popular, but were now the least popular; and the fairly similar tribal groups, the Ngoni and Chewa, had changed places in the popularity league, the latter being the most popular in the 1976 study though they were less popular than the Ngoni when Mitchell conducted his study. These changes are attributable to political circumstances since independence. The Bemba and Ngoni were militarily illustrious formerly. But the Bemba are widely believed now to be cornering envied jobs in the civil service and political positions while the Chewa are the largest group at the door of whom no charge of political adventurism and unorthodoxy can be laid. On the other hand, it is to be noted, most ethnic groups had remained fairly stable in the 'popularity league'.

Buchanan (1952) shows that the view Americans held of Russians was very much less favourable in 1948 than it had been when the Russians were fighting Hitler in 1942. Anant (1975) finds that over a few years in North India attitudes of caste Hindus to Harijans (untouchables) has become slightly more favourable, in line with the official government position. He also showed (1974) that between 3rd December and 14th December 1971 - India during the interim giving armed support to Bangladesh against Pakistan - the stereotype held by Indian students of Americans (America favoured Pakistan) became less favourable and the stereotype of Britons (on India's side) became more favourable. The autostereotype of Indians also became more favourable. Anant does present significance tests, but the result is quite clear. Sinha and Uphadyay (1960) showed that stereotypes of Chinese held by Indians became less favourable after the armed conflict between India and China over the border dispute.

An examination of Bogardus' work (see Ehrlich, 1973) shows that over a few social distance studies in America over 40 years (in 1926, 1946, 1956, and 1966) rank correlations of social distance to 28 ethnic groups shown by white Americans were all greater than .92. In other words, social distance to these groups (which included the English, Russians, black Americans, Jews, Chinese, and Indians) remained very stable over 40 years. But although the rank order of the groups was stable, less social distance was expressed to all of them in each successive testing: this lessening of social distance is related, no doubt, to the increasing social disfavour of prejudice and discrimination.

Finally on a similar note, Karlins, Coffman, and Walters (1969 - the study was done in 1967) repeated the classic study of stereotypes done by Katz and Braly (1933/1961). Both studies were done on students at the high-standing Princeton University. Katz and Braly, it will be recalled from an earlier chapter, presented lists of adjectives to students and asked them to mark those adjectives they thought characteristic of Americans, Chinese, Germans, Negroes (sic), etc., and to specify the five adjectives they thought most typical of the nationalities referred to. In addition, Karlins et al. asked their students to rate the favourableness of the adjectives. While the 1933 students had not apparently commented on the procedure, many of their 1967 counterparts found the exercise unrealistic and insulting, an indication that prejudice on the basis of nationality or race had become far less acceptable during the interval between 1933 and 1967. The remaining results run parallel to the results with the social distance scales mentioned in the last paragraph. By and large, stereotypes of outgroups remain in existence - despite the reluctance to express them. The least number of adjectives chosen which account for half of the total selections for each group provides a crude measure of stereotyping: the correlation between this measure of stereotyping for different groups between 1933 and 1967 is very high - 0.794. In other words, the groups people agreed about in 1933 were still agreed about in 1967. However, in line with the changes in social norms over the period, the favourableness of the stereotypes has increased - in particular, of Jews, Chinese, and Blacks: but again, while the average favourableness has increased, the correlation between the favourableness of the stereotypes of 1933 and 1967 is very high - 0.745. So the groups towards which a relatively favourable prejudice was held in 1933 retained a relatively favourable prejudice in 1967, and the groups towards which there was a relatively unfavourable prejudice in 1933 retained their relatively unfavourable prejudice in 1967. Again, prejudices - particularly to black Americans - has lessened, and this change follows the profound changes in norms over the years.

PRINCIPLE VIII
    Intelligence, education, and social class
    are negatively related to prejudice.

Adorno and the others showed that the E and F scales are negatively related to measures of intelligence in various samples, and the E scale is related negatively to educational attainment. (Intelligence, education, and class, are closely related to one another). The finding that authoritarianism and prejudice on the one hand, and intelligence, education and social class, on the other, are negatively correlated, has been replicated again and again, with a variety of measures of prejudice towards a variety of groups: by Rubenowitz (1963) in Sweden, by Warr, Faust, and Harrison (1967) and by Bagley and Verma (1979) in a large scale survey, in Britain, by Lever (1968) among South African Whites, by Weima (1964) in Holland (the target group here was Catholics), by Bagley (1973) in Holland again (the target group defined in racial/ethnic terms), and Rogers and Frantz (1962) among Rhodesian (Rhodesia is now Zimbabwe) Whites, by Schonbach, Gollwitzer, Stiepel, and Wagner (1981) in Germany, among many others.

(The correlations are not quoted, since their numerical size depends so greatly on factors like the range of education/class scores, and so on. The crucial thing is that they are so consistently sigificant.)

Weller (1964) in the USA, and Weima (1964) in Holland - both these studies have been referred to - found that among less educated respondents authoritarianism accounted for relatively less prejudice than among better educated respondents. (It must not be forgotten, though, that authoritarianism is related to prejudice in all the categories.) Weller found that among his lower social class groups factors like age and (lack of) education accounted for more of the prejudice. This result may be partly attributable to the artifact that variance among the scores of lower class respondents may be constricted (thus lowering the apparent correlation), but it does, as has been said, suggest that simple learning and cultural pressures to accept racist myths do play a larger part. Where cultural pressures to accept racist myths (which, for the most part, are fairly plainly lacking substantiating evidence) is high relative to the capacity to resist this pressure, ethnic prejudice results. Now, as has been pointed out, in South Africa and such places the pressure to accept these myths is high. Among uneducated and less intelligent persons the resistance to the pressure is low, since there is less ability to investigate the truth of these matters. In a large scale study, involving a sample of 1,499 people in the USA, Grabb (1979) found that education was a better predictor of prejudice towards a variety of outgroups than was occupational status or income. On the other hand, Cummings's (1980) study has already been referred to in another context: he found that working in an occupation where competition with Blacks was a potential threat was associated with increased prejudice. The precise nature of the interaction between education, occupational status, intelligence, income, and prejudice, has yet to be sorted out.

PRINCIPLE IX
Children develop similar attitudes and prejudices to those held by their parents and other primary agents of socialization.

This principle is really a corollary of the fourth one, above. It is mentioned here to emphasise the importance of socialization. Presumably, attitudes are acquired from parents by children in two main ways: these are (a) through the child-rearing practices the parents adopt, and (b) through direct learning, and control of behaviour, access to media, contact with members of other ethnic groups, etc.

There is evidence that children tend to have similar attitudes to their parents. Murphy, Murphy, and Newcomb (1937) quote studies which show that children below the age of 17 have virtually identical (as measured by Thurstone scales) attitudes to the church and to communism as their parents (though the difference gets greater as sons and daughters in different samples increase in age). In another study involving 548 families (the parents ranged from 34 to 82 years old), parent-child correlations on attitude to the church, to war, and to communism, were all very significant. In South Africa, Lever (1968) showed Afrikaans speaking white children show a greater social distance to black people than English speaking white children, and it is known (e.g., MacCrone, 1937/1957) that Afrikaans speaking adults show the same tendency. Boshier and Thom (1973) found a significant correlation of +0.27 between C scale scores of adolescents and their parents in New Zealand: the C scale, it will be remembered, correlates with the F scale. Horowitz (1936) found that the children of communists in America did not display race preferences, as one would expect of their parents. Pushkin (see Pushkin & Veness, 1973) found that white London children who consistently preferred white to black dolls in a doll play test tended to have 'very hostile' (to black people) mothers. Marsh (1970) showed that white working class English children between three and seven years old with black foster parents had more favourable attitudes to black children than a control group - a result which must at least in part be due to their socialization. Epstein and Komorita (1966) showed that in a Michigan school children's social distance scores correlated significantly with the social distance which <u>the children thought</u>

their parents would express.

It is not clear what mechanism of socialization is operating in the studies mentioned. Evidence has been quoted showing that, in accordance with the authoritarian personality theory, rigid and demanding socialization practices are associated with prejudice. In the Epstein and Komorita (1966) study, it seemed that children of parents perceived by the children as expressing high social distance, themselves expressed high social distance if their parents were not harshly disciplinarian. Now it is known that moderate punishment leads to the strongest socialization, so it seems clear that children of moderately disciplinarian parents learned their parents' attitude directly. Both the mechanisms of socialization mentioned above, then, seem to be operative, in the acquisition of unfavourable ethnic attitudes.

The consistently found negative correlations between F scale scores and intelligence should lead one to expect - since intelligence is heritable - that authoritarianism (and hence ethnic prejudice) will also be, to a degree, heritable. And so it proves. Tellegen (cited by Goldsmith, 1983) reports a significantly higher correlation between the F scale scores of young adult MZ twins than between DZ twins (MZ: $r=0.61$, $N=231$; DZ: $r=0.37$, $N=106$; p[difference] < .001). Scarr (1984) reports a study of 171 adopted children and their adopted families (all but six were adopted before they were nine months old) and 122 biological families. (The 'children' were young adults at the time of testing.) Using a form of the F scale controlling for acquiescence response bias, she found that the correlation between the F scores of the biological parents and their children was 0.44, whereas that between parents and their adoptive children was 0.06 - a highly significant difference. Corresponding correlations for IQ scores were 0.52 and 0.14. Similarly, the correlations for both F scores and for IQ were significantly higher for biological than for adoptive sibs. Hence the degree of authoritarianism is likely to be fairly similar in children to what it is in parents, and this similarity seems quite largely explicable as being a consequence of the heritability of intelligence.

PRINCIPLE X
Children are able to discriminate at an early age between members of different ethnic groups and may show signs of ethnic attitudes at an early age, but may take time to develop consistent attitudes and preferences.

Many of the studies which indicate that children can discriminate between ethnic groups at an early age have been carried out with white and dark coloured dolls. Some doll preference studies have already been mentioned, in connection with ethnic preferences. Clark and Clark (1958), in a study apparently carried out during 1940-41, presented black children in Northern and Southern states of the USA with brown and white dolls, and asked the children to comply with a number of requests, including: 'Give me the doll that looks like a white child', 'Give me the doll that looks like a coloured child', and 'Give me the doll that looks like a Negro child'. they found that 77% of the three year old children could identify the doll looking like 'white child' and 'coloured child', though the use of the term 'Negro' in the last question introduced some confusion. By the age of seven, all children correctly identified the 'white child' doll and the 'coloured child' doll. Essentially similar results were found by Hraba and Grant (1970) in a repetition of Clark and Clark's study in Nebraska some 30 years later. Marsh (1970) found that 76% of children under four years old in Southern England could correctly identify a picture of a white or black person when asked 'Who looks most like you?', and 'Who looks most like your Mummy and Daddy?'. Milner (1973) found that all the 100 English, 100 Indian and Pakistani, and 100 West Indian (presumably at least some of the latter two groups were of English nationality) five to eight year olds in 'two large British cities' could correctly identify dolls representing an 'English man', and 'Jamaican man' (or 'Indian man' or 'Pakistani man', in the case of the 'Asian' children). Similarly, in Glasgow, Johoda, Thompson, and Bhatt (1972) found that Asian chidren living in Glasgow, as well as white, nearly all gave themselves the correct pigmentation when building identikit pictures of themselves.
    Some evidence for the early beginning of ethnic attitudes was mentioned above during discussion of the fourth principle: it is presumed that

misidentification and preference by minority group children for dolls, pictures, etc. representing dominant group children are in part due to ethnic attitudes. There is other evidence, too. In the author's experience, spontaneous racialist expressions are not unknown among children. Milner (1973) quotes one white boy as saying ' " . . . My Mum and Dad don't like the black ones so I don't either" '. He, like Marsh (1970) and Pushkin (Veness & Pushkin, 1973) all in Britain, and very many studies (e.g., Clark & Clark, 1958; Horowitz, 1936; Criswell, 1939, to name but a few) in America, have shown evidence of ethnic prejudice and preference at an early age - as early as three years old, in some cases.

Attitudes do seem to be very inconsistent at an early age. There is some consistency among adults between attitude and behaviour. There seems, not surprisingly, to be little consistency in attitudes among young children; consistency increases with age. Horowitz (1936) found correlations between different measures of ethnic preferences increased with age (the measures of preference being the children's ranking of pictures of black and of white children in response to questions like 'Who would you like to take home to lunch?', 'Who would you like to play ball with?', etc.). Porter (1971) found that children who appear hostile to ethnic outgroups when questioned, played with them quite happily. Kawwa (1968) found that white London adolescents who had non-white friends expressed no less negative attitudes than those without non-white friends. Wilson (1963) in Massachusetts, found that the internal consistency of some ethnic attitude scales increased with the age of respondents. The work of Jaspers, Van de Geer, Tajfel, and Johnson (1972) with Dutch children in Grades two to six indicates that preferences for different countries grow more consistent between different children (presumably they were all assimilating the cultural stereotypes) with increasing age.

It is not surprising that children's ethnic attitudes are inconsistent and somewhat fuzzy, especially in the light of the work of Piaget and Weil (1951) in Geneva and Jahoda (1962, 1963) in Glasgow on the development of ideas about nationality. Up to the age of six or seven years, children have no conception of nationality: six year old Glaswegian children often chose 'the British' as a liked foreign country. Six year old Genevans did not realize that Geneva was part of

Switzerland, and young Glaswegians take time to learn that Glasgow is in Scotland (so that they are both Glaswegian and Scottish), and that Scotland is in Britain (so that they are both Scottish and British).

Chapter 7

SEX PREJUDICE AND DISCRIMINATION

A prejudice which is worth looking at in some detail, because it is so pervasive, and because it affects so many people in western society and in the world - is sex prejudice. Most such prejudice that has taken the attention of social psychology, and society in general, is anti-women prejudice. The pervasiveness of its social and personal consequences render it worth studying despite its high fashion. This chapter can be looked on as a kind of interlude.

A lot of work has been done on the subject over the last few years, though the passionate demands and denunciations, as well as the conclusions that can be reached relating specifically to this prejudice, are virtually all to be found in the famous tract of Mary Wollstonecraft (1792/1929) and in the calm examination of the topic by John Stuart Mill (1869/1929). Mary Wollstonecraft might be described as an early feminist, and John Stuart Mill, (who wrote on the philosophy of science, economics, and social justice, as well as the classic justifications of democracy and individual liberty), set down all the arguments against sexist prejudice and discrimination which have been made popular by the feminist movement recently.

ARE THERE SEX DIFFERENCES?

Clearly there are - but are they produced by nature or nurture, or by an interaction of the two? What is the extent of the psychological differences, and how susceptible to alteration by change in mores, customs, and folkways? It is not the place of this book to explore these questions in detail, but they have a clear bearing on prejudices about the sexes, and so will very briefly be looked at.

Demographic and Social Differences

Plainly there are demographic and social differences in our society between the sexes. Women, for example, are sometimes talked of as an oppressed minority – but they are not a minority. Though about 106 boys are born for each 100 girls, the mortality rate for males is higher, so that in middle age the numbers even out, and after that age women outnumber men. In the population as a whole (in Britain) there are about 94 men to each 100 women.

There are many differences between the behaviour and styles of life and attitudes of men and women in Britain and other western countries which are well documented. More men smoke than women do, and those who do smoke, smoke more. This difference is diminishing, and in the upper three social classes the rate is about equal (Ramprakash, 1984). There is, surprisingly, little difference in participation in sports between young men and women, but boys watch television more than girls do, while women watch more than men: the differences are not large. A striking sex difference is apparent in crime, both in amount and in type of crime. For women, the most common type of crime is shoplifing, and more women than men are convicted of that offence. On the other hand, for practically every other category of offence more men than women are convicted: about 20 men are convicted in Crown Courts for each woman who is convicted. The ratio of men to women sent to prison in the early 1970s was about 30 to 1 (Central Statistical Office, 1974), but that ratio is now about 15 to 1 (Ramprakash, 1985).

In education, traditionally great sex differences have been diminishing. It is still the case that boys are much more likely than girls to take woodwork and metalwork examinations, and less likely to take home economics. Until 1973, more boys than girls passed O-level examinations, but the trend reversed in that year, and in 1982 915,000 girls passed O-levels against 880,000 boys. It continues to be the case, however, that more boys than girls obtain the higher A-levels, though the difference is diminishing: whereas in 1972, 59% of those obtaining A-levels were boys, in 1982 the proportion had dropped to 53%. Although the proportion of girls is climbing slowly, boys remain heavily preponderant in maths, physics, and chemistry (at O- and A-level). Girls continue to predominate in English, modern languages, and biology, and the gaps between the sexes here are actually broadening. In the United Kingdom in 1982, 61% of university degrees went to men - men predominating in engineering and science, and women in languages - though more women than men went into other forms of higher education. In universities, as in A-level studies, the trend is for the gaps between men and women to narrow.

Married women are increasingly likely to work, and this applies both to married women with and without dependent children. The older the youngest child in a family is, the more likely a mother is to work. About a quarter of women with children under five work, while the proportion of women with children between five and nine working is more than twice that. The proportion of women working at all ages increased between 1971 and 1976.

There remain concentrations of women in certain jobs: the service industries and distributive trades have concentrations of women. There are some jobs which are overwhelmingly done by women: the great majority of typists, canteen assistants, nurses, for instance, are women. Equally, there are virtually no women miners in Britain, and a very small proportion of butchers and painters and decorators are women. On the other hand, the proportion of women in some 'men's' occupations is increasing: in the armed services, for example. And the increase in the proportion of women is particularly marked among the higher professional and managerial occupations. Fogarty, Rapoport, and Rapoport (1971), show that between 1961 and 1966 the proportion of women medical practitioners, engineers, university teachers, accountants, and personnel managers (among other occupations), increased, and there is every reason to suppose this trend is accelerating. Fogarty et al. (1971) show that the overwhelming majority of women graduates of 1960, even those who have children, expect and intend to work, the bulk of them full-time, for most of their lives - except, that is, when their children are young. More educated women are more likely than others to work, and are more likely to have fewer children, and those later in life, than less educated women. Childlessness is itself associated with a tendency to work. Since it is the better educated section of the population which often leads in social change, we may expect to see more women entering other occupations as well. And, as has been said, girls and women are getting more and more education, so the trend for women to work, and to occupy increasing proportions of 'good' jobs is likely to accelerate. Happily, things have changed considerably from the circumstances prevailing in the middle of the last century, when Mill (1869/1929, p. 316) wrote: 'What, in unenlightened societies, colour, race, religion, or in the case of a conquered country, nationality, are to some men, sex is to all women; a peremptory exclusion from almost all honourable occupations, but either such as cannot be fulfilled by others, or such as those others do not think worthy of their acceptance'. In demographic and social matters, the trend is for pronounced differences to give way to increasing similarity.

Psychological Differences

Demographic differences are probably accepted as factual, without demur: psychological differences and their origins are more contentious. A comprehensive review of the literature would be even more out of place than in the last section, and would require a very large amount of space.

A large proportion of experiments in the journals report sex differences incidentally to their main findings. It would be very difficult to induce much from this mass of literature, except that the findings are not always what might be expected. Shapira and Lomranz (1972), for example, show Israeli Arab girls to be more competitive than boys.

A great many differences have been hypothesised - often very dogmatically - and there exists evidence on some of these. Only a few of the more prominent ones need take our time here. The interested reader will find a fairly comprehensive review by Fairweather (1976), and a shorter one by Singleton (1979).

Some gross behavioural differences are incontrovertible: for instance men engage in more violent crime than women (Central Statistical Office, 1974), and observational studies of children, from pre-school ages up, generally show boys to be more physically aggressive than girls, while girls are more verbally aggressive (e.g. Archer & Westeman, 1981). But only at this gross level is any 'fact' relating to sex difference without question, and here as elsewhere, the explanation for the difference is unclear. It may have to do with the roles men and women have in our society, with opportunity, with the tendency shown by Newson and Newson, (1978) among others, for boys to be smacked more than girls are by their parents, or with any number of other factors. The physical punishments administered by parents probably serve as a model, but may themselves be brought about partly by the greater activity and mischievousness shown by boys as compared to girls. When it comes to competitiveness in general, results are far from clear. Shapira and Lomranz's (1972) finding of higher competitiveness in girls than in boys among Israeli Arabs has been referred to. A comprehensive review of the competitiveness literature (Struber, 1981) reveals that it is only among white American children and Indian children (and perhaps Mexican or Mexican-American children) that boys are fairly consistently more competitive than girls. In the other cultures studied, the difference is not evident.

Slightly more controversially, up to 1970 or so, women appeared to be more open to persuasion and to conform in Asch-type situations more than men did, but this difference, according to one reviewer, has diminished since then (Eagly, 1978). A further review and analysis (Eagly and Carli, 1981) confirms that the sex difference in persuasibility and conformity, does exist, though it is quite small. The conclusion is complicated by the possibility that a sex difference accounts in part for this sex difference! Eagly and Carli (1981) found that male experimenters were more likely to report a sex difference than were female experimenters. Hoffman (1977), in a review of sex differences in 'empathy', suggests that women may have a greater tendency than men to put themselves in another's place. Moore and Clautour (1977) found that in a sample of fifteen-year-old London boys and girls, 40 per cent of the girls (compared with 56 per cent of the boys) expressed a preference for a man's life, and 27 per cent (compared with 12 per cent of boys) for a woman's life: the difference is significant. Fogarty et al. (1971) found in a sample of British married people who had graduated from a university in 1960 (the survey was done about eight years after graduation) that a higher proportion of women were dissatisfied with their performance as wives than men were as husbands. And Dion (1975), with a sample of Canadian women students, found that where their failure at a game was ascribed to the actions of male opponents, severe failure resulted in lower self-esteem than mild failure; this difference was not significant where the failure was ascribed to female opponents. There is some evidence, then, for the suggestion that women are lower in self-esteem than men, and some for the suggestion that women's self-esteem is peculiarly vulnerable to knocks by men.

It has often been assumed that the sexual responses of men and women were very different, but the results of Masters and Johnson's (1966) work show that the differences are not so great as had widely been supposed.

Social research does reveal expected sex differences in attitude and role in western society. The lower probability of a woman (than a man) doing science at university, and the higher one of her doing social science or language, is shown by the research of the British Central Statistical Office (1974). Fogarty et al. (1971) show that married women graduates are far more likely than men to find the family their greatest source of satisfaction in life (82 per cent of these women with children say their family is their greatest source of satisfaction), and men are far more likely to say their career is their greatest source of satisfaction. Babladelis, Deaux, Helmreich, and Spence (1983), found that in a large and diverse sample of students in the USA, women regard marriage as more important for themselves than men do. No doubt some of this difference is due to the interrupted nature of most women's careers, but the differences are very great; and most women graduates do intend to return to work when their children have grown up. Men graduates, if their answers to questions are to be believed, are more ambitious - in the sense of wanting to succeed visibly in their careers - than women graduates; while women graduates are more interested in working with people and helping others (see Fogarty et al., 1971, p. 203 and p. 211). Despite what one supposes is the increasingly approving attitude to women working, 1960 British graduates seemed to think that this work should not be allowed to interfere with a husband's 'being looked after in a way he wanted and expected in marriage', and that, if this interference occurs, the wife should work only part-time. And indeed, even in Eastern Europe, traditional attitudes to a woman's role is very much alive (Fogarty et al., 1971, p. 80). In a large scale survey conducted in 1983 (reported by Airey, 1984) the overwhelming majority of married couples reported that the wife still plays the major role in washing and ironing, cooking and cleaning, while the husband sees to the maintenance and repair of the house. The findings are very similar to those in the USA. Of course attitudes are liberalizing all the time and practices are changing - but not all that rapidly, it would seem.

Television - in Britain and the USA certainly - constantly purveys the traditional attitude to sex roles; a mass medium cannot move far ahead of its audience, or it would no longer be a mass medium. Research showing the traditionalist nature of television regarding sex roles is legion. Manstead and McCulloch (1981), as just one example, examined 170 advertisements that went out on commercial television in Britain in one week in 1979. They found that women were overwhelmingly portrayed as product users (rather than producers), shown to be at home (rather than, say, at work), and to advertise domestic products. Morgan (1982) shows that a positive attitude to traditional sex roles is fostered by heavy viewing of television in relatively intelligent girls. (Girls in the lower intelligence/class brackets were highly sexist irrespective of amount of television viewing). For boys, there was also a clear positive correlation between amount of television viewing and positive attitudes to traditional sex roles. In other words, television viewing, conservatism in relation to sex role attitudes (and to other aspects of conservatism as well one would suppose), and intelligence/social class, are intercorrelated (the latter negatively).

Where heat is really generated, however, is in discussion of differences in intelligence. A dogma has long persisted that women are less intelligent than men. In relation to intelligence, as in other spheres, it has been suggested that the variance of the distributions of measurements is smaller for women than for men (see Hutt, 1972), but there appears to be little evidence for this assertion. A myth of long standing, and one that is by no means dead today, is that intelligence is highly correlated with the size of the brain, and that women (and black people of both sexes) have smaller brains than white men. Gustave le Bon, a follower of Paul Broca, wrote in 1879 that the inferiority of women to men was indubitable, and that even 'in the most intelligent races . . . there are a large number of women whose brains are closer in size to

174

those of gorillas than to the most developed male brains' (quoted by Gould, 1978). The refutation had been clearly presented by Mill ten years earlier when he observed that the supposed brain intelligence correlation was very much open to dispute, and must lead to the conclusion that 'a tall and large boned man must on this showing be wonderfully superior in intelligence to a small man, and an elephant or a whale must prodigiously excel mankind' (1869/1929, p. 280).

There does seem to exist, however, fairly firm evidence that men and women differ in certain specific abilities or categories of abilities. Boys and men appear to do better than girls and women on tests involving 'spatial' ability - a vague term, but no precise way of defining it exists just now: examples of 'spatial' tasks are block design and picture completion, and males are likely to do better at these subtests of the WISC than females (Wechsler, 1958); boys are better at arithmetic than girls (e.g. Wechsler, 1958); Fairweather (1976), however, shows that the supposed superiority of girls and women at verbal skills is less well supported. Perhaps it should be noted that the differences between the sexes are small: Wechsler's (1958) figures show the adult sex difference on the arithmetic subtest of the WAIS to be something like one third of a standard deviation. Fairweather also suggests that male superiority at arithmetic may be due to the common apprehension of arithmetic as appropriate to the male sex. As has been noted, the difference between the proportion of boys and girls taking maths and science is diminishing, and, if Fairweather's suggestion is correct, this male superiority may equally be diminishing.

Hence the whole question of sex difference in cognitive abilities remains open. The very existence of sex differences is dubious. Where there is fairly firm evidence - as in the case of arithmetic and spatial abilities - the explanation is very much an open question. That the differences owe at least something to environmental factors, or an interaction between environmental and constitutional factors, is indubitable. And the various hypotheses relating to constitutional-cum-genetic differences cannot be regarded as established; even the currently popular explanation, the hypothesis that cerebral lateralization occurs earlier in girls and that this lateralization is responsible for many sex differences in cognition, cannot (to say the least) be regarded as confirmed.

SEX PREJUDICE

We now approach the core of what is to be said on the subject of women. 'Racism' may be defined as the assumption that people, supposedly belonging to one or other racial group, have certain characteristics which pertain to all or most people of that group, usually with the implicit hypothesis that these characteristics are genetic or constitutional in origin. 'Sexism' can be defined as the assumption that men and women have certain differing characteristics, arising from their sex, and which are implicitly assumed to be genetic or constitutional in origin. A usage that is becoming current in psychology is that 'sex' is taken to refer to genetic differences, real and supposed (such as differences in morphology), and 'gender' to acquired and role differences: to be 'sexist' is to make insufficient distinction. Where there is insufficient evidence for these assumptions, they are prejudices: and, of course, what constitutes sufficient evidence is usually a moot point.

In recent years the feminist or women's liberation movement appears to have had a considerable impact on sexism. Sexist assumptions no longer seem firm and no longer go largely unquestioned. Of course, sceptical people have always been sceptical about these assumptions as about other things - vide Mill's work, written at a time when to champion opposition to sexism was not only unfashionable, but was considered utterly ridiculous.

Sex Stereotypes

Men and women still hold sex stereotypes, and Broverman, Vogel, Broverman, Clarkson, and Rosenkrantz (1972) summarize some recent research in the area. American students were first asked to list characteristics on which men and women differed, and the 122 characteristics mentioned more than once by the original sample were put in the form of bipolar rating scales, and given to other samples of people, who were asked to give ratings of the degree to which the scales characterized men, women, and themselves. On 41 of the items there was substantial agreement as to which pole characterized which sex. Further investigations showed that the agreement about characteristics of men and women was shared by American samples composed of people of different sexes, socio-economic groups, and religions. Williams and Best (1982), drawing on evidence from studies of children and students from 30 countries, ranging from Australia, through England, Israel, Japan, Malaysia, Peru, to Zimbabwe, showed that this conception of men's and women's characteristics was substantially similar across cultures. The set of 'male' adjectives agreed upon in the overwhelming majority of cultures includes the following: active, aggressive, confident, dominant, enterprising, rational, strong, unemotional, and also lazy, reckless, and rude; 'female' adjectives include: affectionate, dependent, dreamy, emotional, gentle, seductive, submissive, talkative, and weak.

Moreover, insofar as this constellation of adjectives is a prejudice (and that depends on whether there is evidence for the validity of the implied stereotype, and whether the stereotype does influence people's judgements of men and women) it is a prejudice against women. Rosenkrantz, Vogel, Bee, Broverman, and Broverman (1968), and Wolff and Taylor (1979), have shown that the social desirability ratings of adjectives produced by people as characteristic of men are higher than adjectives produced as characteristic of women. Of course, it is possible to draw up lists of 'male' and 'female' adjectives which are equal in social desirability, since there is considerable overlap in social desirability ratings, and such a list is presented by Stoppard and Kalin (1978); but more 'male' than 'female' adjectives are socially desirable. Moreover, social desirability and judgements of what characterizes a 'mentally healthy' person were found to be closely related, (judgements were made by '79 practising mental health clinicians: clinical psychologists, psychiatrists, and psychiatric social workers' - Broverman et al., 1972, p. 69): thus 'mental health' seems to imply having largely 'male' characteristics. But there is a confusion here: ratings of characteristics on their desirability for men and for women separately (rather than just their social desirability without specifying either sex) shows that 'male' characteristics are less desirable for women than 'female' characteristics are for men. That is, women ought not to be masculine, but some degree of femininity is acceptable in men. In any case, reviews show that counsellors and psychotherapists are not biased by these notions in practice (Smith, 1980; Whitley, 1979).

That the strength of prejudices in this field can be exaggerated is shown by the finding of Rosenkrantz et al. (1968) that men and women conceive themselves as less characterized by 'male' and 'female' (as the case may be) adjectives than they conceive the average man or woman to be; and this is in spite of the highly socially desirable nature of most 'male' adjectives. Mackie (1980) and Myers and Gonda (1982) found, with large and diverse samples in North America, men and women tended not to describe themselves in terms of the stereotyped 'masculine' and 'feminine' characteristics, when allowed to describe themselves freely (instead of ticking adjectives on a list). Further, Babladelis et al. (1983) found that American women students favoured men with some 'feminine', and women with some 'masculine', characteristics.

There is formal evidence (e.g. Morgan, 1982; Babladelis et al., 1983) that intelligence/social class is positively correlated with 'sexist' attitudes. The F scale is related to 'sexist' attitudes, and the consistently found negative correlation between F and intelligence/social class has been remarked in a previous chapter.

Role and Stereotype

Broverman and her colleagues (e.g., 1972) consistently use the hybrid term 'sex-role stereotype'. They thus fail to distinguish the conceptually distinct terms 'role' and 'stereotype'. Role, of course, refers to a person's rights and duties, to the way a person in a group or society is normally expected to behave by others.

In practice one may expect some overlap between descriptions of a person's role and the stereotype pertaining to the person: a nurse is expected to be sympathetic, though matter-of-fact, and nurses are thought to embody those characteristics in actuality. And that is what has been found concerning role and stereotype in women and men: the role and the stereotype overlap. Stoppard and Kalin (1978) found that on the list of adjectives they used, which were balanced for social desirability, Canadian students thought men and women should be like what they thought men and women were _actually_ like. This similarity true of both desirable and undesirable characteristics, contradictory though that sounds. A case, perhaps, of the mask becoming the face; or the face the mask?

Two widely used questionnaires exist, to measure how far a person is 'masculine', 'feminine', 'androgynous' (Ben Jonson, Thou shouldst be living at this hour!), and 'undifferentiated'. They are the Bem Sex Role Inventory (BSRI), developed by Bem (1974), and the various versions of the Personal Attributes Questionnaire (PAQ, or EPAQ - Extended PAQ) of Spence, Helmreich and colleagues (e.g. Runge, Frey, Gollwitzer, Helmreich, and Spence, 1981). Both contain lists of 'masculine' and 'feminine' attributes, which respondents mark as to whether or not they apply to themselves. 'Androgynous' people are those who score high on _both_ M and F adjectives, while 'undifferentiated' people are those who score low on both. The BSRI and the EPAQ correlate very highly (above 0.7; Lubinski, Tellegen, and Butcher, 1983). The BSRI and the EPAQ have both been validated cross-culturally - e.g., in Israel (Maloney, Wilkof, & Dambrot, 1981) and in Germany (Runge _et al._, 1981), indicating further that sex roles are similarly conceived in a variety of cultures.

A Role Effect

A look at the socially desirable male adjectives shows that they are the characteristics one would associate with worldly success in competition with others. Hence a woman succeeding in this way may be an anomaly to people holding the stereotype, and an anomaly to be denigrated. Feather and Simon (1975) showed that this denigration did indeed occur. In a questionnaire study, upper class girls in a Church of England school in Australia were asked to rate hypothetical men and women who had done well or poorly in a predominantly male occupation, a predominantly female occupation, or an occupation in which neither sex was predominant. They found that whatever the occupation, successful males were evaluated more positively on the semantic differential than unsuccessful males; but successful females were evaluated _less_ positively than unsuccessful ones. Whatever the actual sex of the hypothetical person who failed or succeeded, he or she was rated more masculine if he or she succeeded and more feminine if he or she failed.

Women, it appeared, have a motive to avoid success.
Feather (1975, 1978), has extended and
qualified the conclusions of Feather and Simon
(1975). It was noted that the sample in Feather and
Simon's study was restricted. With a bigger sample
drawn from different social classes, he found an
interaction of social class with reaction to success
or failure of men and women. Respondents of high
social class did indeed evaluate (hypothetical)
successful men more highly than successful women,
and unsuccessful women more highly than
unsuccessful men; and they did suggest that
successful females were more likely to wonder if
they were normal, and if it was all worthwhile, than
successful males; and that unsuccessful women were
less likely to be exercised by these doubts, than
unsuccessful men. But these results did not apply
with respondents of middle and lower social classes.
Hence, women's motive to avoid success does not seem
to be general. Interactions show yet again as the
currents and eddies in psychology's flow. But
there was evidence of an effect, general to the
whole sample: successful women were thought likely
to worry about the reactions of boyfriends, whereas
it was the unsuccessful men who, according to the
sample, would have those sorts of worries.
Further qualification comes from the finding
that there is a relationship between perceived
happiness and success, and unhappiness and failure,
in men and women, and the extent to which the
failure is in a male dominated or female dominated
field. Hypothetical men were judged more likely to
be happier with success, and unhappier with failure,
than women, the more male dominated an occupation
was. And, similarly, the more female dominated an
occupation, the more likely women were to be judged
happy with success and unhappy with failure than
men. But here again it is to be noted that his
sample was different: in this 1975 study his sample
consisted of university students.

Sexist Judgements of Men and Women and their Work
We come now to a question which feminists probably
regard as having a foregone conclusion: does the
sex of the creator of a piece of work affect
judgements of its quality?
Taylor et al. (1978) in a study which has
already been mentioned, showed that where different
groups of subjects heard precisely the same things
said by men and women on a tape, the women were

still rated as less influential, more sensitive, and more warm, than the men. The stereotypes do affect judgements of people in a fairly realistic situation.

Goldberg's study (1968) caught the wave of interest in this question just at its rise, and his article is often quoted as providing an affirmative answer to the question. He asked American girl students to rate six articles in different fields on a number of dimensions relating to their quality. The same article was given to one group of students with an author whose name pointed to his being a man, and to a second group with an apparently female author. Two articles were in the male dominated fields of law and city planning; two were in the female dominated fields of dietetics and elementary school teaching; and two were in the neutral fields of art history and linguistics. The results are obscurely presented, but it seems to be the case that in almost all the fields, even in the female dominated ones, articles attributed to men were rated more highly than the same articles when they were attributed to women. Goldberg presents this as evidence of a pervasive devaluation of women, even by women.

The hypothesis that there is a pervasive devaluation of women in western society has been tested many times, and the evidence does not unequivocally support it. Feather and Simon (1975) had many ratings done relating to men and women in their study of reactions to success and failure in sex-linked occupations, and found with their sample of upper-class Australian girls 'negligible evidence of generalized devaluation of females' (p. 29). Ward (1979) asked students at Durham University and St. Martin's College of Art to evaluate two paintings, each attributed to a male artist for half the students and a female artist for the other half: on most of the dimensions on which the paintings were rated (composition, technique, etc.) the first painting was rated better when attributed to the female artist; with the second painting no main effect for sex of artist was found, but students at the art college were more critical in their ratings of the supposed female artists, while the university students' ratings were more favourable to supposedly women artists. Bradley (1984) examined marks allocated to students' experimental projects in five psychology departments in British universities and polytechnics. She found that second markers, who had not been involved in the supervision of the project, had a clear tendency to allocate women's projects marks closer to the centre than the first marker, but to allocate men's projects marks closer to the extreme. In other words, when the marker was not closely acquainted with the work prior to marking it, s/he was inclined to allocate women mediocre marks, but to give men either good or bad marks. Noel and Allen (1976) asked a sample of Americans (not students) to rate editorials in a student newspaper, and found that when the editorial was attributed to a male author it was rated as of better quality than when attributed to a female author.

Thus the evidence concerning a devaluation of women's work, just because it is a woman's and not a man's, is mixed. Friend, Kalin, and Giles (1979) asked British students to rate several articles, attributed to male and female authors for different groups of students, and found support for the hypothesised devaluation of women; and Moore (1978) found, when examining reviews of books by male and female authors which actually appeared in Contemporary Psychology, that more negative things were said about male authors' books - a contrary finding: but both findings are qualified by an interaction. In Moore's study, the very unusual interaction of sex of rater by sex of author was found, reviewers tending to have more positive things to say about authors of their own sex. A similar finding is reported by Dovidio, Campbell, and Kahn (1982), but only for men and women high on authoritarianism.

The interaction quite commonly found, and the one reported by Friend, et al. (1979), is between sex of the author of a work and the sex congruence of the area to which the work relates. Males are commonly rated better when their work concerns, for instance, city planning or law, and females when their work concerns, for instance, nursing or dietetics. This interaction was not reported by Goldberg (1968), but it is reported by Friend, et al. (1979); by Ferber and Huber (1975), who examined ratings by American students of their college teachers: the possibility here is that male teachers were better at teaching science, and female teachers were better at teaching home economics; and by Mischel (1979) when American students rated articles in different fields attributed to male and female authors - but not when samples of Israeli students and high school pupils rated the articles.

Discrimination on the Basis of Sex

That actual discrimination occurs on the basis of sex is too obvious to need extensive documenting. How much discrimination is justified, and how much is based on prejudice, is a bigger question. Many investigations and experiments have been done to demonstrate discrimination on the basis of sex. For the sake of completeness, two will be referred to here. Rosen and Jerdee (1974a) asked male undergraduate business students to evaluate applicants for various positions, as part of a class exercise. Some students received application forms with the name 'Phillip Lewis', while others received the identical application form, but containing the name 'Phyllis Lewis'. Females were selected for managerial positions less frequently than men with identical backgrounds. The same investigators (Rosen & Jerdee, 1974b) conducted a similar experiment, but with 95 male bank 'supervisors' (who were attending a summer course) as subjects, which makes the situation more closely analogous to 'real life'. The supervisors were given applications as part of a class exercise, for promotion, for leave to attend a conference, and for leave of absence to look after a young child, some receiving applications from male employees, and others from female employees. It was found that males were significantly more likely to be recommended for promotion than female applicants with exactly the same qualifications, that women were discriminated against when it came to recommending leave to attend a conference, and that the supervisors reckoned it more appropriate for women than for men to be given leave of absence for looking after young children.

CONCLUSION

It is plain that there are sex differences in social and demographic matters; and while these are diminishing, they remain a prominent part of our society. There may be some psychological differences - in spatial abilities; for instance, between the _average_ male and the _average_ female, but the larger questions relating to cognitive differences remain open. Stereotypes, which are congruent with sex roles, are common in many societies. But there is no convincing evidence for a pervasive prejudice against women's work, and even evidence for the hypothesis that prejudice is in favour of work in fields congruent with the sex of the author of the work, and against work in sex-incongruent fields, is not overwhelming. That is not to say that prejudice does not occur: but there is no evidence of a <u>pervasive</u> prejudice against women's work. It may be that any prejudice affecting judgements of work, efficiency, etc., in regards to sex shows only in interaction with other factors, or in certain circumstances which have not yet been clearly delineated. On the other hand, discrimination certainly does occur, of a kind which is becoming less and less acceptable. That discrimination does, and prejudice almost certainly does, occur, and is assumed by a large number of people to occur, is sufficient warrant for taking reasonable preventive measures.

Chapter Eight

PREJUDICE IN ACTION

It is very difficult to say very much of great
significance about the prevalence of ethnic
prejudice and discrimination in contemporary society
- other than that prejudices do exist, and
discrimination does occur. No-one needs social
science to tell him or her that: we all know that
there is still some anti-Semitism about, that some
Jews are very ethnocentric, and that stereotypes of
Yorkshiremen, the Scots, Irish, Welsh, non-Whites,
French people, Germans, and so on, are common. And
if we do not know it, reference to various studies
cited in preceding pages provides sufficient
evidence. There is no universal standard on which
to compare attitudes and prejudices; and the
difficulty is increased by the differences between
techniques, samples, and so on, employed by the
various studies that have been done.

Black Britons
There have been black people living in Britain
since late medieval times. In the last two decades
the immigration of black and brown (and, to a lesser
extent, yellow) people into Britain increased
significantly, though emigration has ensured that
there has been a net emigration (i.e., more people
have left the country than have entered it) from the
United Kingdom almost every year since 1950 (see
Thompson, 1975, Chart 1.4, Ramprakash, 1985, chart
1.6). Out of a total population of about 54 million
in Great Britain in 1983, there is a resident
population of just over three million immigrants -
that is, people from overseas. Of these, 1,792,000
are 'white' - mainly from Europe, South Africa, the
Republic of Ireland, and the 'Old Commonwealth'
(i.e., Canada, Australia, and New Zealand). Of the

remainder, 778,000 were born in India, Pakistan, or Bangladesh, and 257,000 were born in the West Indies. It appears that slightly less than three per cent of the population of Britain are 'coloured' immigrants, and slightly more than three per cent are white immigrants. (These figures are culled from Ramprakash, 1985, and are based on 1983 figures.) The situation is one which undergoes quite rapid change. Between 1971 and 1976, there was a net emigration of people of West Indian origin, and this trend has probably continued. On the other hand, in 1976 there were about 160,000 people of Asian descent, but who came from East Africa, in Britain, most of whom immigrated between 1971 and 1976 (Thompson, 1979): this influx has not continued at that pace.

How many coloured people there are in Britain, including coloured Britons, is hard to estimate. Immigrants tend to be young, and men migrate more than women do, initially anyway. Hence there was an imbalance among West Indian immigrants between men and women until recently, though this imbalance has been rectified, and there was and remains a greater imbalance between men and women from the Indian subcontinent though this imbalance only remains significant in size for the middle-aged group (see Ramprakash, 1983, table 13.1).

Partly because they are young, immigrants have more children than the average for all women in Britain (all women include elderly women, of whom there is a far greater proportion among the established population than among migrants): 6.1 per cent of children born in Britain in 1976 were born to immigrants from the New Commonwealth and Pakistan whereas only 2.14 per cent of the total population are from the New Commonwealth. But again, the situation is changing faster than anyone would have predicted. Between 1971 and 1976 the total period fertility rate (i.e. the average number of children per woman that would result if women survived to the end of their reproductive period) of women immigrants both from the West Indies and from Asia dropped, the fertility rate among West Indian women dropping particularly dramatically, from 3.4 in 1971 through between 2.1 and 2.2 in 1976, to 1.8 in 1983. (The total period fertility rate for women born in the UK is 1.7). Among women from Asia and the West Indies, it appears that there are fewer women having very large families. (See Immigrant Statistics Unit, 1978; the Financial Times, 1 February, 1978, Office of

Population, Censuses and Surveys, 1984.) It appears then that women become acculturated, they begin to accept and practice the birth control measures which affect the fertility rates of native English women, and any projection of numbers of black and brown people in Britain in the future must take account of this drop in fertility. 1983 figures (Ramprakash, 1985) give the total number of persons living in Britain who are not of 'white' ethnic origin as just under 2.5 million, or 4.3 per cent of the population.

Figures for 1981 regarding employment tell the expected tale. A far higher proportion of white than non-white men are 'economically inactive', since a greater proportion of white men are retired – there being relatively few non-white men in Britain over retirement age. Unemployment is higher among Asian men than white, and highest among Blacks: the difference is most striking among 16 – 24 year olds, in which age group 38 per cent of Blacks were unemployed on the 1981 figures (Ramprakash, 1983, table 13.8). Ethnic differences in unemployment among women were less striking.

A far higher proportion of Asians (75%) owned their own houses than of Whites (55%) or of Blacks (37%). A far lower proportion of Asians occupied local authority housing (14%) than of Whites (32%) or Blacks (46%).

It may also be interesting to note that, looking at employed men, Blacks are under-represented (compared to Whites and Asians) in the professional and managerial classes, but slightly over-represented in the skilled manual group. And, as an interesting sidelight, the Community Relations Commission (1976) found that more 'coloured' people than white read 'quality' newspapers (34% vs. 19%) at the expense of the Daily Express and the Daily Mail.

Attitudes and Prejudice
Most of what will be said will concern attitudes and prejudice of white Britons regarding black Britons and immigrants. It is very hard, as has been said, to give any adequate answer to a question like 'What is the extent of prejudice and discrimination in Britain?' since no universal scale exists on which to measure these things.

In 1966 and 1967 extensive interviews were carried out in five boroughs with high proportions of coloured residents; these were Lambeth and

Ealing in London, Wolverhampton, Bradford, and Nottingham (see Rose, 1969, chapter 28). Four questions (three to do with accommodation) concerning coloured people were among those asked, and those giving answers hostile to coloured people on three or four of them were deemed 'prejudiced'; those who gave two 'hostile' answers were deemed 'prejudiced-inclined'; one - 'tolerant-inclined'; and those giving none, 'tolerant'. On this basis 10% of the sample were 'prejudiced', 17% 'prejudiced-inclined', 38% 'tolerant-inclined', and 35% 'tolerant'. Now, these phrases are meaningless out of context, and the scale was a poor one (the four questions were of untested reliability and their validity is likely, on the face of it, to be faint), but the results are worth bearing in mind. Banton (1959) surveyed opinions of 300 white people in Ipswich, Coventry, Alcester (in rural Warwickshire), Leeds, Hawick (in the Scottish Border country), and Leith (Edinburgh), in 1956, and concluded that 8% of men and 3% of women were 'unfriendly' towards Blacks, whereas 58% of men and 61% of women were 'friendly' or 'very friendly'. Banton and Rose found women more friendly than men, and the latter found as expected that Conservative voters were significantly more 'prejudiced' than Labour or Liberal voters; and the usual significant relation with education appeared. It is easy to misinterpret short answers to questions: in the Rose survey 53% said that coloured people were inferior to themselves, and 10% of Banton's sample agreed that 'coloured people will always be inferior to white people'. Further probing in both cases revealed that very few actually based their views on racial criteria (5% and 2%), most referring to educational opportunities and so on. In the Rose survey, 30% of the sample said they felt less sympathy for coloured people than for Whites living in poor conditions - but only 10% said that this absence of sympathy would apply even if the coloured in question were born in Britain: in other words, only 10% were using racial criteria.

Ethnicity does play a significant part in children's attitudes to other children. Davey (1983) found, using paper and pencil tests to compare white, West Indian, and Asian children's attitudes to one another, that each group did indicate favourable attitudes to members of their own group and less favourable attitudes to members of the other groups. West Indian and Asian children indicated less prejudice to white children than to

188

each other. On the other hand, it should be noted
that when asked about friendship choices, only a
third of the children in ethnically mixed schools
chose friends exclusively from their own ethnic
group. In a small sample of white, working-class,
English, teenagers, Hewstone and Jaspers (1982)
found that the most striking part of the stereotype
of Blacks was that they are 'athletic' - a positive
attribute.

In the USA, Gaertner and McLaughlin (1983)
found that white students do not attribute negative
characteristics ('lazy', 'dirty', 'stupid') more to
Blacks than to Whites, but they did attribute
positive characteristics ('ambitious', 'smart',
'clean') more to Whites than to Blacks: a subtle
but important way of thinking.

Jackman and Senter (1980) examined the data
from a survey conducted in 1975, of nearly 2000
adults from all over the USA. They found that less
than four per cent of the Whites were willing to
endorse the view that <u>all</u> Blacks are lazy (though
they saw Blacks as lazier in general than Whites);
on the other hand, as many as fifteen per cent of
men and of women agreed that '<u>all</u>' women are
'emotional' and 'talkative'. Stereotypes are less
than categorical, especially negative racial
stereotypes. Kinder and Sears (1981) report - on
data collected in 1969 and 1973 - that few
Californian Whites (about 15 per cent) think Blacks
less intelligent than Whites or support school
segregation (about 10 per cent). On the other hand,
well over half the sample were opposed to 'busing'
(ensuring a racial mix in schools by driving
children to schools not in their neighbourhood);
and opposition to 'positive discrimination' (i.e.
discrimination in favour of Blacks in jobs,
promotions, college places, etc.) was expressed by
73 per cent of the sample. Still, that is a far cry
from blatant prejudice.

Discrimination in Britain and the United States
Unfortunately, discrimination against coloured
people is not uncommon in Britain. Some recent
experiments allow us to gauge its approximate
prevalence in some fields.

Jowell and Prescott-Clarke (1970) sent letters
of application to firms in various English cities
which had advertised jobs in the fields of sales and
marketing, accountancy and office management,
electrical engineering, and secretarial work. Each

firm received two letters, one purporting to come from an immigrant, and one apparently from a native English person. In each case the two applicants had about the same qualifications, and the applicants were matched for age, marital status, and so on. The immigrants were either West Indian, Asians (Pakistanis or Sikhs), Australians or Cypriots, and half had apparently had their secondary schooling in Britain. They found that in 80% of the cases there was no discrimination, in 18% there was discrimination against the immigrant applicant (i.e., the Briton was asked to attend interviews or to send further particulars, while the immigrant was not), and in 2% (three cases) there was discrimination in favour of the immigrant. The level of discrimination does not seem massive, but it must be remembered that this thinning out took place in response to the first letter, and further discrimination may have occurred at the interview or when further particulars were obtained. No discrimination occurred against Australians, whose success rate, like the Britons, was 78%. West Indian and Cypriots had a sucess rate a little lower (69%), and Asians' applications were heavily discriminated against (35% success rate). Immigrants who received their secondary schooling in the U.K. were more successful (70%) than those who had received their schooling abroad (58%), which seems fairly reasonable on the employers' part. It would be very hard for a coloured person to obtain redress under the Race Relations Act, since no firm openly discriminated; they simply wrote a polite and untruthful refusal to the immigrant applicant. The Briton or Australian would be asked to attend interview, for instance, while the other immigrant received a letter saying '. . . we will not be proceeding further with this appointment due to internal reorganization' (Jowell & Prescott-Clarke, p. 411).

McIntosh and Smith (1974) conducted similar experiments to those described above, in 1973 and 1974, and in addition they used immigrant and native actors to make personal applications for jobs and for accommodation, in London and Birmingham. In each area they employed West Indians, Indian, Pakistani, Greek, and white British actors, who applied for unskilled and semi-skilled jobs in person, skilled jobs by telephone responses to advertisements; they also visited estate agents to seek houses to purchase, and replied by 'phone to advertisements for rented accommodation. The apparent ages, experience, earnings, and so on were equivalent; the actors were not activists (which might have made their manner unacceptable to prospective employers), and care was taken to ensure that they appeared to be genuine, eager, applicants.

In 30 cases out of 81 (37%) where one of them was offered an unskilled job, the coloured immigrant was discriminated against, and in seven cases, involving somewhat undesirable jobs, discrimination occurred in 14 out of 65 cases (22%). Coloured immigrants were given inferior treatment in 18 out of 137 cases by estate agents, and in 12 out of 41 (29%) of cases involving rented accommodation. There seems to be no difference in the amount of discrimination against West Indians, Indians, and Pakistanis. In each situation there were a very few cases where the coloured immigrant was favoured. Cases of discrimination against the Greek immigrant were much fewer. Comparison with a fairly similar study done in 1967 (pp. 18-19) indicates that the degree of discrimination had greatly declined in the interval.

Smith and McIntosh (1974) also carried out a similar experiment to that of Jowell and Prescott-Clarke, applying for jobs as salesmen, accountants, management trainees, clerical workers, and secretaries, in towns in various parts of England, in the guise of similarly qualified Britons, and Asian, West Indian, or Italian immigrants. In cases where at least one was offered a job (that is, not counting cases where both were refused: the figures that follow would thus over-estimate discrimination), coloured immigrants were discriminated against in 36% of the cases, and Italian immigrants in 18% of the cases. No differences between discrimination against West Indians and Asians were found. No differences between different areas of England were found. Inspection indicates that coloured women receive less discrimination in applications for secretarial and clerical jobs than is experienced by applicants for accountancy and management posts. A similar experiment carried out by Bagley (1973) with male applicants for accounting posts in Amsterdam, in Holland, found the level of discrimination much lower in Holland than in Britain, and that in Holland black Dutchmen were discriminated against less than white foreigners.

Ballard and Holden (1975) found that coloured graduates of Leeds and Manchester found it difficult to get jobs after graduating, and this difficulty is probably at least partly attributable to discrimination.

Smith (1974) reports surveys of a sample of factories in areas where there is an immigrant or coloured population; information was obtained from management through interviews and questionnaires, and in some factories studies in depth were made. Some of the points to emerge were that, as is quite widely known, some managements operate a quota, allowing a certain number of coloured workers and no more. About half the managers interviewed were prepared to commit themselves to generalizations (i.e., prejudices, when applied to individual people) such as West Indians or Asians are more or less conscientious as manual workers than Whites, though that proportion dropped to 30% or so when non-manual workers were being dealt with. Two foundries were found near one another, one of which discriminated heavily against West Indians, and whose work-force was largely composed of Indians, and the other of which excluded Indians in favour of West Indians! Managers showed an exaggerated fear of the reactions of white workers to the employment of coloured workers - trouble is seldom encountered by management owing to the employment of coloured workers, and even prejudiced workers settle down to possible work relationships with minority group members. The Unions did little in general to foster non-discriminatory practices, and sometimes discriminated themselves; the Rose (1964) survey has found that members of trades unions were no less prejudiced than their non-union peers. Managers seldom had a clearly thought recruitment or discrimination policy, especially in small plants; larger plants were more likely than smaller to have anti-discrimination policies. The 1968 Race Relations Act seemed not to have aroused hostility among managers, though rigorous steps were seldom taken to ensure compliance with it.

Recently, Howitt, Craven, Iveson, Kremer, McCabe, and Rolph (1977), illustrated a degree of discrimination in a minor area, but one which is probably indicative of a tendency to petty discrimination in other areas. They made use of the 'lost letter technique'. They selected 55 Asian and 86 native English households at random in Loughborough. Half of each ethnic category of households were sent a letter addressed to a fictitious 'Mr. Singh', and half were sent a letter addressed to a fictitious 'Mr. Edwards': all had the address of 'The Loughborough Conservation

Society' on the back of the envelope. Asian households returned (i.e. to 'The Loughborough Conservation Society') about 70 per cent of the letters, and it made no difference whether a letter was addressed to an apparently English or an Asian addressee. English households, on the other hand, returned about 88 per cent of letters addressed to an English addressee, but only 56 per cent of letters with an Asian name on them - a significant difference.

Another fairly standard method of measuring (very crudely) discrimination is to have numbers of different ethnic groups ask members of the public for some simple form of help. Sissons (1981) sent white and Asian male and female students out in Brighton, England, to ask for change for a coin. She found that English people gave less help to Asians than to English requesters, but this discrimination occurred only when the requester was of the same sex as the person approached.

In a review of studies of discrimination in helping behaviour in the United States between 1967 and 1978, Crosby, Bromley, and Saxe (1980) found that discrimination - both by Whites and by Blacks - does occur, but is not hugely in evidence. In 55 per cent of the studies no discrimination in favour of own race persons occurred. Discrimination was less likely to occur in face-to-face situations.

Discrimination, on the basis of race and sex, continues to be characteristic of the mass media. Kolbe and LaVoie (1981) examined 19 prize-winning children's books published in the United States between 1972 and 1979. They found that while women appear more frequently than in former years, their roles in the books 'remain those of the stereotype woman in our culture'. Weigel, Loomis, and Soja (1980) looked at television programmes broadcast in the United States in 1978, and found that Blacks are under-represented in television advertisements, and in programmes - especially as when Blacks do appear it is often in specialist, predominantly black, programmes. Where Blacks and Whites interact on American television, Weigel et al. found it was very frequently in job related situations, and very infrequently in intimate situations.

The Race Relations Act of 1976 should have a continuing and notable effect. This act prohibits discrimination on grounds of race between applicants for jobs, in promotions, opportunities for training, in schools, etc., and forbids segregation and incitement to racial hatred. It also sets up a body known as the Commission for Racial Equality which can investigate cases of alleged discrimination and serve non-discrimination notices on bodies suspected of practicing racial discrimination. The law is wide-ranging, defining discrimination very comprehensively:

> A person discriminates against another in any circumstances relevant for the purposes of any provision of this Act if -
>
> (a) on racial grounds he treats that other less favourably than he treats or would treat other persons; or
>
> (b) he applies to that other a requirement or condition which he applies or would apply equally to persons not of the same racial group as that other but -
>
> (i) which is such that the proportion of persons of the same racial group as that other who can comply with it is considerably smaller than the proportion of persons not of that racial group who can comply with it; and
>
> (ii) which he cannot show to be justifiable irrespective of the colour, race, nationality, or ethnic or national origins of the person to whom it is applied; and
>
> (iii) which is to the detriment of that other because he cannot comply with it.

Similarly, the Sex Discrimination Act, 1975, forbids discrimination on the basis of sex in employment, trades unions, and so on, and sets up an Equal Opportunities Commission. In this act, too, discrimination is very broadly defined, and while the act cannot hope completely to eliminate unwarranted sex discrimination, it spreads an aura of official disapproval of such discrimination.

Ulster

The passions and violence in Northern Ireland are too immediate to allow of a detached account of the situation there which might receive general acceptance. Nonetheless, a few short points might be made.

That discrimination is widespread by Catholics (or Republicans) and Protestants (or Loyalists) is not a matter of dispute. This discrimination goes hand in hand with intense prejudice. Protestants have stereotypes of Catholics, as well as abusive names: 'Taigs' or 'Fenians' are 'work-shy, lazy, treacherous' (Beattie, 1979, p. 249), and, in country areas at least, rough (or low class) and superstitious. 'Prods' are 'dour, vengeful' (Beattie, 1979, p. 249), hard-working but money-grabbing, and intellectual philistines. And it is plain that there is some acceptance of some aspects of the other group's stereotypes within each group (principle 4). Wealthy Catholic farmers, for example, refer to the 'laziness' of their poor fellow-Catholics (Harris, 1972, p. 152). These attitudes are well documented in Harris's sociological study of a country area in Northern Ireland. And the stereotypes persist, partly because the groups are in conflict (principle 2), and thus groups need to justify their attitudes, and partly because contact between Protestants and Catholics is small in country areas (Harris, 1972), and almost non-existent in working class town areas (Darby, 1976): principle 3 applies here. Moreover, even among 'loyalists', there is an unflattering stereotype of the English, a prejudice attributable partly to a lack of contact with English people.

> . . . their stereotype of the Englishman reflected in almost every detail the Englishman's war-time stereotype of the Prussian. The Englishman was efficient but ruthless, subservient to rules and regulations to a comical extent, pompous, humourless, and often cruel (Harris, 1972, p. 188).

TRENDS IN PREJUDICE AND DISCRIMINATION

There is every reason to think that in Britain and the United States, ethnic (and sex) prejudice and discrimination are on a continuing downward trend. Even in South Africa the grosser forms of racial prejudice are now frowned upon. Quesnell, van der Spuy, and Oxtoby (1978) compared responses on an anti-Black scale made in 1956 and 1973, by groups of students. While the two samples were in many ways different, the difference in their responses - the 1973 being more positive - is very marked. Melamed (1970) compared scale values for items in MacCrone's (1937/1957) scale measuring attitudes to Blacks in

195

South Africa. Overwhelmingly, the items were found
to be perceived as more negative in 1970 –
indicating that the basic attitude, or adaptation
level, of the sample had become more positive.
These pieces of formal evidence confirm the
observation that crude racism, even in South Africa,
is less common. Indeed the official justification
for the policy of apartheid is based on the notion
of historically and culturally defined groups:
though the major effects, and the rationale in the
eyes of the person in the street, remains
unambiguously racial. In the United States, it is
not so long since overt race discrimination and
gross negative prejudices were the norm. That
certainly is not the case now. Segregation, and
discrimination in many situations, on the basis of
race, are now illegal. In the classic study of
stereotypes Katz and Braly (1933/1961) found that
the wealthy and intelligent young men at Princeton
University harboured clear and well-developed images
of many ethnic groups, and that some of these
stereotypes were so much part of the culture that,
for instance, more than three quarters of their
sample ascribed the trait 'lazy' to black Americans
and 'shrewd' to Jews. A 1967 (Karlins, Coffman,
& Walters, 1969) repetition of the experiment at
Princeton found significantly less agreement about
what traits characterized members of various groups,
that stereotypes of groups denigrated in 1933 (Jews,
'Negroes', Chinese) had become more favourable by
1951 and yet more favourable by 1967; that the
autostereotype (Americans) had become less
favourable; and, most significantly, that there was
an increasing tendency to protest at the task as
unreasonable. Hence overt racial prejudice has
declined. And so too have attitudes unfavourable to
racial mixing: Condran's comparison (1979) of
survey data between 1963 and 1977 shows that white
Americans in general, including persons in the
South, older people, and less educated people
(traditionally the less 'liberal' groups), have
become more inclined to favour racial mixing. In
1977, for instance, over 70 per cent of all the
groups were against school segregation.
    In New Zealand, too, blatant ingroup
preference has declined among Whites relative to
Maoris (Vaughan, 1978). And in Britain (except
Northern Ireland), the trend is for decreasing
racial prejudice and discrimination. The decline in
overt racial discrimination in recruitment for work
between 1967 and 1974 found by McIntosh and Smith

196

(1974) has already been referred to.

These observations give one an optimistic view of the future of race relations. This optimism is reinforced by the finding in the Rose survey that only about 11 per cent of the sample said that the presence of coloured people in Britain was a 'very important' problem; about 34 per cent said it was not at all important. The more recent Community Relations Commission (1976) survey found that only 1 per cent of their two samples spontaneously mentioned race relations or some such thing; even when presented with a list of problems which included 'colour/racial prejudice', only 14 per cent of the white and 13 per cent of the coloured sample endorsed it. The problem was slightly more salient to younger West Indians than older, and less to younger Whites than to older. This survey found that 38 per cent of Whites were optimistic about future race relations in Britain; 52 per cent of coloureds were optimistic. Forty eight per cent of young people were optimistic, and only 26 per cent pessimistic about race relations. A survey done in 1983 (Airey, 1984) found, in the current climate of unprecedentedly high levels of unemployment, 42 per cent of their large sample of white respondendents and 36 per cent of their coloured respondents, thought prejudice would be more widespread 'in 5 years' - figures very similar to those found by the Community Relations Commission eight years before. Opinion polls between 1959 and 1975 show a fairly steady increase in the number of people saying that race relations are getting better, except for the hiccups in 1967 and 1968 when certain politicians were seeking to cultivate and fertilize racism in Britain. With the fact that the young are less prejudiced, and that educational standards are rising (and education goes with tolerance and the absence of prejudice), there seems to be ground for optimism regarding prejudice and race relations in Britain and elsewhere in the world.

On the other hand, two or three points do need to be made. One is that the decline in prejudice, ingroup preference, and so on, has been documented among the traditionally dominant groups. It may be among some groups so far less prominent in world affairs, in-group preferences and prejudices against outgroup members will wax before they wane. A second is that it is likely that we will see temporary 'hiccups' in the declining trend in prejudice and the rising trend of tolerance and harmony. Riots with racial overtones in Britain or the USA, the kind of thing made so vivid by the mass media, or an increase in the level of war in South Africa, which will inevitably have a racial flavour, may temporarily inflame the passions of which reason is so often the slave. In those circumstances, since the information provided by seeing real violence on our television screens is vivid in comparison to the relative pallidness of the information in textbooks like this one (see the earlier chapter on the influence of prejudice on reasoning and judgement), it is easy to suppose that the trend is permanently reversed. Unless very clear, replicable, evidence comes to light, we must continue to believe, on the basis of the kind of evidence presented, that overt prejudice and discrimination are in terminal decline.

Finally, as a prophylactic against rampant optimism, it may be worth noting that, while overt racism is on the way out, there remain somewhat more subtle forms of hostility and discrimination which may overlap with crude racism. These are variations on the theme 'Some of my best friends are --s, but . . .'. The first is 'Some of my best friends are Blacks, but Blacks are unduly favoured these days'. A telephone survey of 1,309 Whites in the USA in 1980 (Kluegel & Smith, 1982) revealed that most Whites thought that racial minorities received preferential treatment and were the subject of 'reverse' (i.e. favourable) discrimination when it came to 'getting ahead', and that over 70 per cent thought Blacks had an average or better chance of 'getting ahead'. Now, there is no easy way of showing whether these views are correct or incorrect, but it is fair to say that it is unlikely that the average black American would give the same estimates. Kluegel and Smith show that the same variables go with the view that Blacks receive very favourable treatment as go with high F scores: older persons, persons of lower education/social class/income, persons from the Southern states, all hold this view.

The second is 'Some of my best friends are Blacks, but I can't stand the working classes'. As Blacks in America and Britain remain predominantly economically badly off, this attitude is one that is indirectly against the majority of Blacks. Giles, Gatlin, and Cataldo (1976) present results which suggest that Whites in Florida who are well educated and wealthy and who dislike racial desegregation in schools, dislike it mainly because it brings members of the lower social classes into contact with their children: that these children from lower social class backgrounds are also predominantly black is of secondary importance.

It appears that Whites in the United States perceive Blacks as fully integrated and unduly favoured in many cases because of the prominence of a small and unrepresentative emergent black middle class. There are some black politicians in positions of power and influence, for example. These are vivid examples, because they are newsworthy, and hence lead to an overestimate of their numbers in the general population. Blacks, and non-Blacks of sympathetic disposition, may feel that if Mr Smith or Ms Jones is discriminated against it makes no difference to Mr Smith or Ms Jones whether it is because he or she is black, or whether it is because he or she is supposedly of inferior class. As far as Mr Smith's or Ms Jones's feelings go, that may be so. But the difference is substantial in its implications. For one thing, all the old 'in the blood' theories – regarding inherent lack of intelligence, inherent laziness, etc. – become more difficult to justify. And for another, a person's class, education, and so on, can change: a person's skin colour cannot. The attitude is more fluid.

If the reader doubts that things are improving, let him or her consider these few quotations, for the article 'Negro' in the Encyclopaedia Britannica, 1911, written by an anthropologist. 'Mentally the Negro is inferior to the white . . . the arrest or even deterioration in mental development is no doubt very largely due to the fact that after puberty sexual matters take the first place in the Negro's life and thoughts. . . . the mental constitution of the Negro is very similar to that of a child . . . often exhibiting in the capacity of servant a dog-like fidelity . . . .' Would it be conceivable that anything like that could be written by an educated person today? Optimism, if not rampant optimism, regarding race attitudes is in order. I am confident that my great-grandchildren will wonder at racism as we wonder at the mindless savagery that sent children up chimneys to bleed and die of the sooty cancer.

Chapter 9

WHAT CAN BE DONE?

This section is written from an unashamedly partisan
standpoint. Like most social psychologists, I abhor
racism and all forms of prejudice, and would like to
see them eradicated from the earth sooner rather
than later. This section is technology rather than
science, and all technology implies value
judgements, inasmuch as the technologist expresses
implied approval for what he or she is bringing
about. So here, based on what has gone before, are
some explicit suggestions for reducing racism and
prejudice.

Change the social climate
    Prejudice is 'caused' by personality factors and by
conformity to norms of prejudice. It follows that
if the norms of a society do not foster prejudice,
prejudice will be reduced. Easier said than done,
perhaps: but a social movement did so in the United
States, political independence did so in many former
British colonies (which were pretty racist before
independence), and Her Majesty's Government has
passed Race Relations Acts in Britain outlawing many
forms of discrimination, and making the official
establishment view of prejudice clear. Smith and
McIntosh's (1973) investigation indicates that less
discrimination was encountered by coloured people
seeking accommodation in 1973 than in 1967, and the
prevalence of discrimination must have been very
much less in 1973, because in 1968
advertisements discriminatory to any ethnic group
were prohibited. The 1968 Race Relations Act, and
changed social climate partly resulting from it,
must be given some credit, and this official policy
has been maintained and widened in scope by the Race
Relations Act 1976 and the Sex Discrimination Act

1975. Similarly, Smith's (1974) investigation of the practice in factories showed that a strong official line led to Whites accepting coloured workers, in spite of previously expressed attitudes and prejudices. When it is not respectable, or accepted, or common practice (i.e., when it is not the norm) to be prejudiced and to discriminate, people will tend not to show prejudice or to discriminate.

Banton (1959) found that people often thought they were less prejudiced than the norm. This 'conservative bias' has often been reported. O'Gorman (1979) looking at large scale surveys done in the USA in 1969, 1970, and 1972, reports that both Blacks and Whites overestimated the general level of support for segregation in the country as a whole. They also found that the overestimation was greater for people stongly in favour of segregation. Similarly, Airey (1984), considering a large scale British survey conducted in 1983, found that a great majority of people considered others to be more prejudiced than themselves: in other words, they misperceived the average (or 'norm') where racism is concerned. People need to be told that most people express reasonably tolerant, non-racist, attitudes. If people know the norm is to be unprejudiced, they will be more likely to act in an unprejudiced way. The saddest thing Mr. Powell did for Britain in the late 1960s was to make it seem normal and respectable to be racist.

Change in social climate can have wider implicatioms. If politicians from minority groups are elected to positions of influence and power, not only do they have the opportunity to act directly against discrimination, but the fact that they are in positions of power and influence affects black people's involvement in the political process and hence the possibility of peaceful change. Abney and Hutcheson (1981) found that in Atlanta, Georgia, following the election of a black mayor, black people came to express greater trust in local government at a time when the national trend was for people to feel more alienated from local government.

Changing the social climate will not change the opinions of deeply prejudiced people in a short time. Members of the British National Party will probably continue to harbour acid prejudices against coloured people for the foreseeable future, but they do lay less emphasis on this aspect of party policy now than formerly. Deeply prejudiced people need outgroups to hate, and coloured people are very convenient targets. Moreover, they seem to be of rigid disposition, and hence are unlikely to change. But they are very conventional, and if convention changes, authoritarians will change with it: perhaps they will find other, less easily injured, targets. Maybe the government should foster the myth that hostile Martians have been observed!

Child rearing practices

It appears that harsh, rigid, child rearing practices tend to form authoritarian personalities. Perhaps encouragement of more relaxed child rearing practices by respected bodies would help in reducing prejudice.

Contact

It has often been supposed that contact with members of other ethnic groups reduces prejudice, and many studies have been done to test this assumption. Results have been mixed. It is plain that contact does not invariably reduce prejudice, as any visitor to South Africa or Rhodesia knows. Pushkin (Pushkin & Veness, 1973) found evidence of ethnic hostility in the London suburb of Willesden, where contact between Whites and Blacks was to be found. Kawwa (1968) found children in Lowestoft where no contact with immigrants was to be had, expressed less unfavourable attitudes to immigrants than children in London, where contact was to be found. Or was it? People can be physically close but have little contact with one another. A visitor to Rhodesia during the war between the black guerillas and the white government told the author that he saw a black and a white soldier chatting at a road-block, and he wondered if they ate lunch together. Even apparently close physical contact can represent (psychologically) great distance! And even contact between people of apparently equal status can be misleading: Riordan and Ruggiero (1980) had to go to considerable lengths to get black American lads to behave as assertively in mixed groups as Whites, in an experimental situation. Cultural differences and expectations can be quite subtle! In Israel it was found that putting people into villages with others of different background did not lead to much contact between them, since people preferred to maintain primary groups with others of like background even if it meant travelling considerable distances,

(Amir, 1969). Again, Amir, Bizman, and Rivner
(1973) found that in most army units, in which
Israeli recruits of Oriental and European ancestry
or origin are mixed, friendships did not develop
between the two groups. They tell us that oriental
conscripts are on average less educated, and less
highly motivated as soldiers.

On the other hand, in the paratroop platoons,
such intergroup friendships did develop, and it is
observed that paratroopers are all highly motivated
volunteers, and highly selected. There is much
evidence that contact is often associated with a
reduction in hostility and prejudice. Marsh (1970)
found evidence that white children with black foster
sibs showed no unfavourable attitudes, in contrast
to a group without black foster sibs. Wiser and
Cook (1975) investigated two schools in Colorado
which had recently become racially mixed. Some
children were taught in the usual classroom
situation, but others were put in small, multiracial
groups of four to six children who worked
cooperatively. After four and a half months in one
school and seven months in the other they found that
white students in the small groups rated
Mexican-Americans equal to Whites on four desirable
attributes, whereas children taught in the
traditional classroom rated Mexican-Americans lower.
(Attitudes to black children, however, were not
affected by this contact, nor were more global
measures of ethnic attitude.) Foley (1976) found in
an American prison that men, black and white, placed
in multiracial dormitories were more likely to
become less racially hostile and prejudiced than men
in segregated two-man cells: this result, in a
setting in which prolonged and intimate contact is
unavoidable, is probably explicable partly in terms
of the contact between men of different races, and
partly in terms of the norms of non-prejudice and
tolerance which had grown up in the dormitories.
Davey (1983) found that both white and black
Londoners in areas where there is a relatively high
concentration of Blacks are more likely to say race
relations are good and improving than those living
in areas where there are few Blacks: Davey
attributes this to the greater contact between black
and white people in the high-concentration areas.
Schonbach et al. (1981) found that the lowering of
prejudice against Turks among German youths brought
about by contact was confined to the well-educated
youths. Malherbe (quoted by Lever, 1968) showed in
1938 that children attending schools in South Africa

with both Afrikaans and English speaking children
showed less social distance to the other language
group than children attending schools attended by
members of only one language group. Luiz and Krige
(1981) found that pleasant and cooperative contact
between white and coloured (mixed race)
school-girls over a couple of separate days made the
race attitudes of both groups more positive, in
contrast to no-contact control subjects.

Following Amir (1969) closely, we can conclude
that contact reduces ethnic prejudice and
unfavourable attitudes when some of the following
conditions obtain:

(a) the groups are of equal status, or
the members of the less prestigious groups
are of higher status;

(b) the social climate and authority
favour reduction in prejudice and the
development of favourable attitudes;

(c) the persons involved are well
educated/intelligent;

(d) the contact is fairly intimate;

(e) the contact is fairly pleasant;

(f) the members cooperate for the
attainment of a common goal;

(g) the contact does not lower the
status of either group;

(h) neither group has practices which
are morally offensive to the other.

Recalling that prejudice is of two types - that
dependent on misinformation and that dependent on
personality factors - we may suppose that contact
works in two ways to reduce prejudice: (a) it
may reduce the misinformation, or the
dependence of people's judgements on the mass media
(which highlight the extraordinary and the bad);
and (b) it may lead to the habituation of anxieties
and other emotions.

Education
Prejudice indicates ignorance of reality, and hence

education is likely to dispel prejudices, to some extent. To the extent that attitudes are dependent on prejudices, education is likely to alter attitudes too. These considerations partly account for the negative relation of education with prejudice that is almost universally found, though they are not the only factors. Verma and Bagley (1973) report an investigation of the effects of teaching about race relations and different cultures on the attitudes of 14-16 year old school children in England; though they say the teacher's 'overt position was one of neutrality' (p. 56), it seems unlikely that his own attitude did not communicate itself, and this may partly account for the positive results found with white girls and black boys. No significant result was found with white boys (whose scores started off very high) or with black girls (whose scores were in any case very low). The postive result with black boys may lead one to think that their self-esteem could do with a fillip. It should be noted, that with reluctant and very hostile students teaching has had the effect of making attitudes more unfavourable in at least one instance (Miller, 1969).

Perhaps we might also include under education the effects of undergoing hostility at the hands of others oneself. Clearly not all such experiences diminish hostility to outsiders, or else there would be no hostility between non-white people in South Africa. But one experiment in North Carolina (Wiener & Wright, 1973), showed that it works sometimes. White children in a class were divided into Oranges and Greens. For one day, the Oranges were discriminated against, refused pudding at lunch, not allowed to help the leader collect books, and so on; and for another the Greens were thus maltreated. On the third day, and two weeks later, the children were more willing to go on picnics with black children, and scored lower on prejudice scales, than a control group. While this result is not conclusive, it is suggestive - though submitting people to hostility on a large scale is clearly not practicable.

Imitation and Contagion

We know that people learn by imitation, and that if people are in doubt about what to do, they often follow a lead provided by someone else. (The social psychological literature on these subjects goes under the headings of 'social learning theory' and 'behavioural contagion'). Not much needs to be added to these well established principles at this stage. By way of illustration, Donnerstein, Mueller, and Wilson, (1979) allowed white students the opportunity of giving electric shocks (as part of a supposed learning experiment) to a black subject. (It is well established that Whites give higher levels of shock to Blacks than to Whites under these circumstances.) White students who had seen a model choose to administer a low level of electric shock in a similar situation administered lower levels of shocks to Blacks than did students who had not seen such a model.

Consistency with other Values

The literature on cognitive consistency does not allow of very clear conclusions. Perhaps the most we can say is that people's attitudes sometimes change in the direction of greater (quasi-logical) consistency with other attitudes where the inconsistency becomes conscious. Hence, it seems likely that quietly pointing out to people who are expressing racist opinions, that their views are inconsistent with the clearly expressed ideas of the Declaration of Independence or with the ingrained British ideas of fairness and sympathy for the 'underdog' may be the best way of dealing with situations where racist opinions are expressed. A change in attitude cannot be expected immediately. There is often a 'sleeper effect': conflicting ideas need time for a degree of reconciliation.

Mass Media

The mass media deserve a special mention because of their influence, though the uses of the mass media in reducing prejudice and unfavourable attitudes are adjuncts of the points made about social climate and education. The mass media can foster a climate in which people of different races live and work together as a normal thing, and my own viewing of British television, particularly children's television, indicates that it is helping to this end. Though I have not undertaken a formal current analysis, it does seem clear that there are more black and brown faces than there were, doing just the same kinds of things as non-Blacks and non-Browns do: programmes for young children, like Playschool, regularly have black actors; and on some American-produced series, black people regularly catch malefactors and rescue pet animals. Happily, this trend is accelerating in Britain. This kind of thing is bound to have a good effect. The media can and do play a big part in presenting information about foreign countries and various ethnic groups, which is a valuable educative function. Both showing black Britons as nothing extraordinary, and by showing something about several ethnic groups, are forms of contact, in a way, which are likely to be beneficial in terms of the principles outlined above. And the media provide powerful models for people to learn from and follow. The inference is clear: the media should be pressured to include members of ethnic minorities in 'ordinary' roles, and to include programmes which have an informational or educational content about minority groups.

Another possible function of the media is to lampoon racists. There is no formal evidence that ridiculing helps, but it seems probable that it does. No-one who saw Charlie Chaplin's film 'The Great Dictator' in 1943 could have remained in awe of Hitler.

Chapter Ten

HYPOTHESES AND CONCLUSIONS

This chapter presents the hypotheses and conclusions
(and two theories) educed and justified in the text.
The chapter is thus a summary of what has gone
before. It also represents, in the presentation of
reasonably clear and testable hypotheses, a statement of a systematic explanation of the phenomena
associated with prejudice. The need for refinement
and improvement is obvious.

HYPOTHESIS 1

People tend to accept as logically valid those
arguments whose conclusions reflect their
prejudices, and as invalid those whose conclusions
contradict their prejudices.

<u>Rider</u>
Some reasons for the distortions that occur in
logic are that people (a) accept a smaller degree of
evidence as implying the truth of propositions they
agree with than of propositions they disagree with
(and conversely, accept a smaller degree of evidence
as implying the falsity of propositions they
disagree with than they of propositions they agree
with; (b) people select, omit, and add to,
premisses, in order to support conclusions
compatible with their prejudices; (c) people alter
the meanings of statements in order to make
statements conducive to the support of their
prejudices; (d) people sometimes simply ignore the
requirements of logic; and (e) people are prone to a
number of errors and error-inducing tendencies
(such as the atmosphere effect, invalid conversion,
probabilistic inference, through which conclusions

conformable to their prejudices come to be drawn.

CONCLUSION 1

Memory (and perception, to a lesser degree) are far less trustworthy and far more malleable than has generally been realized, and far more prone to being shaped by our prejudices.

HYPOTHESIS 2

When making inferences which can be normatively modelled in terms of statistical sampling theory and measures of correlation, people usually perform very poorly when compared with formal statistical procedures and theory.

Riders

Some reasons for the poor intuitive performance in sampling and estimates of correlation are (a) the disproportionate emphasis on information which seems representative, which is readily available, and which is congruent with the theories and orientations of the person - such as the tendency to order events in terms of cause and effect; (b) the common tendencies to stick rigidly to initial estimates, to be conservative when making data-based estimates of correlation and probability, and to be over-confident of estimates; (c) the tendency to code information or data in such a way as to make it congruent with expectation or prejudice, including the tendency to infer such characteristics of other people from their behaviour as conforms with the perceiver's expectations and prejudices; (d) the tendency for memory to be biased to conform with expectation and prejudice; and (e) the tendency to give cases conforming to expectation and prejudice undue emphasis and attention.

CONCLUSION 2

The racism endemic in Anglo-Saxon cultures has historical roots. Briefly, the prejudice against black people is the result of the necessity of trying to reconcile (by rationalization) the economic desirability of owning slaves (and the inhuman cruelty that entailed) with the human desire to maintain a clear conscience.

CONCLUSION 3

Differences in IQ (and other personality factors) are almost certainly explained by genetic <u>and</u> environmental factors, and possibly an interaction between the two, though it is not possible to put a precise figure to the degree to which each of these factors influences intelligence.

CONCLUSION 4

It is not possible to say whether there are genetically based racial differences in intelligence: certainly none has been conclusively shown, and gross differences seem very unlikely.

HYPOTHESIS 3

Much ethnic prejudice, particularly in relatively well educated people, is explained by the theory of the authoritarian personality. The F scale, suitably modified to control for acquiescence response bias, measures authoritarianism.

<u>The Theory of the Authoritarian Personality</u>
Authoritarians have many impulses, desires, feeling, traits, ideas, and so on, which, because of the rigid and harsh socialization they underwent as children, are unacceptable to themselves. These impulses etc. are repressed, and projected onto members of outgroups, who are then denigrated for supposedly having the unacceptable characteristics. Minority groups are typically chosen as projection screens because they are weak and unable to retaliate for this denigration.

<u>Riders to the authoritarian personality theory</u>. The F scale predicts conservative political and social attitudes, conventionality in religion, conformity, desire for prestige, tendency to aggression towards members of outgroups and towards persons with 'undesirable' opinions, and tendency to perceive other people as either <u>good</u>

210

or _bad_ (rather than as having both good _and_ bad characteristics).

HYPOTHESIS 4 (Principle I)

There are two interacting types of prejudice: one is based on personality structure and needs, and the other is based on misinformation – some of it culturally based – and the need to keep cognitive load light.

Corollary. Unconventional persons in our culture are less likely to be ethnically prejudiced than conventional persons.

HYPOTHESIS 5 (Principle II)

When groups are in competition or conflict, or members of one group fear those of another, or sometimes when a person simply recognises that he or she belongs to one particular group as distinct from another, discrimination in favour of the ingroup and unfavourable attitudes to members of the outgroup become the norms in each.

Group Identity Theory

A group is defined as a set of people who feel themselves to belong to the same group, or are felt by others so to belong. People strive for a satisfactory self-image, and a person voluntarily remains a member of a group only as long as being a member enhances his or her self-image. People understand the social environment in terms of groups. In some circumstances people behave as members of groups rather than as individuals, and in these circumstances members of one group will act in a fairly uniform way to members of another group. Social movements arise for or against change when members feel they are marginal, or when members of superior groups feel the elevated position of their group is threatened and/or when members of a lower group cease to accept the legitimacy of their lot or the immutability of the social system.

Rider

The following factors serve to increase discrimination in favour of members of an ingroup:

211

(a) real or imagined personal similarity between members of a group; (b) sharing of a common fate between members of a group; (c) a prominent basis of division into groups.

HYPOTHESIS 5 (Principle III)

The less information we have about a person, the more likely we are to respond to him or her in terms of stereotypes or the prevailing social norms.

HYPOTHESIS 6 (Principle IV)

The socially accepted attitudes and stereotypes of various ethnic groups is widely known to members of a society, and have widespread effects on behaviour.

HYPOTHESIS 7 (Principle V)

Prejudices can be self-fulfilling: belief that a person has certain characteristics or attitudes may itself lead to evidence for that belief.

HYPOTHESIS 8 (Principle VI)

The category of people about which prejudice centres differs from one group to another.

HYPOTHESIS 9 (Principle VII)

Prejudices are at least in part reflections of norms. Consequently they remain relatively stable as long as norms remain stable, and suffer change when norms, e.g., those governing relations between members of different groups, undergo change.

HYPOTHESIS 10 (Principle VIII)

Intelligence, education, and social class, are negatively related to prejudice.

HYPOTHESIS 11 (Principle IX)

Children develop similar attitudes and prejudices

to those held by their parents and other primary
agents of socialization.

HYPOTHESIS 12 (Principle X)

Children are able to discriminate at an early age
between members of different ethnic groups and may
show signs of ethnic attitudes at an early age, but
may take time to develop consistent attitudes and
preferences.

CONCLUSION 5

Stereotypes, which are congruent with sex roles
(which are broadly similar across cultures), are
common to and in many societies. 'Male'
characteristics include: active, aggressive,
confident, dominant, enterprising, rational, strong,
unemotional, - and lazy, reckless, and rude;
'female' characteristics include: affectionate,
dependent, dreamy, emotional, gentle, sensitive,
submissive, talkative, and weak. In general, the
'male' characteristics are regarded as the more
socially desirable.

CONCLUSION 6

There is evidence for some small inherent
psychological differences between the sexes in some
specific abilities. While there are plainly social
and demographic differences between the sexes in
modern societies, there is no convincing evidence
for a pervasive prejudice against women's work, or
even for a prejudice against women's work in
supposedly sex-incongruent areas. It may be that
sex prejudices show themselves in judgements only in
interaction with certain other factors and
circumstances, which have not yet been clearly
delineated.

CONCLUSION 7

Ethnic prejudice and discrimination are commonly
occurring features of British and American society.
Both are declining - not necessarily continuously
and steadily - in amount and degree, and changing in
form. Trends in other parts of the world are less

213

clear.

HYPOTHESIS 13

The following is a list of factors and occurrences which will help bring about reduction in the prevalence of ethnic prejudice:

(a) a change in social climate, such that prejudice becomes contrary to norms;

(b) the widespread adoption of relaxed and tolerant child-rearing practices;

(c) contact between members of different ethnic groups, provided that some or all of the following conditions obtain:

    i.   the groups are of equal status, or the members of the less prestigious group are of higher status;

    ii.   the social climate and authority favour a reduction in prejudice and negative attitudes;

    iii.   the contact is fairly intimate;

    iv.   the contact is fairly pleasant;

    v.   the members of different groups cooperate for the attainment of a common goal;

    vi.   the contact does not demean either group;

    vii.   neither group has norms or practices which are strongly unacceptable to the other.

(d) an increase in education in general, and particularly (in favourable circumstances) education about the customs and histories and circumstances of different ethnic groups.

(e) the mass media use their potential for education, and for setting examples of tolerance and of positive attitudes. The examples of tolerance and postive attitudes may be expected to have an effect through the processes of imitation and behavioural contagion.

REFERENCES

Abney, F. G., & Hutcheson, J. D., Jr. (1981). Race, representation, and trust: Changes in attitudes after the election of a black mayor. Public Opinion Quarterly, 45, 91-101.

Adorno, T.W., Frenkel-Brunswik, E., Levinson, D.J., & Sanford, R.N. (1964). The Authoritarian Personality. New York: Wiley Science Editions. (Originally published, 1950.)

Ainsworth, L.H. (1958). Rigidity, insecurity and stress. Journal of Abnormal and Social Psychology, 56, 67-74.

Airey, C. (1984). Social and moral values. In R. Jowell and C. Airey, eds., British Social Attitudes the 1984 Report, pp. 121-145. Hampshire: Gower.

Ajzen, I. (1977). Intuitive theories of events and the effects of base-rate information on prediction. Journal of Personality and Social Psychology, 35, 303-314.

Alloy, L. B., & Tabachnik, N. (1984). Assessment of covariation by humans and animals: The joint influence of prior expectations and current situational information. Psychological Review, 91, 112-149.

Allport, G. W., & Ross, J. M. (1967). Personal religious orientation and prejudice. Journal of Personality and Social Psychology, 5, 432-443.

Amir, Y. (1969). Contact hypothesis in ethnic relations. Psychological Bulletin, 71, 319-342.

Amir, Y., Bizman, A., & Rivner, M. (1973). Effects of inter-ethnic contact on friendship choices in the military. Journal of Cross Cultural Psychology, 4, 361-373.

Anant, S. S. (1974). The effect of political realignments during an armed conflict on ethnic stereotypes. International Journal of Psychology, 9, 139-144.

Anant, S. S. (1975). The changing inter-caste attitudes in North India: A follow-up after four years. European Journal of Social Psychology, 5, 49-59.

Anastasi, A. (1958) Differential psychology: Individual and group differences in behaviour. (3rd Ed.) New York: Macmillan.

Anderson, L. R. (1968). Some personality correlates of the strength of belief and strength of affect dimensions of the summation theory of attitudes. Journal of Social Psychology, 74, 25-38.

Aptheker, H. (1970). American Negro Slave Revolts. N. Y.: International Publishers.

Archer, J., & Westeman, K. (1981). Sex differences in the aggressive behaviour of school children. British Journal of Social Psychology, 20, 31-36.

Asch, S. E. (1948). The doctrine of suggestion, prestige, and imitation in social psychology. Psychological Review, 55, 250-276.

Babladelis, G., Deaux, K., Helmreich, R. L., & Spence, J. T. (1983). Sex-related attitudes and personal characteristics in the United States. International Journal of Psychology, 18, 111-123.

Bagley, C. (1970). Relation of religion and racial prejudice in Europe. Journal for the Scientific Study of Religion, 9, 219-225.

Bagley, C. (1973). The Dutch Plural Society. London: OUP for the Institute of Race Relations.

Bagley, C., & Verma, G. K. (1979). Racial Prejudice, the Individual and Society. Farnborough: Saxon House.

Bagley, C., Verma, G. K., Mallick, K., & Young, L. (1979). Personality, Self-esteem, and Prejudice. Farnborough: Saxon House.

Bakare, C. G. M. (1977). Metaperceptual congruence as a measure of the 'kernel of truth' in Nigerian interethnic stereotypes. Journal of Social Psychology, 102, 13-25.

REFERENCES

Ballard, R. E. H., & Holden, B. M. (1975). The employment of coloured graduates in Britain. Journal of the Community Relations Commission, 4, 1-12.

Banton, M. (1959). White and coloured. London: Cape.

Bass, B. M. (1955) Authoritarianism or acquiescence? Journal of Abnormal and Social Psychology, 51, 616-623.

Beattie, G. W. (1979). The 'Troubles' in Northern Ireland. Bulletin of the British Psychological Society, 32, 249-525.

Bem, S. L. (1974). The measurement of psychological androgyny. Journal of Consulting and Clinical Psychology, 42, 155-162.

Beswick, D. G., and Hills, M. D. (1972). A survey of ethnocentrism in Australia. Australian Journal of Psychology, 24, 153-163.

Bethlehem, D. (1984). Two cultures in psychology. Bulletin of the British Psychological Society, 37, 113-115.

Bethlehem, D. W. (1969). Dogmatism and allied personality variables related to prejudice in young adults. Unpublished doctoral dissertation, University of London.

Bethlehem, D. W. (1977). Validity of social distance scales: A Zambian study. Journal of Social Psychology, 101, 157-158.

Bethlehem, D. W. (1980). Social psychology as the scientist views it. Bulletin of the British Psychological Society, 33, 445-447.

Bethlehem, D. W., & Kinglsey, P. R. (1976). Zambian student attitudes toward others, based on tribe, class, and rural-urban dwelling. Journal of Social Psychology, 100, 189-198.

Billig, M., & Tajfel, H. (1973). Social categorization and similarity in intergroup behaviour. European Journal of Psychology, 3, 27-52.

Block, N., & Dworkin, G. (Eds.). (1977). The IQ controversy: Critical readings. London: Quartet Books.

Bogardus, E. S. (1925). Measuring social distances. Journal of Applied Sociology, 9, 299-308.

Boshier, R., & Thom, E. (1973). Do conservative parents nurture conservative children? Social Behaviour and Personality, 1, 108-110.

Bourhis, R. Y., Giles, H., & Tajfel, H. (1973). Language as a determinant of Welsh identity. European Journal of Social Psychology, 3, 447-460.

Brett-James, A. (ed.) (1961). Wellington at War 1794-1815: A selection of his wartime letters. London: Macmillan.

Brewer, M. B., & Silver, M. (1978). Ingroup bias as a function of task characteristics. European Journal of Social Psychology, 8, 393-400.

Brewer, M. B. (1979). In-group bias in the minimal intergroup situation: A cognitive-motivational analysis. Psychological Bulletin, 86, 307-324.

Brigham, J. C. (1971). Ethnic stereotypes. Psychological Bulletin, 76, 15-38.

Broverman, I. K., Vogel, S. R., Broverman, D. M., Clarkson, F. E., & Rosenkrantz, P. S. (1972). Sex-role stereotypes: A current appraisal. Journal of Social Issues, 28, 59-78.

Buchanan, W. (1951). Stereotypes and tensions as revealed by the Unesco international poll. International Social Sciences Bulletin, 3, 515-528.

Buckley, R. N. (1979). Slaves in Red Coats. London: Yale U. P.

Budner, S. (1962). Intolerance of ambiguity as a personality variable. Journal of Personality, 30, 29-50.

Chapman, L. J., & Campbell, D. T. (1959). Absence of acquiescence response set in the Taylor Manifest Anxiety Scale. Journal of Consulting Psychology, 23, 465-466.

Chapman, L. J., & Chapman, J. P. (1959). Atmosphere effect re-examined. Journal of Experimental Psychology, 58, 220-226.

Chapman, L. J., & Chapman, J. P. (1969). Illusory correlation as an obstacle to the use of valid psychodiagnostic signs. Journal of Abnormal Psychology, 74, 271-280.

REFERENCES

Chapman, L. J., & Chapman, J. P. (1982). Test results are
what you think they are. In D. Kahneman, P. Slovic, & A.
Tversky (Eds.), Judgment under Uncertainty: Heuristics
and Biases (pp. 329-248). Cambridge: CUP. (Reprinted
from Psychology Today, November 1971, pp. 18-22,
106-110)

Cheyne, W. M. (1970). Stereotyped reactions to speakers with
Scottish and English regional accents. British Journal
of Social and Clinical Psychology, 9, 77-79.

Christie, R., Havel, J., & Seidenburg, B. (1958). Is the
F-scale irreversible? Journal of Abnormal and Social
Psychology, 56, 143-159.

Christie, R., & Jahoda, M. (1954). Studies in the scope and
method of the Authoritarian Personality. Illinois: Free
Press of Glencoe.

Claeys, W. (1973). Primary abilities and field-independence
of adopted children. Behaviour Genetics, 3, 323-338.

Clark, K. B., & Clark, M. P. (1968). Racial identification
and preference in negro children. In E. E. Maccoby, T.
M. Newcomb, and E. L. Hartley (Eds.), Readings in social
psychology (3rd ed.). London: Methuen.

Colman, A. M., & Lambley, P. (1970). Authoritarianism and race
attitudes in South Africa. Journal of Social
Psychology, 82, 161-164.

Community Relations Commission. (1976). Some of my best
friends . . .': A report on race relations
attitudes. London: Author.

Condran, J. G. (1979). Changes in white attitudes towards
Blacks: 1963-1977. Public Opinion Quarterly, 43,
463-476.

Conneau, T. (1977). A Slaver's Log Book. London: Robert
Hale.

Couch, A., & Keniston, K. (1960). Yeasayers and naysayers:
agreeing response set as a personality variable. Journal
of Abnormal and Social Psychology, 60, 151-174.

Craton, M. (1982). Testing the Chains. London: Cornell U. P.

Craton, M., & Walvin, J. (1970). A Jamaican Plantation.
Toronto: Univ. of Toronto Press.

Criswell, J. H. (1939). A sociometric study of race cleavage in the classroom. Archives of Psychology, (No. 235).

Crocker, J. (1981). Judgment of covariation by social perceivers. Psychological Bulletin, 90, 272-292.

Crocker, J. (1982). Biased questions in judgment of covariation studies. Personality and Social Psychology Bulletin, 8, 214-220.

Cronbach, L. J. (1950). Further evidence on response sets and test design. Educational and Psychological Measurement, 10, 3-31.

Crosby, F., Bramley, S., & Saxe, L. (1980). Recent unobtrusive studies of black and white discrimination and prejudice: A literature review. Psychological Bulletin, 87, 546-563.

Cummings, S. (1980). White ethnics, racial prejudice, and labor market segmentation. American Journal of Sociology, 85, 938-950.

Curtin, P. D. (1970). The Atlantic slave trade: A census. Madison: University of Wisconsin Press.

Darby, J. (1976). Conflict in Northern Ireland: The development of a polarized community. Dublin: Gill and Macmillan.

Davey, A. (1983). Learning to be Prejudiced. London: Edward Arnold.

DeVries, D. L., & Edwards, K. J. (1974). Student teams and learning games: Their effects on cross-race and cross-sex interaction. Journal of Educational Psychology, 66, 741-749.

Dion, K. L. (1975). Women's reactions to discrimination from members of the same or opposite sex. Journal of Research in Personality. 9, 294-306.

Donnerstein, E., Mueller, C., & Wilson, D. W. (1979). The effect of models and choice in promoting positive interracial behaviors. Journal of Social Psychology, 109, 49-57.

Douglass, F. (1973). Narrative of the life of Frederick Douglass, an American Slave. New York: Anchor Books. (Originally published in Boston by the Anti-slavery Office, 1845.)

Dovidio, J. F., Campbell, J. B., & Kahn, S. (1982). Authoritarianism and sex-related attributional biases. Journal of Social Psychology, 118, 199-205.

Dreger, R. M., & Miller, K. S. (1968). Comparative psychological studies of Negroes and Whites in the United States: 1959-1965. Psychological Bulletin, 70, (Monograph Supplement No. 3, Pt. 2).

DuBois, P. H. (1939). A test standardized on Pueblo Indian children. Psychological Bulletin, 36, 523. (Abstract.)

Duncan, B. L. (1976). Differential social perception and attribution of intergroup violence: Testing the lower limits of stereotyping of Blacks. Journal of Personality and Social Psychology, 34, 590-598.

Eagly, A. H. (1978). Sex differences in influenceability. Psychological Bulletin, 85, 86-116.

Eagly, A. H., & Carli, L. L. (1981). Sex of researchers and sex-typed communications as determinants of sex differences in influenceability: A meta-analysis of social influence studies. Psychological Bulletin, 90, 1-20.

Edwards, D. W. (1974). Blacks versus Whites: When is race a relevant variable? Journal of Personality and Social Psychology, 29, 39-49.

Ehrlich, H. J. (1973). The Social Psychology of Prejudice. New York: Wiley.

Elkin, S. L., & Panning, W. H. (1975). Structural effects and individual attitudes: racial prejudice in English cities. Public Opinion Quarterly, 39, 159-177.

Elms, A. C., & Milgram, S. (1966). Personality characteristics associated with obedience and defiance toward authoritative command. Journal of Experimental Research in Personality, 1, 282-289.

Encyclopaedia Britannica. (11th edition, 1911). Negro. (Vol. 19). Cambridge: CUP.

Epstein, R. (1965). Authoritarianism, displaced aggression, and social status of the target. Journal of Personality and Social Psychology, 2, 585-589.

Epstein, R., & Komorita, S. S. (1965). Parental discipline, stimulus characteristics of outgroups, and social distance in children. Journal of Personality and Social Psychology, 2, 416-420.

Epstein, R., & Komorita, S. S. (1966). Childhood prejudice as a function of parental ethnocentrism, punitiveness, and outgroup characteristics. Journal of Personality and Social Psychology, 3, 259-264.

Epstein, S., & Fenz, W. D. (1965). Steepness of approach and avoidance gradients in humans as a function of experience: Theory and experiment. Journal of Experimental Psychology, 70, 1-12.

Equiano, O. (1967). Equiano's travels. London: Heinemann. (An abridgement by P. Edwards of The interesting narrative of the life of Olaudah Equiano, or Gustavus Vassa, the African, written by himself, 1789)

Evans, J. St. B. T. (1982). The Psychology of Deductive Reasoning. London: Routledge & Kegan Paul.

Eysenck, H. J. (1962). Response set, authoritarianism and personality questionnaires. British Journal of Social and Clinical Psychology, 1, 20-24.

Eysenck, H. J. (1975). The inequality of man. Glasgow: Fontana Collins.

Eysenck, S. B. G. & Eysenck, H. J. (1964). Acquiescence response set in personality inventory items. Psychological Reports, 14, 513-514.

Fairweather, H. (1976). Sex differences in cognition. Cognition, 4, 231-280.

Feather, N. T. (1964). Acceptance and rejection of arguments in relation to attitude strength, critical ability, and intolerance of inconsistency. Journal of Abnormal and Social Psychology, 69, 127-136.

Feather, N. T. (1967). Evaluation of religious and neutral arguments in religious and atheist student groups. Australian Journal of Psychology, 19, 3-12.

Feather, N. T. (1975). Positive and negative reactions to male and female success and failure in relation to the perceived status and sex-typed appropriateness of occupations. Journal of Personality and Social

Psychology, 31 536-548.

Feather, N. T. (1978). Reactions to male and female success and failure at sex linked occupations: effects of sex and socio-economic status of respondents. Australian Journal of Psychology, 30, 21-40.

Feather, N. T., & Simon, J. G. (1975). Reactions to male and female success and failure in sex-linked occupations: Impressions of personality, causal attributions, and perceived likelihood of different consequences. Journal of Personality and Social Psychology, 31, 20-31.

Feldman, J. M., & Hilterman, R. J. (1975). Stereotype attribution revisited: The role of stimulus characteristics, racial attitude, and cognitive differentiation. Journal of Personality and Social Psychology, 31, 1177-1188.

Ferber, M. A. & Huber, J. A. (1975). Sex of student and instructor: A study of student bias. American Journal of Sociology, 80, 949-963.

Flynn, J. R. (1984a). Banishing the spectre of meritocracy. Bulletin of the British Psychological Society, 37, 256-259.

Flynn, J. R. (1984b). The mean IQ of Americans: Massive gains 1932-1978. Psychological Bulletin, 95, 29-51.

Fogarty, M. P., Rapoport, R., & Rapoport, R. N. (1971). Sex, career and family. London: Allen & Unwin.

Foley, L. A. (1976). Personality and situational influences on changes in prejudice: A replication of Cook's rail-road game in a prison setting. Journal of Personality and Social Psychology, 34, 846-856.

Fransella, F., & Frost, K. (1977). On being a woman. London: Tavistock.

French, E. G., & Ernest, R. R. (1956). The relation between authoritarianism and acceptance of military ideology. Journal of Personality, 24, 181-191.

Frenkel-Brunswik, E. (1948). A study of prejudice in children. Human Relations, 1, 295-306.

Freund, J. E. (1950). The degree of stereotype. Journal of the American Statistical Association, 45, 265-69.

Friend, P., Kalin, R., & Giles, H. (1979). Sex bias in the evaluation of journal articles: Sexism in England. British Journal of Social and Clinical Psychology, 18, 77-78.

Gaertner, S. L. (1973). Helping behavior and racial discrimination among Liberals and Conservatives. Journal of Personality and Social Psychology, 25, 335-341.

Gaertner, S. L. & McLaughlin, J. P. (1983). Racial stereotypes: Associations and ascriptions of positive and negative characteristics. Social Psychology Quarterly, 46, 23-30.

Gaier, E. L., & Bass, B. M. (1959). Regional differences in inter-relations among authoritarianism, acquiescece, and ethnocentrism. Journal of Social Psychology, 49, 47-51.

Galileo. (1962). Sopra le scoperte dei dadi. (Trans. by E. H. Thorne). In F. N. David, Games, Gods and Gambling. London: Charles Griffin.

Garrett, H. E. (1962). The SPSSI and racial differences. American Psychologist, 17, 260-263.

Genesee, F., Tucker, G. R., & Lambert, W. E. (1978). The development of ethnic identity and ethnic role taking skills in children from different school settings. International Journal of Psychology, 13, 39-57.

General Household Survey Unit. (1978). The changing circumstances of women 1971-1976. In Office of Population Censuses and Surveys, Population Trends 13. London: HMSO.

Giles, M. W., Gatlin, D. S., & Cataldo, E. F. (1976). Racial and class prejudice: Their relative effects on protest against school desegregation. American Sociological Review, 41, 280-288.

Goldberg, P. (1968). Are women prejudiced against women? Trans-Action, 5, 28-30.

Goldsmith, H. H. (1983). Genetic influences on personality from infancy to adulthood. Child Development, 54, 331-355.

Goldstein, M., & Davies, E. E. (1972). Race and belief: A

225

further analysis of the social determinants of behavioural intentions. Journal of Personality and Social Psychology, 22, 346-355.

Gould, S. J. (November 1978). Women's brains. New Scientist, 364-366.

Grabb, E. G. (1979). Working-class authoritarianism and tolerance of outgroups: A reassessment. Public Opinion Quarterly, 43, 36-47.

Granberg, D. (1972). Authoritarianism and the assumption of similarity to self. Journal of Experimental Research in Personality, 6, 1-4.

Graves, R. (1960). Goodbye to all that. Harmondsworth: Penguin.

Green, J. A. (1972). Attitudinal and situational determinants of intended behavior towards Blacks. Journal of Personality and Social Psychology, 22, 13-17.

Green, R. T. & Stacey, B. G. (1966). The Response Style Myth: An empirical study involving the F-Scale. Acta Psychologica, 25, 365-372.

Greenwald, H. J., & Oppenheim, D. B. (1968). Reported magnitude of self-misidentification among Negro children - artifact? Journal of Personality and Social Psychology, 8, 49-52.

Haimowitz, M. L., & Haimowitz, N. R. (1950). Reducing ethnic hostility through psychotherapy. Journal of Social Psychology, 31, 231-241.

Hakluyt, R. (1972). Voyages and discoveries: The principal navigations, traffiques and discoveries of the English nation. J. Beeching (ed.). Harmondsworth: Penguin. (Originally published, 1598-1600)

Hall, J. R., & Black, J. D. (1979). Assertiveness, aggressivenes, and attitudes toward feminism. The Journal of Social Psychology. 107, 57-62.

Hamilton, D. L., & Rose, T. L. (1980). Illusory correlation and the maintenance of stereotypic beliefs. Journal of Personality and Social Psychology, 39, 832-845.

Hanley, C. (1962). The difficulty of a personality inventory item. Educational and Psychological Measurement,

$\underline{22}$, 577-584.

Hanley, C. (1965). Personality item difficulty and job satisfaction. Journal of Applied Psychology, $\underline{49}$, 205-208.

Harding, J., Kutner, B., Proshansky, H., & Chein, I. (1954). Prejudice and ethnic relations. In G. Lindzey, (ed.), Handbook of social psychology. Reading, Mass.: Addison-Wellesley.

Harris, D. B., Gough, H. G., & Martin, W. E. (1950). Children's ethnic attitudes: II. Relationship to parental beliefs concerning child training. Society for Research in Child Development, 21, 169-181.

Harris, R. (1972). Prejudice and tolerance in Ulster. Manchester: Manchester University Press.

Harris, R. J., & Monaco, G. E. (1978). Psychology of pragmatic implication: Information processing between the lines. Journal of Experimental Psychology: General, 107, 1-22.

Hastorf, A. H., & Cantril, H. (1954). They saw a game: A case study. Journal of Abnormal and Social Psychology, $\underline{49}$, 129-134.

Hazlitt, W. (1970). Selected writings. R. Blythe (Ed.). Harmondsworth: Penguin.

Hazlitt, W. (1970) Men and manners: Sketches and essays. Ward Lock reprints. (Originally published, 1852.)

Hearnshaw, L. S. (1979). Cyril Burt: Psychologist. London: Hodder.

Heaven, P. C. L., & Bezuidenhout, F. J. (1978). Multidimensionality of social distance among white students in South Africa. Journal of Social Psychology, 106, 275-276.

Heaven, P. C. L., & Nieuwoudt, J. M. (1981). Authoritarian attitudes in South Africa. Journal of Social Psychology, 115, 277-278.

Heinemann, W., Pellander, F., Vogelbusch, A., & Wojtek, B. (1981). Meeting a deviant person: Subjective norms and affective reactions. European Journal of Social Psychology, 11, 1-25.

Henle, M. (1955). Some effects of motivational processes on cognition. Psychological Review, 62, 423-432.

Henle, M. (1962). On the relation between logic and thinking. Psychological Review, 69, 366-378.

Henle, M., & Michael, M. (1956). The influence of attitudes on syllogistic reasoning. Journal of Social Psychology, 44, 115-127.

Henley, S. H. A., Dixon, N. F., & Cartmell, A. E. (1977). A note on the relationship between authoritarianism and acceptance of military ideology. British Journal of Social and Clinical Psychology, 16, 287-288.

Hepburn, C., & Locksley, A. (1983). Subjective awareness of stereotyping: Do we know when our judgments are prejudiced? Social Psychology Quarterly, 46, 311-318.

Hewstone, M., Fincham, F., & Jaspers, J. (1981). Social categorization and similarity in intergroup behaviour: a replication with 'penalties'. European Journal of Social Psychology, 11, 101-107.

Hewstone, M., & Jaspers, J. (1982). Explanations for racial discrimination: The effect of group discussion on intergroup attributions. European Journal of Social Psychology, 12, 1-16.

Himmelweit, H. T., & Swift, B. (1971). Adolescent and adult authoritarianism reexamined: Its organization and stability over time. European Journal of Social Psychology, 1, 357-384.

Hoffman, M. L. (1977). Sex differences in empathy and related behaviours. Psychological Bulletin, 84, 712-722.

Holmes, D. S. (1968). Dimensions of projection. Psychological Bulletin, 69, 248-268.

Holmes, D. S. (1974). Investigations of repression: Differential recall of material experimentally or naturally associated with ego-threat. Psychological Bulletin, 81, 632-653.

Hoogvelt, A.M.M. (1969). Ethnocentrism, authoritarianism, and Powellism. Race, 11, 1 -12.

Horowitz, E. L. (1936). Development of attitude to the word

Negro. Archives of Psychology, (No. 194).

Hovland, C. I., & Janis, I. L. (1959). Personality and persuasibility. New Haven: Yale University Press.

Hovland, C. I., & Sears, R. (1940). Minor studies in aggression: VI, Correlation of lynchings with economic indices. Journal of Psychology, 9, 301-310.

Howitt, D., Craven, G., Iveson, C., Kremer, J., McCabe, J., & Rolph, T. (1977). The misdirected letter. British Journal of Social and Clinical Psychology, 16, 285-286.

Hraba, J., & Grant, G. (1970). Black is beautiful: reexamination of racial preference and identification. Journal of Personality and Social Psychology, 16, 398-402.

Hume, D. (1898). Essays moral, political, and literary. (Vol. 1). T. H. Green & T. H. Grose (eds.). New York: Longmans. (First published, 1741)

Hume, D. (1955). An Inquiry Concerning Human Understanding. Indianapolis: Bobbs-Merrill. (Original work published 1748)

Hutt, C. (1972). Males and females. Harmondsworth: Penguin.

Immigrant Statistics Unit. (1978). Marriage and birth patterns among the New Commonwealth and Pakistani population. Population Trends, 11, 5-9. London: HMSO.

Inhelder, B., & Piaget, J. (1958). The Growth of Logical Thinking from Childhood to Adolescence. (A. Parsons and S. Milgram, Trans.) London: Routledge.

Iwawaki, S., Eysenck, S. B. G., & Eysenck, H. J. (1977). Difference in personality between Japanese and English. Journal of Social Psychology, 102, 27-33.

Jackman, M. R., & Senter, M. S. (1980). Images of social groups: Categorical or qualified? Public Opinion Quarterly, 44, 341-362.

Jackson, D. N., & Messick, S. J. (1957). A note on 'ethnocentrism' and acquiescent response sets. Journal of Abnormal and Social Psychology, 54, 132-135.

Jackson, D. N.,   Messick,   S., & Solley, C. M.   (1957).   How
    'rigid' is the 'authoritarian'? Journal of Abnormal and
    Social Psychology, 54, 137-140.

Jahoda, G. (1962). Development of Scottish children's ideas
    and attitudes about other countries. Journal of Social
    Psychology, 58, 91-108.

Jahoda, G. (1963). The development of children's ideas about
    country and nationality Part I: The   conceptual
    framework. British Journal of Educational Psychology,
    33, 47-60.

Jahoda, G., Thompson, S. S., & Bhlatt, S. (1972). Ethnic
    identity and preferences among Asian immigrant
    children in Glasgow: A replicated study. European
    Journal of Social Psychology, 2, 19-32.

James, W. (1892). Psychology. London: Macmillan.

Janis, I. L., & Frick, F. (1943). The relationship between
    attitudes towards conclusions and errors in judging
    logical validity of syllogisms. Journal of Experimental
    Psychology, 33, 75-77.

Jaspers, J. M. F., Van der Geer, J. P.,   Tajfel, H., &
    Johnson, N. (1972). On the development of national
    attitudes in children. European Journal of Social
    Psychology, 2, 348-369.

Jefferson, T. (1954). Notes on the State of Virginia, (W.
    Peden, Ed.). Chapel Hill: Univ. of North Carolina
    Press. (Originally published 1787)

Jennings, D. L., Amabile, T. M., & Ross, L. (1982). Informal
    covariation assessment: Data-based versus theory-based
    judgments. In D. Kahneman, P. Slovic, & A. Tversky
    (Eds.), Judgment under Uncertainty: Heuristics and
    Biases. (pp. 211-230). Cambridge: CUP.

Jensen, A. R. (1974). Kinship correlations reported by Sir
    Cyril Burt. Behaviour Genetics, 4, 1-28.

Jensen, A. R. (1972). Genetics and education. London,
    Methuen.

Jensen, A. R. (1969a). How much can we boost IQ and
    scholastic achievement? In Harvard Educational Review
    (Ed.). Environment, heredity and intelligence.
    Cambridge, Mass.: Harvard Educational Review.

REFERENCES

Jensen, A. R. (1969b) Reducing the heredity-environment uncertainty. In Harvard Educational Review (Ed.). Environment, heredity and intelligence. Cambridge, Mass.: Harvard Educational Review.

Jinks, J. L., & Fulker, D. W. (1970). Comparison of the biometrical genetical, MAVA, and classical approaches to the analysis of human behaviour. Psychological Bulletin, 73, 311-349.

Jones, E. E., & Davis, K. E. (1965). From acts to dispositions: The attribution process in person perception. Advances in Experimental Social Psychology, 2, 219-266.

Jones, W. J., & Russell, D. (1980). The selective processing of belief disconfirming information: European Journal of Social Psychology, 10, 309-312.

Jordaan, K. (1974). The origins of the Afrikaners and their language, 1652-1720: A study in miscegenation and creole. Race, 15, 461-495.

Jordan, W. D. (1968). White over black: American attitudes toward the negro, 1550-1812. Baltimore: Penguin.

Jowell, R., & Prescott-Clarke, P. (1970). Racial discrimination and white-collar workers in Britain. Race, 11, 397-417.

Juel-Nielson, N. (1965). Individual and environment: A psychiatric-psychological investigation of monozygotic twins reared apart. Acta Psychiatrica Scandinavica, 40. (Supplement No. 183)

Kahle, L. R., & Berman, J. J. (1979). Attitudes cause behaviors: A cross-lagged panel analysis. Journal of Personality and Social Psychology, 37, 315-321.

Kahneman, D., & Tversky, A. (1973). On the psychology of prediction. Psychological Review, 80, 237-251.

Kahneman, D., & Tversky, A. (1982). On the psychology of prediction. In D. Kahneman, P. Slovic, & A. Tversky (Eds.), Judgment under Uncertainty: Heuristics and Biases (pp. 48-68). Cambridge: CUP. (Reprinted from Psychological Review, 1973, 80, 237-251)

Kamin, L. J. (1977). The science and politics of I.Q. Harmondsworth: Penguin.

REFERENCES

Karlins, M., Coffman, T. L., & Walters, G. (1969). On the
fading of social stereotypes: Studies in three
generations of college students. Journal of Personality
and Social Psychology, 13, 1-16.

Katz, D., & Braly, K. W. (1961). Verbal stereotypes and
racial prejudice. In E. E. Maccoby, T. M. Newcomb, & E.
L. Hatley (Eds.). Readings in social psychology (3rd
ed.). London: Methuen. (Originally published, 1933.)

Kawwa, T. (1968). A survey of ethnic attitudes of some
British secondary school pupils. British Journal of
Social and Clinical Psychology, 7, 161-168.

Kerpelman, L. C. (1968). Personality and attitude correlates
of political candidate preference. Journal of Social
Psychology, 76, 219-226.

Kinder, D. R., & Sears, D. O. (1981). Prejudice and politics:
symbolic racism versus racial threats to the good life.
Journal of Personality and Social Psychology, 40,
414-431.

Kirby, A. (1980). A critical comment on 'The social ecology
of intelligence in the British Isles'. British Journal
of Social and Clinical Psychology, 19, 333-336.

Klein, P. S., Levine, E., & Charry, M. M. (1979). Effects
of skin colour and hair differences on facial choice of
kindergarten children. Journal of Social Psychology,
107, 287-288.

Kluegel, J. R., & Smith, E. R. (1982). Whites' beliefs about
Blacks' opportunity. American Sociological Review,
47, 518-532.

Kohn, P. M. (1974). Authoritarianism, rebelliousness, and
their correlates among British undergraduates. British
Journal of Social and Clinical Psychology, 13,
245-255.

Kolbe, R., & LaVoie, J. C. (1981). Sex-role stereotyping in
preschool children's picture books. Social Psychology
Quarterly, 44, 369-374.

Kruglanskie, A. W., & Freund, T. (1983). The freezing and
unfreezing of lay-inferences: Effects on impressional
primacy, ethnic stereotyping, and numerical anchoring.
Journal of Experimental Social Psychology, 19,
448-468.

Kulik, J. A. (1983). Confirmatory attribution and the perpetuation of social beliefs. Journal of Personality and Social Psychology, 44, 1171-1181.

Kutner, B. (1958). Patterns of mental functioning associated with prejudice in children. Psychological Monographs, 72, (Whole number 460).

Lady Nugent's Journal. (1966). (P. Wright, Ed.). Kingston: Institute of Jamaica.

Lambert, W. E., & Klineberg, O. (1959). A pilot study of the origin and development of national stereotypes. International Social Science Journal, 11, 221-238.

Lambley, P. (1974). Racial attitudes and the maintenance of segregation: A study of voting patterns of white, English-speaking South Africs. British Journal of Sociology, 25, 494-499.

LaPiere, R. T. (1934). Attitudes versus actions. Social Forces, 13, 230-237.

Leavitt, E. T. (1956). Water-jar einstellung test and rigidity. Psychological Bulletin, 53, 347-370.

Leavitt, H. J., Hax, H., & Roche, J. H. (1955). 'Authoritarianism' and agreement with things authoritative. Journal of Psychology, 40, 215-221.

Lederer, G. (1982). Trends in authoritarianism: A study of adolescents in West Germany and the United States since 1945. Journal of Cross-Cultural Psychology, 13, 299-314.

Lever, H. (1968). Ethnic attitudes of Johannesburg youth. Johannesburg: Witwatersrand University Press.

Lichtenstein, E., Quinn, R. P., & Hover, G. L. (1961). Journal of Abnormal and Social Psychology, 63, 636-638.

Lippmann, W. (1956). Public Opinion. N. Y.: Macmillan. (Original work published 1922)

Liverpool and slavery: An historical account of the Liverpool-African slave trade. By a genuine 'Dicky Sam'. Newcastle-upon-Tyne: French Graham. (Originally published in Liverpool by A. Bowker and Son, 1884)

233

Locke, J. (1960). Two treatises of government. P. Laslett (Ed.). London: CUP. (First published 1690)

Locksley, A., Ortiz, V., & Hepburn, C. (1980). Social categorization and discriminatory behavior: Extinguishing the minimal intergroup discrimination effect. Journal of Personality and Social Psychology, 39, 773-783.

Loehlin, J. C., Lindzey, G., & Spuhler, J. N. (1975). Race differences in intelligence. San Francisco: Freeman.

Loftus, E. F., Miller, D. G., & Burns, H. J. (1978). Semantic integration of verbal information into a visual memory. Journal of Experimental Psychology: Human Learning and Memory, 4, 19-31.

Loftus, E. F., & Palmer, J. C. (1974). Reconstruction of automobile destruction: An example of the interaction between language and memory. Journal of Verbal Learning and Verbal Behavior, 13, 585-589.

London, P., & Lim, H. (1964). Yielding reason to social influence: Task complexity and expectation in conformity. Journal of Personality, 32, 75-89.

Lubinski, D., Tellegen, A., & Butcher, J. N. (1983). Masculinity, femininity, and androgyny viewed and assessed as distinct concepts. Journal of Personality and Social Psychology, 44, 428-439.

Luchins, A. S., & Luchins, E.H. (1959). Rigidity of Behavior. Oregon: Univ. of Oregon Books.

Luiz, D., & Krige, P. (1981). The effect of social contact between South African white and colored adolescent girls. Journal of Social Psychology, 113, 153-158.

Lynn, R. (1977). the intelligence of the Japanese. Bulletin of the British Psychological Society, 30, 69-72.

Lynn, R. (1978). Ethnic and racial difference in intelligence: International comparisons. In R. T. Osborne, C. E. Noble & N. Wegl (Eds.), Human variation: The biopsychology of age, race, and sex. New York: Academic Press.

Lynn, R. (1979). The social ecology of intelligence in the British Isles. British Journal of Social and Clinical

Psychology, 18, 1-12.

Lynn, R. (1980). The social ecology of intelligence in France. British Journal of Social and Clinical Psychology, 19, 325-331.

Lynn, R. (1982, 20 May). IQ in Japan and the United States shows a growing disparity. Nature, 297, 222-223.

MacCrone, I. D. (1957). Race attitudes in South Africa: Historical, experimental, and psychological studies. Johannesburg: Witwatersrand University Press. (Originally published for the Witwatersrand University Press by O.U.P., 1937)

Mackie, M. (1980). The impact of sex stereotypes upon adult self imagery. Social Psychology Quarterly, 43, 121-125.

Mac Greil, Micheal. (1977). Prejudice and Tolerance in Ireland. Dublin: College of Industrial Relations.

Maloney, P., Wilkof, J., & Dambrot, F. (1981). Androgyny across two cultures: United States and Israel. Journal of Cross Cultural Psychology, 12, 95-102.

Mann, J. W. (1967). Inconsistent thinking about group and individual. Journal of Social Psychology, 71, 235-245.

Mann, L. (1973). Attitude towards My Lai and obedience to orders: An Australian Survey. Australian Journal of Psychology, 25, 11-21.

Manstead, A. S. R., & McCulloch, C. (1981). Sex-role stereotyping in British television advertisements. British Journal of Social and Clinical Psychology, 20, 171-180.

Marlowe, D., & Crowne, D. P. (1961). Social desirability and response to perceived situational demands. Journal of Consulting Psychology, 25, 109-115.

Marsh, A. (1970). Awareness of racial differences in West African and British children. Race, 11, 289-302.

Masters, W. H., & Johnson, V. E. (1966). Human sexual response. London: Churchill.

Matarazzo, J. D., & Wiens, A. N. (1977). Black intelligence test of cultural homogeneity and Wechsler Adult

Intelligence Scale scores of black and white police applicants. Journal of Applied Psychology, 62, 57-63.

McBride, L., & Moran, G. (1967). Double agreement as a function of item ambiguity and susceptibility to demand implications of the psychological situation. Journal of Personality and Social Psychology, 6, 115-118.

McCauley, C., & Stitt, C. L. (1978). An individual and quantitative measure of stereotypes. Journal of Personality and Social Psychology, 36, 929-940.

McDougall, W. (1913). An introduction to Social Psychology (7th ed.). London: Methuen.

McGee, R. K. (1962a). The relationship between response style and personality variables: I. The measurement of response acquiescence. Journal of Abnormal and Social Psychology, 64, 229-233.

McGee, R. K. (1962b). The relationship between response style and personality variables: II. The prediction of independent conformity behaviour. Journal of Abnormal and Social Psychology, 65, 347-351. (b).

McGee, R. K. (1962c). Response style as a personality variable: by what criterion? Psychological Bulletin, 59, 284-295.

McGranahan, D. V. (1962). A comparison of social attitudes among American and German youth. Journal of Abnormal and Social Psychology, 59, 284-295.

McGranahan, D. V., & Janowitz, M. (1946). Studies in German youth. Journal of Abnormal and Social Psychology, 41, 3-14.

McIntosh, N., & Smith, D. J. (1974). The extent of racial discrimination. London: P.E.P.

Meehl, P. E. (1954). Clinical versus Statistical Prediction. Minneapolis: Univ. of Minnesota Press.

Melamed, L. (1970a). Mac Crone's race attitudes scale - thirty years after. Psychologia Africana, 13, 202-208.

Melamed, L. (1970b). The relationship between actions and attitudes in a South African setting. South African Journal of Psychology, 1, 19-24.

Mercer, N., Mercer, E., & Mears, R. (1979). Linguistic and

cultural affiliation amongst young Asian people in Leicester. In H. Giles & B. Saint-Jaques (Eds.), Language and ethnic relations (pp. 15-26). Oxford: Pergamon.

Middleton, R. (1976). Regional differences in prejudice. American Sociological Review, 41, 94-117.

Milgram, S. (1974). Obedience to authority: An experimental view. London: Tavistock.

Mill, J. S. (1929). The subjection of women. London: Dent.

Miller, B. J. (1973). Cross-cultural research in the perception of pictorial materials. Psychological Bulletin, 80, 135-150.

Miller, H. (1969). The effectiveness of teaching techniques for reducing colour prejudice. Liberal Education, 16, 25-31.

Miller, M., & Hewitt, J. (1978). Conviction of a defendant as a function of juror-victim racial similarity. Journal of Social Psychology, 105, 159-160.

Milner, D. (1973). Racial misidentification and preference in 'black' British children. European Journal of Social Psychology, 3, 281-295.

Mintz, A. (1946). A re-examination of the correlations between lynchings and economic indices. Journal of Abnormal and Social Psychology, 41, 154-160.

Mischel, H. N. (1974). Sex bias in the evaluation of professional achievements. Journal of Educational Psychology, 66, 157-166.

Mischel, W. (1965). Predicting the success of peace corps volunteers in Nigeria, Journal of Personality and Social Psychology, 1, 510-517.

Mitchell, H. E., & Byrne, D. (1973). The defendant's dilemma: Effects of jurors' attitudes and authoritarianism on judicial decisions. Journal of Personality and Social Psychology, 25, 123-129.

Mitchell, J. C. (1956). The Kalela Dance. (Rhodes-Livingstone paper No. 27). Manchester: Manchester University Press.

Mitchell, J. C. (1962). Some aspects of tribal social distance. In A. A. Dubb (Ed.), The multi-tribal society. (Proceedings of the 16th conference of the Rhodes-Livingstone Institute). Lusaka, Zambia: Rhodes-Livingstone Institute.

Mogar, R. E. (1960). Three versions of the F scale and performance on the semantic differential. Journal of Abnormal and Social Psychology, 60, 262-265.

Montagu, A. (1963). Race, science, and humanity. New Jersey: van Nostrand.

Moore, M. (1978). Discrimination or favouritism? Sex bias in book-reviews. American Psychologist, 33, 936-938.

Moore, T., & Clautour, S. E. (1977). Attitudes of life in children and young adolescents. Scand. J. Psychol., 18, 10-20.

Morgan, J. J. B., & Morton, J. T. (1944). The distortion of syllogistic reasoning produced by personal convictions. Journal of Social Psychology, 20, 39-59.

Morgan, M. (1982). Television and adolescents' sex role stereotypes: A longitudinal study. Journal of Personality and Social Psychology, 43, 947-955.

Moulton, J., Robinson, G. M., & Elias, C. (1978). Sex Bias in Language Use: 'Neutral' pronouns that aren't. American Psychologist, 33, 1032-1036.

Mummendey, A., & Schreiber, H-J. (1983). Better or just different? Positive social identity by discrimination against or by differentiation from outgroups. European Journal of Social Psychology, 13, 389-397.

Munsinger, H. (1978). Reply to Kamin. Psychological Bulletin, 85, 202-206.

Murphy, G., Murphy, L. B., & Newcomb, T. M. (1937). Experimental social psychology (Rev. ed.). New York: Harper.

Myers, A. M., & Gonda, G. (1982). Empirical validation of the Bem Sex-Role Inventory. Journal of Personality and Social Psychology, 43, 304-318.

Mynhardt, J. C. (1980). Prejudice among Afrikaans- and English-speaking South African students. Journal of

Social Psychology, 110, 9-17.

Nadler, E. B. (1959). Yielding, authoritarianism, and authoritarian ideology regarding groups. Journal of Abnormal and Social Psychology, 58, 408-410.

Newson, J., & Newson, E. (1978). Seven years old in the home environment. Harmondsworth: Penguin.

Nisbett, R. E., & Borgida, E. (1975). Attribution and the psychology of prediction. Journal of Personality and Social Psychology, 32, 932-943.

Noel, R. C., & Allen, M. J. (1976). Sex and ethnic bias in the evaluation of student editorials. Journal of Psychology, 94, 53-58.

Norman, R. D. (1963). Intelligence tests and the personal world. New Mexico Quarterly, 33, 153-184.

Nosanchuk, T. A. (1980). The psychologic of implication. Journal for the Theory of Social Behaviour, 10, 39-55.

Office of Population Censuses and Surveys. (1984). Population Trends, 38. London, HMSO.

O'Gorman, H. J. (1979). White and black perceptions of racial values. Public Opinion Quarterly, 43, 48-59.

Olmedo, E. L., & Padilla, A. M. (1978). Empirical and construct validation of a measure of acculturation for Mexican Americans. Journal of Social Psychology, 105, 179-187.

Orpen, C. (1970). Authoritarianism in an 'authoritarian' culture: The case of Afrikaans speaking South Africa. Journal of Social Psychology, 81, 119-120.

Orpen, C. (1971). Authoritarianism and racial attitudes among English speaking South Africans. Journal of Social Psychology, 84, 301-302.

Orpen, C., & Pors, H. (1972). Race and belief: A test of Rokeach's theory in an authoritarian culture. International Journal of Psychology, 7, 53-56.

Orwell, G. (1962). Boys' weeklies. In Inside the Whale and other essays. Harmondsworth: Penguin.

Paige, J. M. (1970). Changing patterns of anti-white

attitudes among Blacks. *Journal of Social Issues*, 26, 69-86.

Parliamentary Intelligence. (1815, 22 June). *The Times*.

Parry, J. H., & Sherlock, P. M. (1971). *A short history of the West Indies*. (3rd ed.). London: Macmillan.

Peabody, D. (1961). Attitude content and agreement set in scales of authoritarianism, dogmatism, anti-Semitism, and economic conservatism. *Journal of Abnormal and Social Psychology*, 63, 1-11.

Peabody, D. (1966). Authoritarianism scales and response bias. *Psychological Bulletin*, 65, 11-23.

Peabody, D. (1968). Group judgements in the Phillipines: evaluative and descriptive aspects. *Journal of Personality and Social Psychology*, 10, 290-300.

Peterson, C. R., & Beach, L. R. (1967). Man as an intuitive statistician. *Psychological Bulletin*, 68, 29-46.

Pettigrew, T. F. (1958). Personality and sociocultural factors in intergroup attitudes: a cross-national comparison. *Journal of Conflict Resolution*, 2, 29-42.

Piaget, J., & Weil, A. M. (1951). The development in children of the idea of the homeland and of relations with other countries. *International Social Science Bulletin*, 3, 561-578.

Pike, E. R. (1967). *Human documents of the Victorian golden age (1850-1875)*. London: Allen and Unwin.

Porier, G. W., & Lott, A. J. (1967). Galvanic skin responses and prejudice. *Journal of Personality and Social Psychology*, 5, 253-259.

Porter, J. D. R. (1971) *Black child, white child*. Cambridge, Massachusetts: Harvard University Press.

Porteus, S. D. (1950). *The Porteus maze test and intelligence*. Palo Alto: Pacific Books.

Porteus, S. D. (1965) *Porteus maze test: Fifty years' application*. Palo Alto: Pacific Books.

Prentice, N. M. (1957). The influence of ethnic attitudes on reasoning about ethnic groups. *Journal of Abnormal and*

Social Psychology, 55, 270-272.

Press, L., Burt, I., & Barling, J. (1979). Racial preferences among South African white and black preschool children. Journal of Social Psychology, 107, 125-126.

Pushkin, L., & Veness, T. (1973). The development of racial awareness and prejudice in children. In P. Watson (Ed.), Psychology and race. Harmondsworth: Penguin.

Pyszczynski, T. A., & Greenberg, J. (1981). Role of disconfirmed expectancies in the instigation of attributional processing. Journal of Personality and Social Psychology, 40, 31-38.

Quattrone, G. A., & Jones, E. E. (1980). The perception of variability within in-groups and out-groups: Implications for the law of small numbers. Journal of Personality and Social Psychology, 38, 141-152.

Quesnell, R. J., van der Spuy, H. I. J., & Oxtoby, R. (1978). Changes in racial prejudice and authoritarianism of white South Africans 1956 - 1973. In H. I. J. van der Spuy and D. A. F. Shanley (Eds.), The Psychology of Apartheid (pp. 83-88). Washington, DC: University Press of America.

Ramprakash, D. (Ed.). (1983). Social Trends No. 13. London, HMSO.

Ramprakash, D. (Ed.). (1985). Social Trends No. 15. London: HMSO.

Ray, W. S. (1965). Mild stress and problem solving. American Journal of Psychology, 76, 227-234.

Ray, J. J. (1980a). Authoritarianism in California 30 years later - with some cross-cultural comparisons. Journal of Social Psychology, 111, 9-17.

Ray, J. J. (1980b). Racism and authoritarianism among white South Africans. Journal of Social Psychology, 110, 29-37.

Ray, J. J. (1982). Attitude to the death penalty in South Africa - with some international comparisons. Journal of Social Psychology, 116, 287-288.

Revlin, R., & Leirer, V. O. (1978). The effects of personal biases on syllogistic reasoning: Rational decision from personalized representations. In R. Revlin & R. E. Mayer (Eds.), Human Reasoning (pp. 51-81). New York: Wiley.

Riordan, C., & Ruggiero, J. (1980). Producing equal status interracial interaction: A replication. Social Psychology Quarterly, 43, 131-136.

Roberge, J. J. (1970). A reexamination of the interpretations of errors in formal syllogistic reasoning. Psychonomic Science, 19, 331-333.

Robb, J. H. (1954). Working Class Anti-Semite. London: Tavistock.

Rogers, C. A., & Frantz, C. (1962). Racial themes in Southern Rhodesia. New Haven: Yale University Press.

Rokeach, M. (1960). The open and closed mind. N.Y.: Basic Books.

Rokeach, M. (1961). Belief versus race as determinants of social distance: comment on Triandis's paper. Journal of Abnormal and Social Psychology, 62, 187-188.

Rorer, L. G. (1965). The great response-style myth. Psychological Bulletin, 63, 129-156.

Rorer, L. G., & Goldberg, L. R. (1965). Acquiescence and the vanishing variance component. Journal of Applied Psychology, 49, 422-430.

Rose, E. J. B. (1969). Colour and citizenship: A report on British race relations. London: Oxford University Press.

Rosen, B., & Jerdee, T. H. (1974a). Effect of applicant's sex and difficulty of job on evaluations of candidates for managerial positions. Journal of Applied Psychology, 59, 511-512.

Rosen, B., & Jerdee, T. H. (1974b). Influence of sex role stereotypes on personnel decisions. Journal of Applied Psychology, 59, 9-14.

Rosenberg, M. J. (1960). An analysis of affective-cognitive consistency. In C. I. Hovland & M. J. Rosenberg (Eds.), Attitude organization and change. New Haven: Yale University Press.

Rosenkrantz, P., Vogel, S., Bee, H., & Broverman, I.

(1968). Sex-role stereotypes and self-concepts in college students. Journal of Consulting and Clinical Psychology, 32, 287-295.

Ross, E. A. (1908). Social psychology: An outline and source book. N.Y.: Macmillan.

Rubenowitz, S. (1963). Emotional flexibility-rigidity as a comprehensive dimension of mind. Stockholm: Alquist and Wiksell.

Rundquist, E. A. (1967). Item response characteristics in attitude and personality measurement: A reaction to L.G. Rorer's 'The great response-style myth'. (Technical Bulletin STB 67-16.) San Diego, California: U.S. Naval Personnel Research Activity.

Runge, T. E., Frey, D., Gollwitzer, P. M., Helmreich, R. L., & Spence, J. T. (1981). Masculine (instrumental) and feminine (expressive) traits: A comparison between students in the United States and West Germany. Journal of Cross-Cultural Psychology, 12, 142-162.

Sagar, H. A., & Schofield, J. W. (1980). Racial and behavioral cues in black and white children's perceptions of ambiguously aggressive acts. Journal of Personality and Social Psychology, 39, 590-598.

Samelson, F. (1964). Agreement set and anti-content attitudes in the F-scale. Journal of Abnormal and Social Psychology, 68, 338-342.

Sanger, S. P., & Alker, H. A. (1972). Dimensions of internal-external locus of control and the women's liberation movement. Journal of Social Issues, 28, 115-129.

Scarr, S. (1984). The transmission of authoritarianism in families: Genetic resemblance in social-political attitudes? In S. Scarr (Ed.), Race, Social Class, and Individual Differences in I.Q., pp. 399-427.

Scarr, S., & Carter-Saltzman, L. (1982). Genetics and intelligence. In R. J. Sternberg (Ed.), Handbook of Human Intelligence, (pp. 792-896). Cambridge: Cambridge University Press.

Scarr, S., & McCartney, K. (1983). How people make their own environments: A theory of genotype-environment effects. Child Development, 54, 424-435.

Scarr, S., & Weinberg, R. A. (1976). IQ test performance of black children adopted by white families. American Psychologist, 31, 726-739. (Reprinted in S. Scarr, ed., Race, Social Class, and Individual Differences in I.Q., pp. 109-135. London: Lawrence Erlbaum.

Scarr, S., & Weinberg, R. A. (1977). Intellectual similarities within families of both adopted and biological children. Intelligence, 1, 170-191. (Reprinted in S. Scarr, ed., Race, Social Class, and Individual Differences in I.Q., pp. 319-340. London: Lawrence Erlbaum.)

Scarr, S., & Weinberg, R. A. (1978). The influence of 'family background' on intellectual attainment. American Sociological Review, 43, 674-692. (Reprinted in S. Scarr, ed., Race, Social Class, and Individual Differences in I.Q., pp. 357-383. London: Lawrence Erlbaum.)

Schonbach, P., Gollwitzer, P., Stiepel, G., & Wagner, U. (1981). Education and Intergroup Attitudes. London: Academic Press.

Secord, P. F. (1959). Stereotyping and favourableness in the perception of the negro. Journal of Abnormal and Social Psychology, 59, 309-315.

Shaklee, H., & Mims, M. (1982). Sources of error in judging event covariations: Effects of memory demands. Journal of Experimental Psychology: Learning, Memory, and Cognition, 8, 208-224.

Shapira, A., & Lomranz, J. (1972). Cooperative and competitive behaviour of rural Arab children in Israel. Journal of Cross-Cultural Psychology, 3, 353-359.

Sharma, R. (1971). The measured intelligence of immigrant children from the Indian subcontinent resident in Hertfordshire. Unpublished Ph.D. Thesis: University of London.

Sherif, M. (1967). Group conflict and cooperation: Their social psychology, London: Routledge.

Sherwood, J. J., & Nataupsky, M. (1968). Predicting the conclusions of negro-white intelligence research from biographical characteristics of the investigator. Journal of Personality and Social Psychology, 8, 53-58.

Shomer, R. W., & Centers, R. (1970). Differences in attitudinal responses under conditions of implicitly manipulated group salience. Journal of Personality and Social Psychology, 15, 125-132.

Shuey, A. M. (1966). The testing of Negro intelligence. (2nd ed.). N.Y.: Social Science Press.

Siegel, S. (1954). Certain determinants and correlates of authoritarianism. Genetic Psychology Monographs, 49, 187-229.

Singleton, C. H. (1979). Sex differences. In B. M. Foss (ed.) Survey of Psychology, London: Allen & Unwin.

Sinha, A. K. P., & Uphadhyaya, O. P. (1960). Change and persistence in the stereotype of university students toward different ethnic groups during the Sino-Indian border dispute. Journal of Social Psychology, 52, 31-39.

Sissons, M. (1981). Race, sex and helping behaviour. British Journal of Social Psychology, 20, 285-292.

Smedslund, J. (1963). The concept of correlation in adults. Scandinavian Journal of Psychology, 4, 165-173.

Smith, C. E. (1964). The effect of anxiety on the performance and attitudes of authoritarians in a small group situation. Journal of Psychology, 58, 191-203.

Smith, C. R., Williams, L., & Willis, R. H. (1967). Race, sex, and belief as determinants of friendship acceptance. Journal of Personality and Social Psychology, 5, 127-137.

Smith D. J. (1974). Racial disadvantage in employment. London: PEP.

Smith, D. J. (1976). The facts of racial disadvantage: A national survey. London: PEP.

Smith, M. L. (1980). Sex bias in counselling and psychotherapy. Psychological Bulletin, 87, 392-407.

Snyder, M., & Swann, W. B. Jr. (1978). Hypothesis-testing processes in social interaction. Journal of Personality and Social Psychology, 36, 1202-1212.

Snyder, M., Tanke, E. D., & Berscheid, E. (1977). Social perception and interpersonal behavior: On the self-fulfilling nature of social stereotypes. Journal of Personality and Social Psychology, 35, 656-666.

Snyder, M., & Uranowitz, S. W. (1978). Reconstructing the past: some cognitive consequences of person perception. Journal of Personality and Social Psychology, 36, 941-950.

Stankov, L. (1977). Some experiences with the F scale in Yugoslavia. British Journal of Social and Clinical Psychology, 16, 111-121.

Stebbing, L. S. (1961). A modern elementary logic (Rev. ed.). London: Methuen. (First published 1943)

Steiner, I. D. (1954). Ethnocentrism and tolerance of trait inconsistency. Journal of Abnormal and Social Psychology, 49, 349-354.

Steiner, I. D., & Johnson, H. (1963). Authoritarianism and 'tolerance of trait inconsistency'. Journal of Abnormal and Social Psychology, 67, 388-396.

Stoppard, J. M. & Kalin, R. (1978). Can gender stereotypes and sex-role conceptions be distinguished? British Journal of Social and Clinical Psychology, 17, 211-217.

Strongman, K. T., & Woosley, J. (1967). Stereotyped reactions to regional accents. British Journal of Social and Clinical Psychology, 6, 164-167.

Strube, M. J. (1981). Meta-analysis and cross-cultural comparison: Sex differences in child competitiveness. Journal of Cross-Cultural Psychology, 12, 3-20.

Taft, R. (1956). Intolerance of ambiguity and ethnocentrism. Journal of Consulting Psychology, 20, 153-154.

Taft, R. (1966). From Stranger to Citizen. London: Tavistock.

Tajfel, H. (1978). Differentiation between social groups. London: Academic Press.

Tajfel, H., Billig, M. G., Bundy, R. P., & Flament, C. (1971). Social categorization and intergroup behaviour. European Journal of Social Psychology, 1, 148-178.

Tajfel, H., & Wilkes, A. L. (1963). Classification and quantitative judgement. British Journal of Psychology,

54, 101-114.

Tajfel, H., Jahoda, G., Nemeth, C., Rim, Y., & Johnson, N. B. (1972). The devaluation by children of their own national and ethnic group: two case studies. British Journal of Social and Clinical Psychology. 11, 235-243.

Tajfel, H., Nemeth, C., Jahoda, G., Campbell, J. D., & Johnson, N. (1970). The development of children's preference for their own country: A cross-national study. International Journal of Psychology, 5, 245-253.

Taylor, D. M., & Guimond, S. (1978). The belief theory of prejudice in an intergroup context. Journal of Social Psychology, 105, 11-25.

Taylor, D. M., & Jaggi, V. (1974). Ethnocentrism and causal attribution in a South Indian context. Journal of Cross-Cultural Psychology, 5, 162-171.

Taylor, S. E., Fiske, S. T., Etcoff, N. L., & Ruderman, A. J. (1978). Categorical and contextual bases of person memory and stereotyping. Journal of Personality and Social Psychology, 36, 778-793.

Teasdale, T. W., & Owen, D. R. (1984, 14 June). Heredity and familial environment in intelligence and educational level - a sibling study. Nature, 309, 620-622.

Thistlethwaite, D. (1950). Attitude and structure as factors in the distortion of reasoning. Journal of Abnormal and Social Psychology, 45, 442-458.

Thomas, D. R. (1975). Conservatism, authoritarianism and child-rearing practices. British Journal of Social and Clinical Psychology, 14, 97-98.

Thompson, E. J. (Ed.). (1975). Social Trends No. 6. London: HMSO.

Thompson, E. J. (Ed.). (1979). Social Trends No. 9. London: HMSO.

Thouless, R. H. (1959). Effects of prejudice on reasoning. British Journal of Psychology, 50, 290-293.

Triandis, H. C. (1967). Toward an analysis of the components of inter-personal attitudes. In C. W. Sherif & M. Sherif (Eds.), Attitude, ego-involvement, and change.

N.Y.: Wiley.

Triandis, H. C., & Davies, E. E. (1965). Race and belief as determinants of behavioural intentions. Journal of Personality and Social Psychology, 2, 715-725.

Triandis, H. C., & Vassiliou, V. (1967). Frequency of contact and stereotyping. Journal of Personality and Social Psychology, 4, 316-328.

Triandis, H. C., Davis, E. E., & Takezawa, S. I. (1965). Some determinants of social distance among American, German and Japanese students. Journal of Personality and Social Psychology, 2, 540-550.

Triandis, H. C., Loh, W. D., & Levin, L. A. (1966). Race, status, quality of spoken English, and opinions about civil rights as determinants of interpersonal attitudes. Journal of Personality and Social Psychology, 3, 468-472.

Tversky, A., & Kahneman, D. (1982). Belief in the law of small numbers. In D. Kahneman, P. Slovic, & A. Tversky (Eds.), Judgment under Uncertainty: Heuristics and Biases (pp. 23-31). Cambridge: CUP. (Reprinted from Psychological Bulletin, 1971, 76, 105-110.

Vaughan, G. M. (1964). The development of ethnic attitudes in New Zealand school-children. Genetic Psychology Monographs, No. 70.

Vaughan, G. M. (1978). Social change and intergroup preferences in New Zealand. European Journal of Social Psychology, 297-314.

Vaughan, G. M., Tajfel, H., & Williams, J. (1981). Bias in reward allocation in an intergroup interpersonal context. Social Psychology Quarterly, 44, 37-42.

Vaughan, G. M., & White, K. D. (1966). Conformity and authoritarianism reexamined. Journal of Personality and Social Psychology, 3, 363-366.

Verma, G. K., & Bagley, C. (1973). Changing racial attitudes in adolescents: An experimental English study. International Journal of Psychology, 8, 55-58.

Vernon, P. E. (1969). Intelligence and cultural environment, London: Methuen.

Vidulich, R. N., & Kaiman, I. P. (1961). The effects of information source and dogmatism upon conformity behavior. Journal of Abnormal and Social Psychology, 63, 639-642.

Vidulich, R. N., & Krevanick, F. W. (1966). Racial attitudes and emotional response to visual representations of the negro. Journal of Social Psychology, 68, 85-93.

Vine, I. (1974). Stereotypes in the judgement of personality from handwriting. British Journal of Social and Clinical Psychology, 13, 61-64.

Walker, M. (1978). The National Front (2nd ed.). London: Fontana/Collins.

Ward, C. (1979). Differential evaluation of male and female expertise: Prejudice against women? British Journal of Social and Clinical Psychology, 18, 65-69.

Ward, J. R. (1979). A planter and his slaves in eighteenth-century Jamaica. In T. C. Smout (Ed.), The Search for Wealth and Stability. London: Macmillan.

Ward, W. C., & Jenkins, H. M. (1965). The display of information and the judgment of contingency. Canadian Journal of Psychology, 19, 231-241.

Warner, L. G., & DeFleur, M. L. (1969). Attitude as an interactional concept: Social constraint and social distance as intervening variables between attitudes and actions. American Sociological Review, 34, 153-169.

Warr, P. B., Faust, J., & Harrison, G. J. (1967). A British ethnocentrism scale. British Journal of Social and Clinical Psychology, 6, 267-277.

Weatherley, D. (1963). Maternal response to childhood aggression and subsequent anti-Semitism. Journal of Abnormal and Social Psychology, 66, 183-185.

Wechsler, D. (1958). The measurement and appraisal of adult intelligence, (Fourth edition). Baltimore: Williams & Williams.

Weigel, R. H., Loomis, J. W., & Soja, M. J. (1980). Race relations on prime time television. Journal of Personality and Social Psychology, 39, 884-893.

Weiland, A., & Coughlin, R. (1979). Self-identification and preferences: A comparison of white and Mexican-American first and third graders. Journal of Cross-Cultural Psychology, 10, 356-365.

Weima, J. (1964). Authoritarian personality, anti-catholicism and the experience of religious values. Social Compass, 11, 13-25.

Weller, L. (1964). The relationship of personality and non-personality factors to prejudice. Journal of Social Psychology, 63, 129-137.

Whitley, B. E., Jr. (1979). Sex roles and psychotherapy: A current appraisal. Psychological Bulletin, 86, 1309-1321.

Wiener, M. J., & Wright, F. E. (1973). Effects of undergoing arbitrary discrimination upon subsequent attitudes toward a minority group. Journal of Applied Social Psychology, 3, 94-102.

Williams, J. E., & Best, D. L. (1982). Measuring sex stereotypes: A thirty-nation study. Beverly Hills: Sage.

Wilson, G. D. (1973). Development and evaluation of the C-scale. In G. D. Wilson (Ed.), The Psychology of Conservatism (pp. 49-70). London: Academic Press.

Wilson, G. D., & Bagley, C. (1973). Religion, racialism, and conservatism. In G. D. Wilson (Ed.), The Psychology of Conservatism (pp. 117-128). London: Academic Press.

Wilson, G. D., & Patterson, J. R. (1968). A new measure of conservatism. British Journal of Social and Clinical Psychology, 7, 264-269.

Wilson, N. (1970). Legal attitudes to slavery in eighteenth century Britain: English myth, Scottish social realism and their wider comparative context. Race, 11, 463-475.

Wilson, R. S. (1983). The Louisville twin study: Developmental synchronies in behavior. Child Development, 54, 298-316.

Wilson, W. C. (1963). The development of ethnic attitudes in adolescence. In R. E. Grinder (Ed.), Studies in Adolescence. London: Collier-MacMillan.

Wiser, P. L., & Cook, S. W. (1975). The impact of cooperative learning experiences on cross-ethnic relations and attitudes. <u>Journal of Social Issues,</u> <u>31</u>, 219-245.

Wolff, L., & Taylor, S. E., (1979). Sex, sex-role identification, and awareness of sex-role stereotypes. <u>Journal of Personality,</u> <u>47</u>, 177-184.

Wollstonecraft, M. (1929). <u>The rights of woman.</u> London, Dent. (Originally published 1792)

Ziegler, M., King, M., King, J. M., & Ziegler, S. M. (1972). Tribal stereotypes among Ethiopian students. <u>Journal of Cross-Cultural Psychology,</u> <u>3</u>, 193-201.

Zuckerman, M., & Eisen, B. (1962). Relationship of acquiescent response set to authoritarianism and dependency. <u>Psychological Reports,</u> <u>10</u>, 95-102.

NAME INDEX